THE BASICS OF BLOCKCHAIN

Bettina Warburg, Bill Wagner PhD, and Tom Serres

Copyright © 2019 Animal Ventures LLC

All rights reserved.

Edition 1.0

ISBN: 978-1-08-991944-5

Table of Contents

About the Authors ... 9
   Bettina Warburg ... 9
   William Wagner, Ph.D. ... 11
   Tom Serres ... 12
Acknowledgements ... 14
Preface ... 18
Chapter 1 – Blockchain Fundamentals ... 21
   Learning Objectives ... 21
   Let's Get Going... ... 22
   A Foundational Change in Trade? ... 23
   Blockchain Fundamentals ... 27
      Defining Blockchain ... 27
      Elements of a Blockchain ... 32
      Qualities of Blockchains ... 36
   Blockchain and Economics ... 38
      Lowering Uncertainty in Trade ... 39
      Changing the Role of the Firm: A Nexus of Smart Contracts? ... 40
   Blockchain Technology ... 44
      The Origins of Bitcoin and Blockchain ... 44
      Types of Blockchains ... 46
      Evolving the Blockchain Stack ... 49
      Hurdles for Blockchain Adoption ... 50
   Business of Blockchain ... 52
      Use Cases ... 53
      Enterprise Blockchain Platforms ... 57
   Ethical and Other Issues with Blockchain ... 61
   Chapter Summary ... 63
   Key Terms ... 64
   Questions for Further Discussion ... 65
Chapter 2 – The Technology Behind Blockchain ... 66
   Learning Objectives ... 66
   Blockchain in Action –Are You Ready for a Blockchain Phone? ... 67
   Review of the Blockchain Technology Stack ... 67
   Monetizing the Blockchain ... 70
      Monetizing the Core Infrastructure ... 70
      Monetizing Middleware ... 72
      Monetizing the Decentralized Economy ... 73
   An Example: KoffeeKoin ... 74
   What is a Blockchain Wallet? ... 76
   Sorting Blocks ... 80
   Say Hello to My Little Friend –SHA-256! ... 81
      Rewarding Miners ... 86
      Consensus ... 87
   So, You Want to Be a Miner... ... 90
      Evolution of Mining Technology ... 91

Mining Pools	92
Cloud Mining	94
Economics of Mining	95
Can You Still Make Money with a Low-end Machine?	97
Blockchain as a Service (BaaS)	98
Information Technology Use Cases for Blockchain	99
Storage	99
IPFS	100
Edge Computing	101
Web 3.0 and Blockchain	102
Obstacles in Blockchain Technology	103
Sybil Attacks	103
Key Management	104
Scalability	104
Dispute Resolution	105
Updating and Governance	105
Ethical and Other Issues with Blockchain	106
Chapter Summary	107
Key Terms	108
Questions for Further Discussion	109
Chapter 3 – Bitcoin and Crypto-assets	111
Learning Objectives	111
Blockchain in Action – CryptoKitties?!	112
What Are Crypto-assets?	112
Cryptocurrencies	113
Crypto-commodities	114
Other Crypto-tokens	116
What Are ICOs?	119
Top Ten Cryptocurrencies by Market Capitalization	120
Bitcoin	121
Implications of Forks for Cryptocurrencies	125
Altcoins	128
Ethereum (ETH)	128
Ripple (XRP)	129
Bitcoin Cash (BCH)	130
EOS (EOS)	131
Litecoin (LTC)	131
Cardano (ADA)	132
Stellar / Chain (XLM)	133
IOTA (MIOTA)	133
Tronix (TRX)	135
Up-and-Coming Cryptos to Watch	137
Zcash (ZEC)	137
Monero (XMR)	137
Dfinity (DFN)	138
Popular Cryptocurrency Scams	139
FOMO-based ICOs	139
Fake Exchanges	140

Mining Pools	141
Cybercrime and Cryptocurrencies	142
What Makes a Good Token Project?	143
Leadership	143
Community	143
Mission	143
Security and Law	144
Exert Caution	144
Digital Token Exchanges	145
Coinbase	147
Bitstamp	148
Kraken	149
Decentralized Exchanges	149
OTC Crypto Exchanges	150
Adoption Rate of Bitcoin	150
Financial Modeling for Cryptocurrencies	152
Blockchain Analytics	156
Regulatory Considerations	159
Ethical and Other Issues with Blockchain	160
Chapter Summary	161
Key Terms	162
Questions for Further Discussion	163
Chapter 4 – Ethereum and Smart Contracts	165
Learning Objectives	165
Blockchain in Action – Ethereum in Space	166
Basics of Ethereum	166
Ethereum Foundation	167
Ethereum Virtual Machine (EVM)	169
What is Ether? What is Gas?	170
What Is a Smart Contract?	172
History of Smart Contracts	174
Roadmap of Ethereum	176
Casper	177
Plasma	178
Governance	178
On-chain Versus Off-chain Versus Side Chain?	180
Mining Ethereum	182
Ethereum Versus Bitcoin	183
DAOs and DACs	185
Ethical and Other Issues with Blockchain	188
Chapter Summary	189
Key Terms	191
Questions for Further Discussion	192
Tutorial: Developing a Dapp for Ethereum	193
Overview	193
Running a Token Dapp	194
Publishing and Using Your Token with MetaMask	211
How to Write a Smart Contract	218

Basics of Blockchain

Going Forward and Best Practices	223
Chapter 5 –Project Management, Use Cases, and Hyperledger	**225**
Learning Objectives	225
Blockchain in Action –Making Giving Better	226
Project Management: Developing a Use Case	227
Identify a 10-Year, 5-Year, and 2-Year Vision	227
Identify Beachhead(s)	228
Map the Technical Ecosystem	229
Develop a Hypothesis and KPI	229
Sketch Out Prototype Ideas	231
Project Management: Lifecycle for Dapps	232
Do You Need a Blockchain?	233
Evaluating Consensus Mechanisms	234
Identifying a Suitable Blockchain Platform	238
Design Architecture	239
Configuring a Blockchain Application	240
Building APIs	241
Building Administrative and User Interfaces	242
Testing and Scaling	242
Roles in a Blockchain Project	243
Blockchain Project Manager	244
Blockchain Developer	244
Blockchain Quality Engineer	245
Blockchain Legal Consultant	245
Blockchain Web/UI Designer	245
Use Cases	247
Cross-functional Blockchain Use Cases	249
Blockchain for Identity Management	250
Blockchain Use Cases for Asset Tracking	252
Blockchain for Internet of Things (IoT) Integration	255
Functional Area Blockchain Use Cases for Business	256
Finance	256
Marketing/Sales	257
Supply Chain Management (SCM)	258
Accounting	260
Use Cases for Human Resources	261
Use Cases for Specific Industries	264
Insurance	264
Real Estate	266
Healthcare	267
Energy	268
Ethical and Other Issues with Blockchain	269
Chapter Summary	271
Key Terms	272
Questions for Further Discussion	273
Tutorial: Introduction to Hyperledger and Interactive Example	274
Overview	274
Why Enterprise Blockchains?	274

Technical Overview of Hyperledger Fabric	275
Implementing a Textbook Marketplace in Hyperledger	280
Final Remarks	290
Chapter 6 –The Future of Blockchain	292
Learning Objectives	292
Blockchain in Action –Using Blockchain to Fight Fake News	293
Blockchain in the Future	293
Adoption of Blockchain	297
Blockchain Maturity Models	299
Barriers to Adoption	300
The Continuing Evolution of Blockchain	301
Scalability	302
Regulatory Issues	304
Interoperability Issues	307
The Next Wave of Decentralized Computing	307
Blockchain Hardware	308
Quantum-Resistant Blockchains	309
Blockchain and AI	310
What Is AI?	310
Blockchain and Society	313
Blockchain Revolution and Legal Services	314
Blockchain and Government	315
Blockchain and Globalization	318
Blockchain: Job Killer or Opportunity Generator?	319
Leadership in a Blockchain World	321
Ethical and Other Issues with Blockchain	324
Chapter Summary	326
Key Terms	327
Questions for Further Discussion	328
Tutorial: AI and Blockchain	329
Overview	329
Interactive Example: Using AI to predict coffee sales	329
Using the Contract	336
Final Remarks	338
Table of Figures	340
Chapter 1	340
Chapter 2	340
Chapter 3	341
Chapter 4	342
Chapter 5	343
Chapter 6	344
Glossary	345

About the Authors

Bettina Warburg

Bettina Warburg is a Co-Founder and Managing Partner of *Warburg Serres Investments*, an early stage venture capital fund focused on the decentralization of trade and Blockchain Technology. She is a Co-Founder and Managing Partner of *Animal Ventures*, an investment advisory firm that builds and invests in tech startups, educates executives, and designs new ways for Fortune 500 companies to commercialize and leverage emergent technologies. These emergent opportunities include technologies such as Blockchain, Artificial Intelligence, Additive Manufacturing, and the Internet of Things. Animal Ventures has extensive experience in industries such as food, pharmaceuticals, healthcare, trucking, shipping, logistics, online marketplaces, and fin-tech in and around the broader world of supply chain activities.

She is one of the first speakers at TED to unpack the topic of blockchain, and her talk, *"How the Blockchain will radically transform the economy,"* has been seen by over 5 million people, making it the most viewed TED talk on the topic of Blockchain to date. Bettina's collaboration with *Wired Magazine* to help explain Blockchain at 5 levels of difficulty has also been seen by over 2 Million people.

She was executive producer of a show called *Tech on Politics* which featured interviews with some of the greatest minds in technology, media, venture capital, and government. Discussions rove over the convergence of technology, politics, and government.

Bettina lectures each semester as an Adjunct Professor at the *University of Texas School of Information in Austin*, and is co-author of *Asset Chains: The Cognitive, Friction-free, and Blockchain enabled Future of Supply Chains*, as well as *The Basics of Blockchain*. She has given talks at TED, Wired, IBM Think, VMWare,

The Business Council, Credit Suisse Latin American Investment Conference, Smart Cities, Merck & Co's Annual Technology Innovation Conference, The Skoll World Forum, Salzburg Global Seminar, San Francisco's City Innovate Summit, and numerous other conferences and universities around the world. Bettina's work has been cited in publications such as Wired Magazine, BBC News, The Atlantic, Center for Public Impact, ICMA.org, and the San Francisco Chronicle. Bettina received her MSc from Oxford University and BS from Georgetown University's School of Foreign Service, and developed a keen interest in global governance and cultural diplomacy.

William Wagner, Ph.D.

Dr. Bill Wagner is Associate Chair of Accounting & Information Systems at Villanova University, and a researcher at Animal Ventures. He has been a professor of Information Systems at Villanova University since 1991. Bill received his Ph.D. in MIS from the University of Kentucky in 1992. While at Villanova he has developed over 30 new MIS courses, including "Enterprise Systems", "Mobile Application Development" and "Applied Artificial Intelligence." Dr. Wagner has also taught courses on Database Management, Enterprise Systems and Applications, CRM and Data Analytics, Big Data, Decision Support, and Applied AI.

In 2004 he was identified as an "industry thought leader" by SAP. In 2015, Bill was the recipient of the Meyer award for Innovation, Creativity, and Entrepreneurship and was a co-winner of the 2011 Global Consortium of Entrepreneurship Center's award for Excellence. He is the coordinator for the SAP University Alliance and has helped many students get started in IT consulting careers. He has been involved in several startups and was CTO of a mobile application development firm. He has supervised dozens of graduate and undergraduate independent studies, and many of his students have successfully pursued advanced graduate degrees.

Bill has received numerous awards including the Tonkinson Award for Innovative Curriculum, 2001, The Villanova Institute for Teaching and Learning grant for distant learning, 1999, The Villanova Summer Research Grant, 1999; The Carpenter Scholarship, The College of Business and Economics (MBA Program), The University of Kentucky, 1987, The Hagen Fellowship, The College of Arts and Sciences, University of Kentucky, 1983, and was a Member of Agora Excavation Staff, Athens, Greece, 1981.

He has co-authored four books and over 35 journal articles in IT-related fields that have been published in top journals.

Tom Serres

Tom Serres is a Co-Founder and Managing Partner of *Warburg Serres Investments*, an early stage venture capital fund focused on the decentralization of Trade and Blockchain Technology. He is a Co-Founder and Managing Partner of *Animal Ventures*, an investment advisory firm that builds and invests in tech startups, educates executives, and designs new ways for Fortune 500 companies to commercialize and leverage emergent technologies. These emergent opportunities include technologies such as Blockchain, Artificial Intelligence, Additive Manufacturing, and the Internet of Things. Animal Ventures has extensive experience in industries such as food, pharmaceuticals, healthcare, trucking, shipping, logistics, online marketplaces, and fin-tech in and around the broader world of supply chain activities.

Tom lectures each semester as an Adjunct Professor at the *University of Texas School of Information in Austin*, and is Co-Author of *Asset Chains: The Cognitive, Friction-Free, and Blockchain-enabled Future of Supply Chains*, as well as *The Basics of Blockchain*. He is an entrepreneur with experience and expertise in a wide variety of sectors.

Prior to his brief deployment at the Boston Consulting Group, Tom started his first company, *Rally* — the largest political fundraising platform in the United States. Rally garnered widespread attention for raising the largest online-only Series A funding round ever and was recognized as one of the most promising companies of 2013. While serving as Founder and CEO of Rally, Tom was named one of America's Most Promising CEOs under 35 by *Forbes*.

Tom previously hosted a show called *Tech on Politics* which featured interviews with some of the greatest minds in technology, media, venture capital, and government. Discussions rove over the convergences of technology, politics, and government.

Tom attended the University of Texas at Austin McCombs School of Business, and is an occasional writer and speaker on these topics; he and his work can be found in such diverse outlets as *Wired*, *CNN*, *Bloomberg*, and *CNBC*.

Acknowledgements

Learning to Unlearn

In today's fast-paced world of technological innovation, *unlearning* is as important as learning. To appreciate massive technological shifts occurring in the world, sometimes you have to unlearn the old to adopt the new. Blockchain and its impact on the decentralization of our economy is no different. This book will provide you with some of the early building blocks to dive in head first – allowing you to lose yourself in the rabbit hole many of us have come to love. Take the red pill, and we'll show you how deep the rabbit hole goes!

We have been navigating the world of blockchain, the decentralized economy, the future of supply chain, and industry 4.0 for almost a decade. During that journey, we have met a number of people that have helped shape our vision of the future and inspired our continued efforts.

The following names are in no particular order and is likely not an exhaustive list of the people that drove us to dedicate several years toward the creation of this textbook. It's important to note, that this textbook is just the beginning. It is version 1.0, and likely the first of many iterations. It's intended to support a holistic education for a wide variety of disciplines on a complex topic that, once fully understood, will change the way many think about the world.

If there's one thing that has catalyzed us further and further down the rabbit hole, it's the people involved in this nascent technology space. This community is home to some of the most incredible human beings we've ever met. We've had the opportunity to share in the innovation battles of some amazing thinkers who, in the beginning, were often laughed out of rooms and referred to as fringe. Today, they are world-class entrepreneurs, researchers, thinkers, and in some cases...billionaires. We have enjoyed watching them grow and sharing in the ups and downs from these same growing pains. In many ways, we are lucky to have been early enough in an industry to meet and work with some of its earliest movers and shakers.

To that end, huge hugs and thanks to the following people who have inspired us over the years:

Our co-author, Dr. William Wagner, who is always persistent and optimistic about the future. Our family for its immense support, especially Madison, Scott and Cynthia, Marie and Michael, and Max and Nagila. Our friends and partners at Animal Ventures, including Tracey Perkins, Jimmy Hester and Adrian Armaselu and Swathi Chandrashekar for their work on the tutorials, Garrett Conaty, Nicolas Walker, Trevor Cobb, John Fitch, Justin Holmes, Tate Ryan-Mosley, Tristan Mace, and Ezra Tollett. Our network of guides and entrepreneurs, including Celestine Schnugg (Boom Capital), R.Jay Magill, Dominic Williams (Founder of Dfinity), Fabian Vogelsteller (Founder of Lukso), Marjorie Hernandez (Founder of Lukso), Jutta Steiner (Founder of Parity and Polkadot), Gavin Wood (Founder of Parity and Polkadot), Vlad Zamfir (Ethereum Researcher), Vitalik Buterin, (Founder of Ethereum), Gustav Simonsson (Co-Founder of Orchid Labs), Byron Gibson (Stanford Center for Blockchain Research), Ken Kappler (Co-Founder of Parity), TJ Saw (Co-Founder of Parity), Jeff Wilke (Co-Founder of Ethereum), Heiko Hees (Founder of BrainBot), Elizabeth Stark (Co-Founder of Lightning Labs), Sarah Meiklejohn (UCL), Pia Mancini (Democracy Earth), Peter Todd, Nick Szabo, Yaniv Tal (Graph Protocol), Tim Swanson (Post Oak Labs), and Akseli Virtanen (ECSA). Lisbeth McNabb (Linux Foundation), Craig Kennedy (Merck & Co), Quentin Roach (Merck & Co), Paul Cocuzzo (Merck & Co), Jacob Lustig (Merck & Co), Chuck Hammel IV and Chuck Hammel III (PITT-OHIO), Kevin Humphries (FedEx), Dale Chrystie (FedEx), Don Fike (FedEx), Thierry Fabing (AXA), Roland Scharrer (AXA), Mike DiPetrillo (VMWare), Nicolas Harle, and Andrew Walduck. Reid Hoffman (Greylock Partners/LinkedIn), Mike Maples (Floodgate Capital), Kevin Kelly (Author of The Inevitable), Eric Ries (Author of The Lean Startup), John Occhipinti (Wheelhouse Partners), Bruce Armstrong (Khosla Ventures), Hilary Armstrong, Dick Boyce (TPG Capital), Mark Kingdon, Suzanne and Elliott Felson, Joel Flory (VSCO), Matt Galligan (Picks & Shovels Co), Chris Hutchins (Grove), Kevin Rose, Nicolas Michaelson (Systemic Ventures), Clint Nelson (Startup Weekend), Frank Nouyrigat (Startup Weekend), Scott Nolan (Founders Fund), Naval Ravikant (Angel List), Karen Richardson, Satya Nadella, Greg Shaw, Michael and Xochi Birch (Bebo), and the researchers at the Institute for the Future. Dean Eric Meyer (University of Texas School of Information), Cassie Alvarado (University of Texas School of Information), Don Tapscott (Author of Blockchain Revolution), DCI and MIT Media Lab, and John Clippinger. Karen Roth, Bruno Guissani (TED), Anthony Cowell (KPMG), Jon and Sylvia Duncanson, Lynne Bairstow, and Danilo Sierra (Mimosa Agency), Keegan Caldwell (Caldwell LLP), David Belt (New Lab), Scott Cohen (New Lab), General David Petraeus (KKR), and Dr. Brandon Chicotsky.

– Tom and Bettina

Thanks to all my students who gave feedback on the content and to my wife, Susan, for her patience with yet another big project.

— 	Bill

Preface

This text is intended as a current survey of blockchain technology, helping guide readers through some of the context around this important innovation from an economic perspective, a business and industry perspective, as well as a technical perspective. It is rooted in our practical experience of working with the technology hands-on with clients, students, and industry leaders.

However, this text is by no means exhaustive, and improvements and changes are occurring every day in how blockchain technology evolves and is interpreted by society, including regulators. The majority of this text was drafted in late 2018. Throughout the text we have aimed to provide dates where possible, to ensure clarity about when different events occurred or were reviewed for this text. Topics such as "top 10 crypto-assets" are naturally time-conditional and should be treated as a snapshot rather than current market assessment. Between editions of this text, we encourage readers to look to additional sources as they continue their learning journeys.

As authors, we believe in having skin-in-the-game. We are each – individually and through various entities – owners of crypto-assets representing several networks. In writing this text, we strived to ensure that it remains (like us) blockchain-agnostic, and we do not intend this text to endorse any one network, startup, or project over others.

Following are a few important notes on structure and style for readers to get the most out of this book. Each chapter aims to be self-contained and modular. Feel free to skip around to the topics that interest you most, or that you are covering in a given course. While each chapter contains suggested "Questions for Further Discussion," we encourage you to check out our additional instruction material at http://animalventures.com/blockchain including powerpoints, testbanks, and more. If you'd like to engage with us on using this material for teaching purposes, please reach out on the contact form provided on the website.

Regarding style and terminology, we have used the following general rules:

- Text boxes are utilized throughout chapters to offer color commentary or additional information.

- Chapters 4, 5, and 6 each ends with a hands-on tutorial that furthers the technical content featured in that chapter. These are hopefully useful to readers getting started on applying concepts or for more visual/tactical learners.

- **Bolded terms** are key terms and are featured in the glossary section.

- All blockchain networks are capitalized while their tokens are lowercased (e.g. the Bitcoin network allows for the transfer of bitcoin), unless specifically against company design

- We prefer to use the abbreviation *Dapp* for decentralized applications, but DAapp and dApp can be found elsewhere in blockchain literature and are equally accurate.

Chapter 1 – Blockchain Fundamentals

Learning Objectives

- Understand a technical definition of blockchain, including its main traits
- Be able to describe blockchain technology as a part of the broader story of trade
- Explain blockchain technology to your clients, friends, and business colleagues
- Identify which aspects of blockchain technology seem most important and relevant to you
- Understand where blockchain is going, how it works, and how to start preparing for it
- Discuss some of the most important use cases and enterprise platforms

Let's Get Going...

Take yourself back to 1994. The Internet has arrived but is still referred to as an "information superhighway." Computers are mostly desktops, used primarily by scholars and scientists, and require floppy disks to store or move information. Business transactions are still performed largely on paper or via fax. Mosaic (also known as Netscape Navigator), the early commercial web browser created by Marc Andreesen, was just launched in 1993; in only a few decades the world began to build businesses, power government services, and much of our social lives via "the Web." It can be hard to remember what our economy looked like before the advent of companies such as Facebook, Google, and Amazon. A time before smartphones in our pockets —connected to distant parts of the world – powered much of our daily activity. But imagining the last few decades of transition is helpful, because today a new technology is undergoing that same journey: blockchain. Like the Web back in its mid-1990s infancy, today blockchain technology is trying to imagine its own future.

Development of the Internet required popular understanding of new terms and philosophies. Concepts like the "information superhighway" helped people begin to imagine the new global communications infrastructure we would all eventually grow accustomed to utilizing in our daily lives. Similarly, the recent introduction of blockchain technology is immersing people in new language and concepts. One major conceptual hurdle is distinguishing between a digital economy like we have today, based on using the Internet to send and receive messages online, and a digital economy built on an infrastructure where transactions are synchronized to form a consistent global database. The latter is referred to as a "decentralized economy," and the shift to it is sometimes called a move from an "Internet of information" to an "Internet of value." For this reason, blockchain is poised to radically transform how humans and machines engage in economic activity.

The aim of this book is to guide readers through the basics of blockchain technology. It is geared towards the complete newcomer to blockchain technology. Even for the most informed technologists, blockchain is a very difficult and often dense subject matter to fully internalize and understand. So it is very worthwhile to take some time try to appreciate both the opportunities and challenges of this new technology. The text is designed to help you unpack the ideas and better understand what the most important considerations will be in and around this new technology. It takes a comprehensive approach to this complicated subject, covering the economics, technology, and business of blockchain.

A Foundational Change in Trade?

Even though blockchain is a technological innovation that combines many disciplines – such as cryptography, distributed systems architecture, computer science, and economics – it also represents a very social innovation. If we look back over the course of human history, even back to our earliest agrarian days, people have always needed to gather in groups for basic survival. To facilitate this, we have had to learn how to work together to share information and resources such as food and clothing. In early economies, barter was one of the first ways to distribute goods and services, and it actually still accounts for about 30% of modern trade. Often, barter is based upon people's reputations in their respective communities and requires a certain amount of confidence in each other that neither will try and cheat. Trade in these days was largely based on informal rules and constraints, everything from individual reputations and agreements to cultural norms.

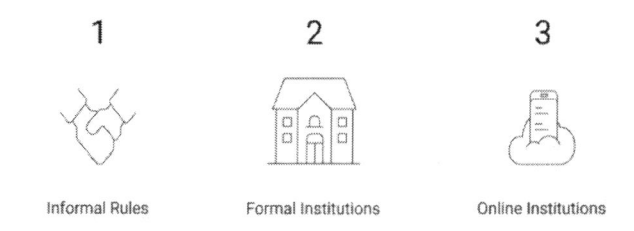

Figure 1-1: Animal Ventures diagram of agrarian to digital-era trade

A foundational change occurred in how people share goods and services with the advent of a standardized currency. Currency removed the necessity of trying to come up with different goods that represented an equivalent amount. Gold, silver, and bronze were good materials to use for standardized currency since they required a substantial amount of work to mine and mint. These metals were also easy to move and hard to counterfeit since they could be measured according to standard weight. Nonetheless, both barter and cash transactions still have significant deficiencies. Each party might have misrepresented their side of the deal (for example, if a sheep died on the way to its new owner, or a cow hide was not tanned properly) and they might have to resort to some kind of primitive arbitration to resolve their dispute. In terms of foundational changes, the introduction of currency represents a more formal institution that we developed in order to help lower uncertainty in our trade and expand our ability to transact at a greater scale.

As commercial transactions increased in frequency and complexity, they necessitated the invention of writing in order to maintain records and allow for accountability. The first historical examples of writing date back to Sumer about five thousand years ago.

Banking in ancient Sumer was developed enough, in fact, that the Code of Hammurabi (1754 BCE) even contained some rudimentary banking regulations. In order to log proof that individuals had paid their taxes to the central government, these transactions were recorded, and copies were kept in a central library or repository. In this sense, writing can be seen as an early example of information technology. Both writing and the introduction of standardized currency were foundational changes to how humans conducted trade. Even with these institutions in place, there could be low confidence in transactions. In order to trade, a person would need a certain level of trust that the person recording the transaction would not make a mistake or fraudulently enter a different transaction, and that the records of the transactions would not be destroyed somehow. Many instances occurred where the central authority abused its power to tax and ultimately ruined the local economy.

There is also evidence that early banks were created to store valuables. In ancient Sumer, temples would loan out seed grain to farmers and get repaid when the crops were grown and sold. The Greek city-states used temples as treasuries for gold and silver from which coins were minted and civic expenses paid. These early temple-banks were protected and trusted by citizens since they were run by the priesthood and connected to their shared religious belief system. Indeed, this system worked well even into the Middle

Ages when the Knights Templar made a fortune operating as the banking system for pilgrims making the arduous trek to the holy land in the Middle East. They functioned as middlemen that enabled travelers to access their money via a line of credit, instead of having to carry a fortune on their persons and risk robbery or worse. This simple "technology" enabled people to travel across borders and the Knights Templar accumulated great wealth by providing this service. With the introduction of banks and treasuries, we began to inculcate more formalized institutions for coordinating economic activity and lowering uncertainty in transactions at scale.

The next foundational change in how we did business was an improvement in how transactions were recorded. Italian bankers in the cities of Genoa and Florence began recording financial transactions using a system of **double-entry bookkeeping** dating back to 1340 CE. A Franciscan monk and colleague of Leonardo da Vinci, Luca Pacioli, became famous as the "father of accounting" after he published a mathematics text in 1494 CE, which codified double-entry accounting for the rest of the world. This technique was a huge step forward because it provided an error detection mechanism for accounts. By making sure that the debits on the left side equaled the credits on the right, this ensured transparency for all stakeholders and allowed them to quickly see an accurate picture of a firm's financial performance at any point in time. 500 years later double-entry bookkeeping is still widely employed and is often credited with enabling the expansion of commerce during the Industrial Revolution and beyond. Of course, errors can still occur when the wrong ledger accounts have been debited and credited, even though accounts technically "balance."

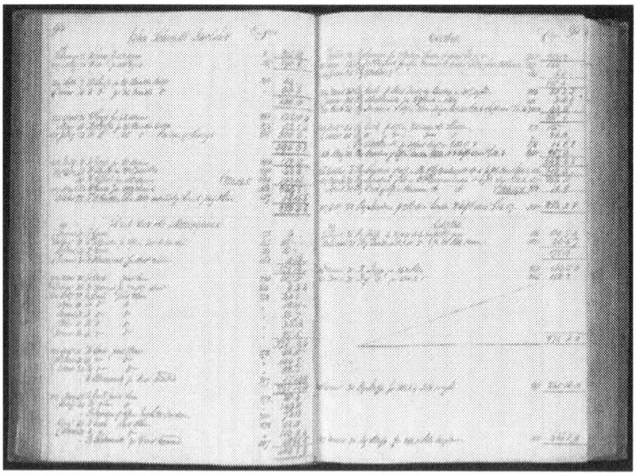

Figure 1-2: Example of double-entry ledger from J. and H. Hadden and Company Limited

If we fast-forward a bit, modern improvements in telecommunications and computing allowed banks to grow dramatically and spread their operations globally in the 20th Century. And web technology has further enabled a higher degree of "transparency" between buyers and sellers. Consumers can now search the Internet for information on products and services and reduce the need for trusted middlemen to manage a transaction. Instead, transactions largely began to take place through platform marketplaces like Amazon, eBay, and Alibaba. This leap in digital innovation has helped to lower the costs to the consumer in many different areas of business and has dramatically expanded global commerce today. The modern expansion in global business has also been significantly spurred by improvements in credit card technology. However, while opening up global transactions for consumers, credit cards are also highly vulnerable to fraud and identity theft, especially for online transactions. Though it's difficult to determine the exact cost of global credit card fraud, Nilsen estimates the 2016 cost of this fraud at $24.71 billion, and these costs are absorbed by banks through credit card processing fees.[1] The growth in hacking and identity theft is also well documented and represents the fastest growing crime in the United States. 16.1 million

---

[1] HSN Consultants, Inc., The Nilson Report, October 2017, Issue 1118, page 6.

https://nilsonreport.com/upload/content_promo/The_Nilson_Report_Issue_1118.pdf

consumers were victimized by identity theft in 2017, which led to another $16.8 billion in financial losses in the U.S. alone.[2] And this problem is growing as more and more of our transactions go digital. The number of middlemen involved in commercial transactions has decreased with digitization, but middlemen have by no means been eliminated in our transition to the Internet. For the moment, we still rely on institutions like banks to manage the risk of digital identities and payments.

This was not meant to be an exhaustive history of commerce, but rather an illustration of how trade has evolved over the years and an introduction to core concepts such as **uncertainty**, **trust**, **transparency**, **value**, **work**, **currency**, and **ledgers**. Understanding how past technological innovations and institutions have expanded and improved commerce will help us to better evaluate whether blockchain represents a similar foundational change for business today.

Blockchain Fundamentals

Defining Blockchain

If you google blockchain, you will quickly be presented with a confusing array of metaphors and definitions all of which attempt to "define" the term. What the best responses to this query agree on: a blockchain is a ***decentralized database that coordinates agreement on an append-only history of transactions across a peer-to-peer network***. This definition contains some very complex ideas that will require a fair amount of effort to unpack.

---

[2] "Facts + Statistics: Identity theft and cybercrime," Insurance Information Institute, accessed June 15, 2019, https://www.iii.org/fact-statistic/facts-statistics-identity-theft-and-cybercrime

Decentralized Database

A database is simply a collection of data or information. A phonebook, for example. A **decentralized database** is one where there is no single, centralized storage of data and no single authority or system administrator. Decentralized databases generally have multiple readers and multiple writers such as when multiple servers on a network provide data to clients. An additional form of information architecture is a **distributed database**, where all the nodes on the network contain information and they are equal and have equal rights. Blockchains are intermittently referred to as both decentralized and distributed, since they often have both qualities (independent nodes and full replication and rights). For the remainder of this text we will keep to the terminology of decentralization.

Google's search engine is an example of a very large, **centralized database**, since Google acts as the central administrator. Another example of a centralized database that everyone has experience with is a bank. We trust banks with our money, knowing that our funds will be accessible when we want them. We also trust that the banks will maintain an accurate record of their customers' accounts. Everything is centralized in the bank's database and it is the keeper of the "truth." Essentially, the bank acts as the administrator for the database that logs the details of its customer accounts. As proven by accounts of fraud such as the 2016 Wells Fargo banking scandal, where millions of checking and savings accounts were opened on behalf of clients without their consent, banks have at times misrepresented these details.

If a bank were to use a decentralized database, it would mean that all of the nodes on the network have a complete copy of all of the banking records. No one node on the network could exert control over all of the other nodes managing information in the database. No central authority would control the system as it would if the bank were the sole administrator. If we turn to a non-banking example, a centralized encyclopedia database is represented by the Encyclopedia Britannica or even the early digital encyclopedia known as Encarta. In both cases, the data was held and appended by one central authority figure – its publisher. Then Wikipedia came along and introduced a decentralized database architecture for encyclopedic information. There could now be multiple readers and writers to the system. So when we describe a blockchain as a decentralized database, the main point is that there is no single arbiter over the system or data.

History of Transactions

Let's tackle another piece of our initial definition, the fact that a blockchain coordinates agreement around a "**history of transactions**." A key feature of blockchain technology is that it is really a specialized kind of database, called a distributed ledger. A ledger is different from what most people think of as a database. Ledgers are designed to keep track of **transactions** as opposed to other data. It's one of the reasons people get confused about "what goes on the blockchain" because talking about storing information makes it sound like a database similar to your use of a USB drive that holds all your files. Instead, the data being coordinated or synced are the most current transactions and accounts; more like a snapshot of your "Finder" view on your computer's hard-disk.

Peer-to-Peer Network

Blockchain is one manifestation of **Distributed Ledger Technology** (DLT). All variations of DLTs share two core features: running on a **peer-to-peer (p2p) network** and using a **consensus protocol** among the peers (or nodes) in order to come to an agreement about the database, instead of relying on a centralized administrator to perform this function. This is why our definition describes blockchains as including a "**peer-to-peer network**." The database is held locally by all the peers that participate as a full node on the network. These nodes function as a community of verifiers for the database. In many ways, you can think of this peer-to-peer network as a group of independent computers that are acting as one. The middleman function that institutions like banks have performed to help us transact with greater certainty is performed collectively on blockchain networks instead, and secured as a shared history.

"Coordinates agreement" and "append-only"

We have covered the beginning and end of the definition of blockchains. But what is most unique about this technology is found in the middle part of our definition, that the technology enables storing a history of transactions that is "**agreed-upon and append-only**." To explain this concept we need to dig into how blockchains coordinate agreement. When participants run blockchain software, it contains protocols that describe how the participants come to consensus, or agreement, on the transaction history. The verification process that all the nodes use to come to consensus is important because it replaces the authority held by a central administrator in a traditional database. This functionality also means that blockchains are community-verified, which roughly translates to "we can all check it," as participants in the network.

An everyday example of this dynamic might be when a homeowner's association (HOA) comes to consensus on a proposal to employ a new trash service and assume associated fees. For blockchains, coming to consensus can be achieved in a number of ways, which we will explore further in later chapters. But essentially, a consensus mechanism allows many participants to maintain one truth together by using protocols, instead of each maintaining separate truths and trying to reconcile them. This is one of the *most difficult concepts* for newcomers to blockchain to grasp. The use of consensus mechanisms actually helps to avoid many of the common disputes related to commercial transactions such as missing payments.

And what, you ask, do we mean when we describe blockchain databases as "append-only"? This means that the transactions being recorded and held locally by each node (or computer) can only be added to, not deleted. Records can be appended to reflect changes and the current state of the network, but the database is, in effect, immutable or permanent. This system is akin to the stamps you find at the beginning of a library book: you can see who checked out a book previously and when, and this data accrues over time to describe the current custodian of a book without deleting the previous history of check-outs.

Which Kinds of Transactions?

To get the most benefit from understanding blockchain, it's very important to consider what we mean when we refer to "**transactions**." Our focus has been on economic transactions, including buying and selling goods and services, or less common activities such as returning a purchase or calling customer support. And transactions in our definition should encompass a broad set of activities, some of which are financial, but not all. It can encompass behavior as simple as liking something on Facebook or exchanging phone numbers among friends. What is essential is that, as a database of transactions, a blockchain needs to know the accounts involved and the transaction information itself.

A common transaction that is analogous to those that take place on blockchains is writing a check. When you write a check, you are essentially delineating the terms of a transaction or deal, "I agree to pay X dollars to Ms. K." You also sign the check with your personal signature, to authenticate it. The check features a bunch of numbers that represent your account with a bank, and in order to execute the transaction, the bank(s) involved use this information to transfer funds from one account to another. Once you have used up a given checkbook, you are left with all the carbon-copies of the transactions you made (with the details blacked out). This is similar to what happens on a blockchain. A transaction is described and signed.

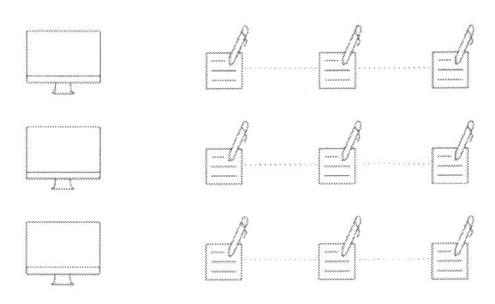

Figure 1-3: Visualizing the checkbook analogy of blockchain transactions

The public key (or account) is referenced alongside your signature in order to cue up the transaction. But instead of banks working in the background to move funds and compare accounts across their separate ledger databases, this transaction gets executed by one database – a set of blockchain software being run by a network of computers. The carbon copies are a similar concept to a "block" of data, which represents all the transactions made over a period of time, that are lumped together (in the case of blockchain, using cryptography). While writing a check is a financial transaction, it is interesting to note that the terms of a deal could just as easily be any data transaction that we agree upon. The check is a written document describing a contract of sorts, or an agreement on terms. This is why, along with describing blockchains as unlocking an **Internet of value**, some people also refer to blockchains as an "Internet of agreements" that describe and execute transactions across a network.

Elements of a Blockchain

Throughout this discussion of blockchain technology, there have been many mentions of different components of a blockchain application such as **nodes**, **community of verifiers**, and **peer-to-peer network**. At times this can be confusing because it is unclear who plays which role in a typical blockchain. Let's dive deeper into some of the roles and functions that go into blockchain architecture.

Nodes

Any computer connecting to a blockchain network is a node participating in the network. Now if you want to be a more active participant in the blockchain and become a member of the "community of verifiers," you have to become a **full node**. To become a full node, you must have a computer (hardware) connected to a blockchain network and you must download a complete copy of the blockchain (software) onto your computer. As of the writing of this text, the size of the Bitcoin blockchain download was over 200 GB and growing. It could take several days to download a complete copy of the Bitcoin blockchain. A full node includes the complete copy of the blockchain and also works to fully validate both the transactions and the blocks. To operate as a full node on a blockchain application certainly requires a high-powered computer setup, including lots of Remote Access

Memory (RAM), large quantities of free space on your hard drive, and a good broadband connection. One user can operate multiple nodes on a blockchain, and there also exist "partial nodes" that point to full nodes for their data.

In order for blockchain applications to grow, it is very important that there are a lot of nodes on the network. The more independent nodes there are, the more control of the network is decentralized and replicated, fostering greater blockchain security. Some people and organizations volunteer to use their spare computing resources to help run a blockchain by functioning as full nodes. These full nodes are what we referred to earlier as the "peer-to-peer network" because they have agreed to take on the role of verifying that transactions and blocks are accurate.

Blocks

Any full node participating on a blockchain can gain the right to package the transactions as they occur into a **block**. As a reference point, blocks on the Bitcoin blockchain are currently about 1 MB in size and take about ten minutes to create. Once a block is created, it is linked to the previous block using a special address as well as cryptography. Grouping these connected blocks into a chain is why the database is called a blockchain, and it represents a chronological history of all the events that occurred in the network. Looking at transactions in a blockchain you will mostly see numbers and letters, representing the alphanumeric address associated with the transaction, as well as the hash (or compression) of the previous blocks.

Public and Private Keys

The ability to use addresses when transacting on a blockchain allows the network to verify transactions without necessarily revealing lots of personal information. Instead, asymmetric cryptography built into the blockchain system allows individuals to use a private key to unlock their address while only sharing a public key with the others involved in the transaction. Essentially, transactions on a blockchain transfer value between public keys. It is this combination of **transparency** and **public-key identities** that ensures that users maintain their "trust" in the transactions logged on the blockchain system. You can think of these as analogous to a safety deposit box at a bank – to unlock the box, there is the bank's key (public) and the customer key (private) that only the customer has access to. Similarly, with an address on a blockchain network, you have a public portion of your account address and a private portion that allows you (and only you) to unlock access to it for making transactions. To perform transactions on a blockchain, you need to digitally sign your transactions with your private key.

Mining

As part of the "community of verifiers," a full node helps validate a blockchain database through a practice called **mining**. Miners are nodes that perform a certain amount of computational work – racing with each other to solve a mathematical puzzle – in order to help keep the network going. Every time a miner successfully solves the puzzle, they win the right to contribute the newest block of transactions to the blockchain. The winning miner sends out a message to the entire network, and receives newly minted tokens as an incentive in exchange for the service of helping maintain the database by mining.

Tokens or Coins

One of the ingenious things about blockchain technology is that it was developed using some elements of game theory and economics. In order to motivate people to participate in a blockchain as a full node and help secure the history of transactions in the database, these systems include an incentive structure that uses "**digital tokens**." A digital token is just a way of representing value on a blockchain application.

Consensus through Proof of Work

How do you create agreement and a shared reality across nodes in a blockchain system? It turns out there are a number of combinations that can produce consensus, and the designs differ depending on which blockchain is being used. Generally speaking, consensus is reached by combining consensus protocols (or mechanisms) with **Sybil control mechanisms**. To be clear, **Proof of Work** and **Proof of Stake** (covered in later chapters) are both Sybil control mechanisms, and cannot achieve consensus on their own. What they do achieve is a way to prevent Sybil attacks, which is when a single adversary controls multiple nodes on a network and has undue influence on that network.

For now, we can focus on describing the consensus created using Proof of Work, since this is the design used by Bitcoin and is the most longstanding. To make decisions, the Bitcoin blockchain uses Proof of Work coupled with the "heaviest/longest" chain selection rule to achieve consensus. Proof of Work alone allows you to fend off spam, but it does not lead to agreement without the incentive for miners to continue mining on the longest chain. In Proof of Work, what happens across the network is essentially a grand competition between all of the nodes running the blockchain software. They are competing to solve a large mathematical puzzle, and whichever node solves the puzzle first, wins the right to package the latest transaction data into a block, around which the remaining nodes form consensus (this competition is the act of mining).

The computational work to solve this puzzle costs energy, and therefore, part of its structure is to incentivize participants with a reward for performing the winning computation (for the Bitcoin network the reward is a fraction of a Bitcoin token). This is coded into the protocols of the blockchain in order to achieve several outcomes. One outcome is that Proof of Work creates some randomness for articulating which node wins the right to package the next block of transactions. Since the nodes are competing, this means that it will be hard to predict and therefore hard to coerce a winning participant to change parts of the block of transactions. If we looked at email as an analogy, Proof of Work can be used to add a hash to an email header proving that a certain amount of computational work was spent in order to send the email. A spammer is unlikely to do this work, since spamming relies on the ability to send a large number of messages at low cost. This system also means an email recipient can verify that an email isn't spam by using the hash.

Proof of Work uses a lot of energy, but it is also one of the most established means of generating consensus in public permissionless blockchains today, since it does not require trust across participants, just that they are engaged in the protocols that help bring about consensus. In short, Proof of Work is the anti-spamming feature of a blockchain, giving participants the ability to verify the effort of other participants.

Qualities of Blockchains

So far we have covered important underlying concepts and definitions for blockchain technology. Next, we'd like to break down the general features and qualities that makes this new infrastructure interesting and useful.

We will cover the following five key features:
- Security
- Resiliency
- Immutability
- Transparency
- Verifiability
- Permissibility

As outlined earlier in this chapter, each new block on a blockchain is cryptographically **secured** through hash functions, and when a new block is mined, the blockchain is immediately synchronized with the rest of the network. Due to the decentralized nature of a blockchain network, for someone to hack or tamper with a blockchain, a majority of the nodes would need to be compromised, which is called a "**51% attack**." But accomplishing this kind of network takeover requires a massive amount of computing power and cost. This means that the larger the network gets, the more difficult it is to alter any transactions stored on its blockchain, making the chance of fraudulent transactions on the blockchain very low.

The fact that all the nodes on the network contain exact copies of the entire blockchain also means that the system has been designed to be very **resilient**. If one node goes down or decides to quit, the other nodes will continue to perform all the functions necessary to keep the network going. The fact that blockchains are decentralized peer-to-peer networks also means that the computers behind the nodes may be located all over the world; making it highly unlikely that the system will go down due to power failures, geopolitical issues, weather, or other technical issues. This quality of system resilience is also sometimes referred to as "fault tolerance."

Another key quality of a blockchain is that it is designed to be append-only, or "**immutable**." This just means that once a block of transactions has been added to the chain it cannot be deleted or changed. If transactions could be easily deleted or changed after the fact, then this would be a source of disputes among the participants. It would be hard to keep a shared reality across all participants, and there would be very low certainty in the transactions logged. Blockchain technology was designed to allow only for reading and writing data onto the blockchain; new transactions can be linked or appended to the end of the blockchain but once they are accepted and verified by the community, no changes can be made to existing blocks. This means that the history of ownership for a particular asset recorded on the blockchain can be easily tracked. Think about an example in today's world where we need to track the records and ownership of an asset, and how that might differ if we used a reliable database structure to point to those records. For instance, if you have had to pay for title insurance when buying real estate, you likely experienced how costly the process of tracking and recording asset ownership can be.

Public permissionless blockchains (like the Bitcoin network) have proven to be a stable design and most of the issues with hacking have been limited to individual user accounts or exchanges, where tokens are held centrally. In 2010, shortly after the introduction of Bitcoin, some hackers exploited a bug in the Bitcoin program to generate 92 billion Bitcoin. Realizing the error, the system developers performed a major update to the software and essentially restarted it from its last pre-attack log. Since then, core developers have worked to iron out bugs and ensure no major attacks on the network as a whole have been perpetrated.

This story also reveals another important aspect of blockchain technology: **transparency**. All of the transactions stored in a blockchain are visible to all of its participants. This is true whether the transactions are huge or infinitesimally small payments. This ensures that everything which has been verified as true by the consensus of the participating nodes can be seen by everyone participating in the blockchain. The history of transactions is also easy to see because each transaction is "**time-stamped**." This time-stamping feature is part of the chronology of blocks and is crucial for allowing participants to accurately verify transactions. While the transparency of a blockchain to its participants is a feature, it can also be seen as a nuisance. Not all data needs to be visible to everyone so long as you can maintain **verifiability** of transactions. Therefore, people are working on different innovations and tweaks to blockchain structures that allow for levels of transparency or privacy to coexist with verifiability. This is true in particular for the personal data of the individuals involved in a given transaction. Depending on the sensitivity of a transaction it may make sense to use a blockchain for verifiability but make sure that data such as health records or identity are protected. One way to deal with who sees what on a blockchain, is to leverage **permissibility** as part of a blockchain design. Some blockchains are permissionless, while others allow for scoping of who participates, making them "permissioned." Both verifiability and permissibility are present in current iterations of blockchain, but these characteristics are also being achieved differently by developers.

Blockchain and Economics

Blockchain technology is intimately connected to the field of economics. This is true for two distinct reasons. First, blockchains create a shared reality that is used for many kinds of economic transactions: between individuals, firms, and even objects. Secondly, the incentives baked into blockchain architecture (e.g. earning fractional token rewards for mining) require analysis from an economic perspective to make sure the system is not gamed or threatened by externalities. **Game theory** – or deriving mathematical models for how rational actors will behave when one person's loss represents another's gain – is related to the incentive structures of blockchains as well. While we don't spend significant time covering crypto-economics and game theory, this section reviews blockchain's influence on ideas about value transfer between individuals and organizations.

Lowering Uncertainty in Trade

Blockchain technology has at times been characterized as a "distributed trust network" because of its reliance on many nodes instead of a central authority. From an economic standpoint, this kind of network can potentially replace some of the trusted third parties, or institutions, that have acted as trust brokers in our transactions to date. **Value** in economic terms is generally referred to as a measure of the benefit of a good or service and is usually measured in units of some currency. The basic idea of blockchain is that we can use technology to disintermediate the institutions to transfer value directly. In some ways, this looks more similar to our early agrarian transactions, where we could trade through barter in a more direct, one-to-one model. For example, instead of using a bank or marketplace platform as a brokering source of trust, we can use a network like the Bitcoin blockchain to directly transfer value between two accounts.

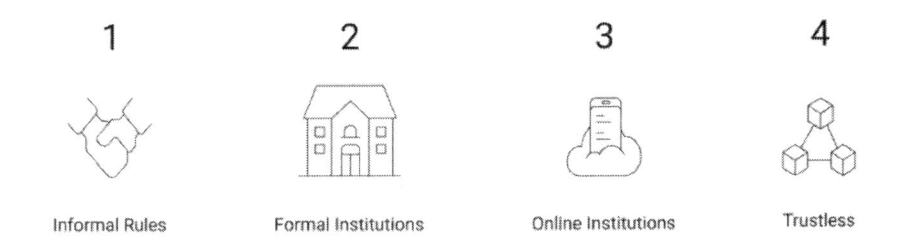

1	2	3	4
Informal Rules	Formal Institutions	Online Institutions	Trustless

Figure 1-4: Progression to one-to-one trade at scale using blockchain technology

If we follow this logic further, we could use blockchain technology to further reduce uncertainty about transactions by using it to encode business logic. Beyond just buying and selling something of value on a blockchain, the network could be used to share the terms of a contract between two parties on the blockchain and make sure that the contract is executed correctly.

As an analogy, this might be similar to when you have an escrow account set up by a mortgage company. Under the terms of the mortgage contract, an escrow account is set up to automatically disburse funds when taxes or insurance payments are due; usually every quarter. For a blockchain, the funds are locked up until the terms of that transaction are met and the payment is triggered through code. The mortgage process itself could be considered a use case for blockchain technology, and some companies are working on replacing the management of mortgages (and its inherent fees), with automated execution without error using the technology of blockchain.

Changing the Role of the Firm: A Nexus of Smart Contracts?

Beyond using blockchains as a tool for minimizing trust in transactions where we usually used an intermediary like a bank, we can also think about their use in performing traditional functions of a company. Some economists view a company or a firm as a collection of contracts. A contract is generally the terms of an agreement between parties that is legally enforceable. If you've ever looked at an org-chart for a company, this becomes fairly clear. A company can be thought of as a large organizational chart that indicates all of the roles, responsibilities, and agreements between members of the firm. This is an extension of the New Institutional Economics ideas espoused by Nobel prize-winning economist, Ronald Coase. If we could write out all of these rules on paper, then we could also write these rules and terms as computer-readable code.

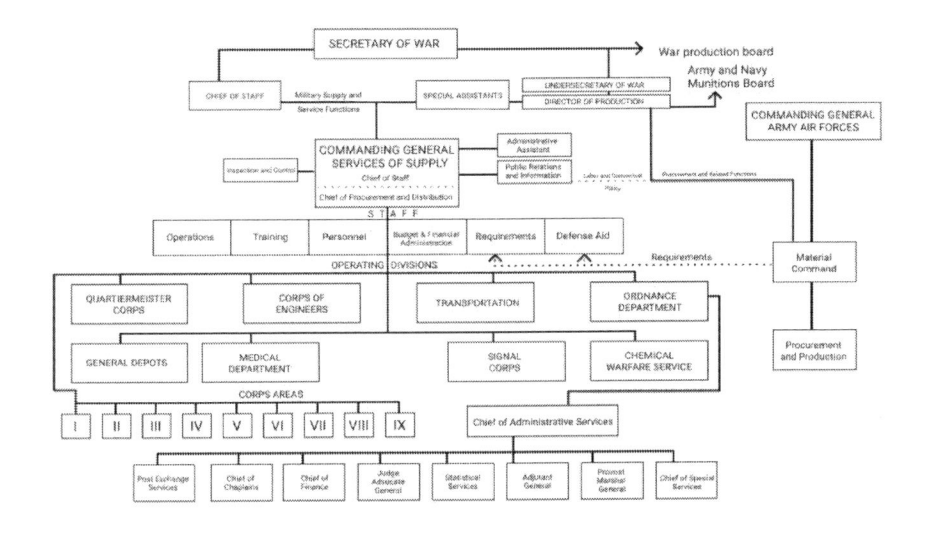

Figure 1-5: Example of a massive organizational chart; army service forces supply

We can use blockchain technology to encode these relationships and agreements and take the place of the firm to some extent. This is the essence of the **smart contract**. A smart contract is basically a small computer program that runs on a blockchain. It contains a series of "if-then" statements that execute automatically when certain conditions are met. We are not arguing that smart contracts are themselves legal contracts. Rather, if we think back to the checkbook example, there are means of writing the terms of simple deals. These are often called "self-executing" or "self-enforcing" contracts because we use the blockchain to execute the contracts automatically and accurately instead of blindly trusting the customer or paying lawyers to enforce them. If the Bitcoin network as a first application of blockchain helped lower our uncertainty for financial transactions, the extension of blockchain into securing smart contracts is a way to lower uncertainty by coding the rules of various transactions into autonomous, if-then or "**programmable transactions**," that a blockchain executes.

A simple example of a smart contract could be a bet between two people. Let's say that Ava and Barry root for two different football teams and that those two teams are playing each other tonight. Ava and Barry could write a contract that says they will each put up some units of a cryptocurrency like bitcoin, and when the system finds the sports results next via some application programming interface (API), the winner will automatically be paid the amount of the bet.

Decentralized Autonomous Organizations!

Take this idea one step further and imagine a collection of smart contracts that could be used to create a set of interlocking rules for a digital corporation. This is what is termed a **Decentralized Autonomous Organization** or "DAO." Sometimes DAOs are also interchangeably called DACs (Decentralized Autonomous Corporations). These digital-only entities are designed to run and maintain all their transactions and rules on a blockchain using smart contracts. Because of the structure of the blockchain, individuals participating in a DAC or DAO are essentially participating in automated businesses. Other than participating in a DAC or DAO through private key digital signatures, these structures can potentially take over many functions that would usually require a board, or other governing body. Some examples of attempts to create DAOs include DASH, and "The DAO." DASH is a cryptocurrency started in 2014 which attempts to operate as a self-governing DAO, funding itself by allocating 10% of mining fees associated with its cryptocurrency propagation to the DAO. As a second example, "The DAO" was crowd-funded in 2016 and built on the Ethereum platform. It was designed to be a traditional venture fund that accepted proposals for projects to be built on Ethereum and grow the ecosystem of innovation for the platform. Its main difference from a traditional fund was that its "code was law," and the smart contract code governing The DAO enabled owners of DAO-tokens to vote on submitted projects through the blockchain and then automatically appropriate funds to those winners. The DAO encountered a lot of controversy, and the U.S. Security and Exchange Commission (SEC) has determined that it may be in violation of securities law.

Considering our modern-day experience, Uber is a great example of how a smart contract could improve current digital services. Uber made a $50 billion business out of connecting drivers with riders in an easy to use mobile app. Uber helped lower uncertainty in transacting between strangers, opening up new kinds of transportation options. But would it be possible to do the same thing and lower our uncertainty – without using Uber as the middleman – by replacing the company's functionality using smart contracts? Uber adds value by creating a trusted marketplace for transporting riders from point A to B.

This involves setting standards of payment, processing transactions, providing feedback mechanisms on drivers and riders, marketing and using algorithms to optimize routes, time, and rates. If we could create a smart contract template that contains the necessary terms of agreement between riders and drivers, it might be possible to disintermediate Uber itself. This standard template could define how a rider and driver could transact business without knowing specific details about each other. And, it could be run on a permissioned blockchain with a vetting procedure (or necessary conditions) in place to establish some credentials for both riders and drivers. So the next Uber might be a company that creates all the templates for the smart contracts that would connect riders with drivers and possibly even autonomous vehicles, allowing these identities to engage in transactions autonomously. This whole discussion of DAOs and DACs doesn't mean to imply that organizations will all disappear or become indistinguishable, but just that they may evolve to include more self-executing functions for tasks that lend themselves to this kind of automation. It may also mean that the marketplaces we have grown accustomed to (that already rely heavily on automation through algorithms) may become more templated and decentralized themselves.

To recap, blockchain technology introduces a newer means of lowering uncertainty in our transactions. And since transactions are basic elements of economics, blockchains should push us to rethink some of the implications of automating business logic. What will it mean to lower our uncertainty in transactions even further or in new ways? They should even cause us to rethink some of the units of organization, like the firm, that we have relied on to broker trust and lower uncertainty and cost for centuries. Instead, implementing blockchain technology leads to new questions about how organizational technology will evolve to create both opportunities and challenges in scaling economic transactions for humans and machines.

Blockchain Technology

The Origins of Bitcoin and Blockchain

The idea of blockchain technology was first described in a groundbreaking paper by a mysterious character called **Satoshi Nakamoto** in October of 2008. This nine-page paper was entitled "Bitcoin: A Peer-to-Peer Electronic Cash System" and laid out the idea of a new peer-to-peer concept for digital cash. Various groups, from cypherpunks and crypto-anarchists to researchers and academics had been working on pieces of this puzzle for decades. For instance, David Chaum pioneered early work on **digital cash** with his 1988 product "DigiCash" and Adam Back gave the world Hashcash in 1997. Others, such as Turing-award-winner Leslie Lamport, who invented Paxos in 1989, contributed massive work on distributed computing concepts such as state replication under unreliable communication between nodes in a network ("faults"). Technical concepts explored throughout the 1980s and 1990s are leveraged by Bitcoin. These include cryptographic concepts such as **hash chains** that allow for a recorded chronology of events (think of how GitHub runs its chronological versioning) and **Merkle trees** for verifying consistency of large data sets. Much research emerged on Byzantine Fault Tolerance and other network attack scenarios. Proof of Work as a spam deterrent was introduced by Cynthia Dwork and Moni Naor in their research from 1992. But Nakamoto's paper pulled all of these ideas together, offering a complex and original proposal to solve a long-standing challenge: the "**double-spend problem**." The paper unleashed a decentralized database architecture where trust is diffused across a set of dynamically changing database maintainers, and incentivized with digital cash, and led to the development of Bitcoin as the first popular cryptocurrency.

But what is the **double-spend problem** and why were people looking to solve it? If you think about the Internet today, it is largely a structure for sending and receiving messages. Your email is a set of messages sent and received between your address and someone else's. If you send an email, you have no way of controlling that it is the only copy out there; that someone hasn't forwarded your email and continued to share it. Similarly, if you see an image on the Internet, it is easy enough to download and use it. While an Internet of information is a valuable communication infrastructure for sending and receiving messages, it is hard to control the content or create and enforce unique value for processes like commerce.

Now think about how we do commerce with cash. If you have a dollar in your wallet you know that it is unique because it has a serial number printed on it. You also have a certain degree of trust in the government that they are not just reprinting the same dollar. When you physically hand that dollar bill to someone else, they know that they have received the unique unit of value that used to be in your wallet. Essentially, they know that you cannot turn around and spend that same dollar on something else, because it is now in their possession and not yours. In the digital world, it is extremely easy to just copy and paste exact copies of things over and over. If you offered to give someone $100 for something you found on eBay, they can't be sure that you will transfer a unique digital equivalent of the $100 that you promised. In the real world this kind of promise would be similar to entering a candle store at the mall and promising that you had $100 in your pocket to buy candles, and while the cashier is ringing up your purchase, you walk into a clothing store and tell them the same thing. This is largely why we use credit cards and banks to guarantee that online transactions are legitimate today. And even the transactions run through those institutions face massive amounts of fraud and abuse. People will use a credit card to spend more than they actually have in their account. Credit card companies try to limit their losses by setting limits on how much each user is pre-approved to spend. Bitcoin solves the double-spend problem through the use of **time-stamps** and **cryptography**.

> **The Mysterious Satoshi Nakamoto**
>
> It is generally acknowledged that Satoshi Nakamoto is a pseudonym used by whoever invented Bitcoin. To date, it isn't publicly known whether Satoshi was a man, woman, group of people or a visitor from another planet, although Satoshi self-identified as "he/him." Since "Satoshi" ended his involvement in the Bitcoin project in 2010, much effort has gone into tracking down this person. At one time, Satoshi was very active in some of the alt-coin forums and people have gone so far as to analyze the times of his postings to see what time zone Satoshi was working from. Satoshi also left another clue in a note attached to the original (genesis) block which he first mined to kick off the whole Bitcoin blockchain. The note makes reference to a January 3, 2009 article in the London Times about a recent bailout of the banks.
>
> While Nakamoto's contributions through the publication of the Bitcoin whitepaper, early online forum engagement, and deployment of the Bitcoin implementation were pivotal to the creation of blockchains as we know them, the relevant concepts were in progress and early pioneers deserve due credit for laying much of the groundwork. One such character is Nick Szabo, who drafted early papers on topics like BitGold, and coined the term "smart contract."
>
> The list of people with the necessary knowledge to develop something like Bitcoin is fairly small and includes experts in cryptography, cyberpunks, etc. Potential candidates have been sought out by the press and confronted, but most of these individuals have denied being Satoshi. The handful of people who have claimed that they were Satoshi, such as an Australian named Craig Wright, have failed all basic tests that would help corroborate such a claim. Since Satoshi's Bitcoin wallet currently holds almost one million bitcoin (which have never been spent), the ultimate proof would be for a person to provide the private key needed to unlock billions of dollars-worth of bitcoin!

Types of Blockchains

If we think back to the early Internet era, we saw growth in the use of company "intranets" after the public Internet emerged – a way for private organizations and groups to transact on this new technology and learn without doing business out in the open. While the original blockchain applications were designed to be public, the technology is also being used as infrastructure that powers more private transactions and experiments. And within the broad categories of public and private blockchains, there are numerous subcategories and variants.

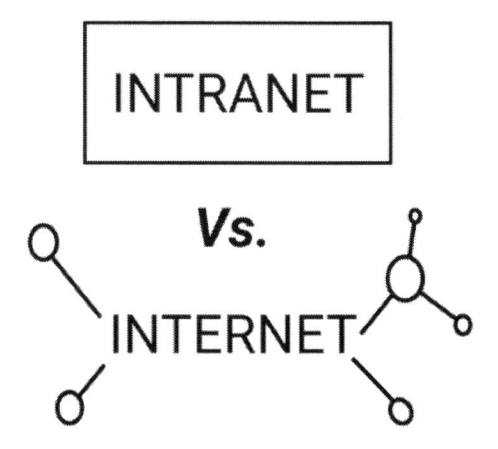

Figure 1-6: The rise of the Internet versus company intranets

Public blockchains, like the Bitcoin network, allow anyone to write onto the blockchain or read from the blockchain. Essentially, participation is completely open and voluntary. In this sense, a public blockchain is similar to Wikipedia, since anyone can post or edit a page on the site. And like Wikipedia, there is a community of verifiers who reach a consensus about the validity of the transaction. If a member of the blockchain repeatedly tries to submit invalid transactions, the blockchain community will start ignoring that particular node. Also, you can see a history of all the changes in ownership of an asset on the blockchain, just as you can see a record of all the edits to a particular article on Wikipedia.

As blockchain technology evolved, it became clear that its basic technology architecture could be modified to suit different situations. Businesses started to become especially interested in creating **private blockchains** so that they could enjoy the operational benefits of blockchain technology (e.g. a shared reality) without opening themselves and their data to the world. In a private blockchain the reading and writing capabilities are scoped to a set of participants, and not publicly accessible. Eventually, some of these private blockchains may migrate to becoming more public, but in the early stages, it makes sense to experiment in a more controlled sandbox rather than run the risk of transmitting or broadcasting sensitive data while still learning how to leverage this technology effectively. For that reason, applications in healthcare, financial services, digital identity, and supply chain management are being developed using private blockchain architectures. As an example, IBM has made this a big part of its corporate strategy and is actively promoting the Hyperledger framework for this kind of enterprise work.

Another qualifier often used for blockchains is whether they are permissionless or permissioned. This refers to how a blockchain's participants are scoped: **permissionless blockchains** allow for *anyone* to participate as a node by installing the software and copying the blockchain onto their computers, such as in the case of Bitcoin; **permissioned blockchains** are scoped to a much narrower set of trusted or semi-trusted participants. The enterprise blockchains described above as "private" are also considered "permissioned" blockchains, because the nodes are scoped to a known and approved set of participants; whether the members of a single organization, or diverse firms in a consortium, or any number of agreed upon participants. The main reason you would describe a blockchain with both qualifiers is the rare case of *public permissioned* blockchains, which represent a scenario where the database is visible to anyone (read and verify functions), but the *write* function is limited to a set of known participants. Generally speaking, when we describe a public blockchain (like Bitcoin or Ethereum) it is permissionless, and when we describe private blockchains (for enterprise) they are permissioned. Whether public, private, permissioned or permissionless, a blockchain still requires digital replicas of a ledger that are verified and shared among the participating nodes on a peer-to-peer network, however it is scoped.

Businesses, governments, and civil society groups today are increasingly experimenting with building consortia around blockchains as a shared technology resource. For example, many banks are investing heavily in permissioned DLTs/blockchains in order to cut their operational costs, believing this kind of database architecture will allow them to transact across a shared truth or reality rather than comparing their separate databases with one another regularly. In these cases, the ledger is distributed and verified by a preselected set of nodes. These nodes might represent different organizations such as industry or governmental groups. Some industries have very strong industry consortia and these have taken the lead in developing federated or consortia blockchain applications. For example, insurance companies must negotiate payments and coverage when two parties have an accident but have differing coverage from multiple, possibly overlapping insurance companies. To solve this complex problem, insurance companies have joined to create the BlockRisk framework. Using the consortia model means that they can more efficiently share claims information while not disclosing anything proprietary or giving control to a single company. Similar consortia are being formed and piloted in financial services (Digital Asset Holdings), banking (R3), and governance.

Evolving the Blockchain Stack

The technology stack of blockchains is not that dissimilar to the stack from our current digital age. We have a core infrastructure, middleware layer, and application layer. Our current Internet uses protocols such as TCP/IP, SMTP and HTTP to create a communication infrastructure on which we build APIs and libraries, on top of which we build applications like email, ride-sharing tools, and mobile apps. Blockchains have core infrastructure defined by the protocols of the Bitcoin network or Ethereum network, upon which clients create middleware and a means of talking to the core technology layer, and then smart contract-based applications are built on top.

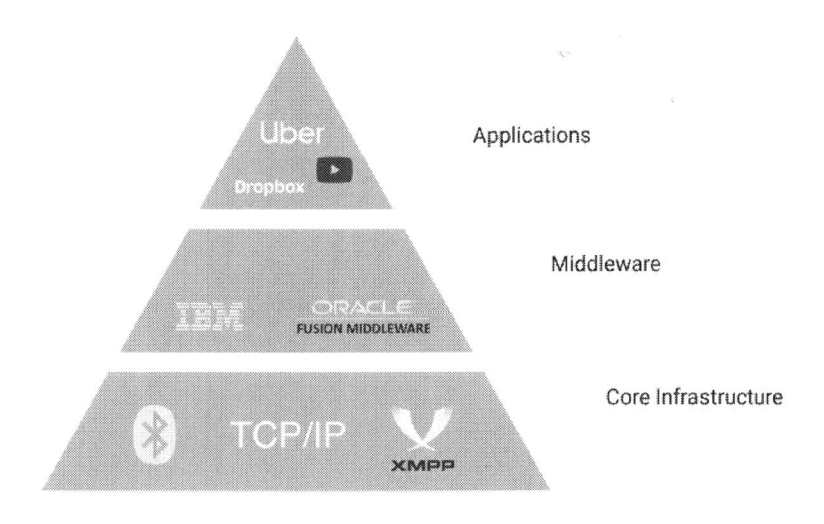

Figure 1-7: Simplified tech stack of the Internet

The applications that are developed using blockchain technology are called **Dapps**, which is short for "decentralized applications." Dapps are applications that are designed to run on peer-to-peer networks of computers as opposed to just running on a single computer. You can think of this as decentralized software. Not all Dapps were designed using blockchain technology. One of the first was a simple music sharing Dapp called Napster that was developed and used in the 1990s. Napster was a free program that allowed users to share their music libraries over a peer-to-peer network. It quickly grew to include 30 million active members. Like many blockchain Dapps, it operated in a gray area of legality and eventually had to shut down due to copyright issues. Bitcoin is an example of the first Dapp that was developed using blockchain technology. Many industries are creating their own blockchain frameworks and Dapp standards in order to take advantage of this new technology.

Hurdles for Blockchain Adoption

You may be wondering where all of this emergent technology is headed? How will blockchains begin to evolve and what are some key hurdles being worked on today to make them more usable and viable as technology solutions? The protocol layer of blockchain technology is already beginning to change. Bitcoin led to the development of Ethereum – a more generalized blockchain that uses smart contracts to program transactions – and now third-generation blockchains are emerging such as Dfinity. Entrepreneurs and technologists are tweaking the original model of Bitcoin to optimize for privacy (Zcash), transaction throughput and scalability (Litecoin), programmable transactions (Ethereum), chain interoperability (Cosmos, Plasma, Polkadot), and enterprise-oriented constructs (Corda, Hyperledger Fabric, etc). We will dig into many of these newer iterations in later chapters.

For now, we can focus on the main hurdles to broader adoption that are currently being worked on through diverse approaches. Here are some of the main challenges that need to be overcome:

1. Blockchains are not scalable. Scalability is part of a trilemma faced by all blockchains today, balancing against decentralization and security. One

scalability concern is that a blockchain cannot process more transactions than a single node can, meaning more nodes does not make a blockchain more efficient. Every node processes all transactions and stores all states of a blockchain. This is currently why Ethereum is limited to ~7-15 transactions per second, and Bitcoin to ~3-7 transactions per second, while centralized services like Visa operate a much greater volume of transactions. Scalability is a hurdle for mainstream blockchain usage for enterprises and consumers alike.[3] Additional solutions to scalability concerns are approaches for off-chain transactions that settle on-chain, and other second layer mechanisms.

2. <u>Blockchains pose privacy and confidentiality risks in transactions.</u> While public blockchains are exactly as they sound – visible to all, there are advances in cryptography that allow for the proof of information without revealing it, known as Zero-Knowledge Proofs. These proofs, and other uses, such as Secret Stores, are beginning to provide options for how to construct blockchains that allow for much greater privacy in transaction data. Additionally, privacy is a constraint that can be addressed by way of governance choices. Depending on the blockchain design being used (private/permissioned) you can delineate how and what information is visible to whom.

3. <u>Blockchains are not interoperable</u>. The idea that blockchains will move toward an interoperable "Internet of blockchains," relies on the ability for contracts and transactions to reference one another across different blockchain architectures. Today, this interoperability is being advanced through research on parent-child chain formations (e.g. Plasma) and inter-chain settlement layers (e.g. Polkadot). While there is no single solution, the need to make blockchains more interoperable will be important for enterprise usage in the long term.

---

[3] GitHub Ethereum Wiki, Sharding FAQs, updated August 22, 2018, https://github.com/ethereum/wiki/wiki/Sharding-FAQs

Basics of Blockchain

> **Welcome to the world of cyberpunks, cypherpunks, and crypto-anarchists!**
>
> From the earliest days of blockchain innovation, the emerging field has attracted a wide variety of adherents. Many of them were interested in how technology could be used as a vehicle for political and social change. Cyberpunks grew out of sci-fi literature and generally represent a dystopian future world where technology is everywhere and people have adapted to it. Movies like Blade Runner, Robocop, and 12 Monkeys are good examples of the cyberpunk genre in film. Cypherpunks combined the word "cipher" with "cyber" and are more focused on issues related to maintaining individual rights and privacy in a technology-soaked world. From the beginning they were drawn to blockchain because of how it uses cryptography to maintain anonymity and undercut central authorities. The typical cypherpunk is more technical-oriented and might focus on writing actual software to help maintain individual privacy.
>
> Julian Assange of Wikileaks fame is probably the most famous of the cypherpunks. Another group, known as crypto-anarchists, want to use cryptography to protect against government surveillance and censorship. They associated themselves with blockchain and cryptocurrency technology early in their development out of a desire to develop an alternative to the centralized banking and financial systems. They are similar to extreme libertarians. And by making it difficult to collect taxes and regulate commerce, they are hoping to reduce or even eliminate the power of the state over individuals.

Business of Blockchain

Both large and small businesses around the world are beginning to experiment with blockchain technology. New startups are emerging that offer blockchain-based products, and consultants are working at the intersection of the two to analyze and inform use cases. Just as with the rise in the dot-com business sector, and the growth in Big Data and cloud computing, we are seeing blockchain horizontally affect almost every industry. In this section, we cover some of the use cases of blockchain technology as well as enterprise-level approaches to date.

Use Cases

Once you start doing research on blockchain, you will inevitably encounter many different blockchain "use cases." Developing use cases is sometimes a formal text description of a new application created at the beginning of the development process. It describes how users will interact with the application but is free of technical jargon. The more comprehensive use cases may even include some flow charts and/or financial projections in order to better make the case for that particular application. In the context of blockchain applications, we typically think of a "use case" as a thumbnail description of the application and the problem it is attempting to solve. This section will outline some of the major categories of blockchain use cases.

Asset Tracking

Just about every business has some kind of asset that must be managed and tracked. These assets can be tangible things such as food, rare minerals, vehicles, and real estate. Or they can be intangible assets like patents, trademarks, copyrights, brands, and even the infamous "goodwill." Significant time and resources are spent trying to manage assets so that people can get the most return from them. In order to properly track an asset, we first must be sure that the asset's identity matches what we have recorded for it. In this sense, every business has some kind of supply chain – a set of relationships and transactions for an asset along its lifecycle. For a tangible asset, it may be important to accurately know its identity, provenance and certification. Consider Walmart, for example. They may receive a food alert related to an E-coli outbreak affecting romaine lettuce that they have sold in their stores. Once they learn about the outbreak, they need to quickly trace this lettuce back to the actual farm where it was grown and packed. The lettuce may have been contaminated somewhere along the supply chain, too, so they need to identify all the different touch-points for the lettuce in question. Likewise, they need to be able to identify who purchased the romaine lettuce that was contaminated. Walmart today has excellent systems for tracking items in its supply chains, which are some of the best in the world. However, the company can still take weeks to get down to the granularity of the actual farmer or purchaser of the lettuce. Supply chain recalls are costly and time-consuming. Blockchain technology offers major improvements in all the areas of asset tracking.

The concept of **asset tracking** on a blockchain is a very powerful thing for businesses. It means that we have the ability to quickly and efficiently track assets such as conflict-free diamonds, pharmaceuticals, artwork, land, and food all the way from the producer to the consumer. Tracking can include the provenance (or source of the items), attributes of the item itself for authentication, and any special certifications or transaction history that asset may acquire along the way. Tracking an asset through a blockchain means that the complete history of the asset can be made available to anyone we wish to share this with. Let's say that Tina is a songwriter and she records a new song. This song is an asset for Tina. She could notarize the intellectual property of her song using a blockchain, and it would be verified and assigned a unique identifier. Now, the provenance of this song will be stored forever on this immutable blockchain. Tina can accept money from Ralph in exchange for the right to download or access her song, and the transaction of this asset transfer becomes a part of the blockchain application. While this may sound like a gimmick, the musical artist Imogen Heap licensed her 2016 song Tiny Human using an Ethereum-based smart contract, managing royalties and her own profits directly without a record label in the middle of her transactions to fans or even Digital Service Providers (like Spotify or iTunes). While it was an early experiment, her project has turned into an ecosystem for creatives called Mycelia, and similar endeavors are underway at the Berklee Open Music Initiative. The ability to track assets in new ways leveraging blockchain can open up a huge improvement in our ability to prove ownership and the history of all kinds of valuable assets, both physical and digital. The old adage that "possession is nine-tenths of the law" will no longer be true, since we can have much greater confidence in our blockchain records to authenticate transactions.

Identity Management

Identity management use cases are also very powerful and somewhat controversial. In the blockchain world we can think about "identity" in terms of the identity of an individual and also the identity of an object. Think about all the times each day that your identity is checked. Maybe you are purchasing something online or getting gas. It could be that you are going through security at your local airport. You may just be logging into your email server to check your email. These are all cases where your personal identity may be checked. You can even quickly sign into many of your online applications using your email account or the technology behind something like Facebook Connect. The problem with some of the identity verification tools is that we still cannot be sure that someone else isn't just using your Facebook information or email account to access other accounts. Facebook only asks a few questions from you when you set up your account, rather than verifying that you are indeed who you claim to be. But if we imagine that a governing body has certified your identity on an identity blockchain application, then there would no longer be any question about you being who you say you are. You wouldn't have to prove your identity over and over again.

The real power of identity management on a blockchain is that other blockchain applications can leverage (or reference) the current state of your identity to create whole new applications. The need for a verifiable identity online is related to another similar concept in business called **Know Your Customer** (KYC). There are times such as tracking donations, when the government actually requires that organizations keep records of the identities of people for tax purposes and to flag potential money laundering and terrorism-financing. Unfortunately, every company that engages with you financially needs to track this kind of transaction information itself to comply with the laws around KYC, meaning you as a consumer must enter it and share it repeatedly. Blockchain could simplify this tremendously. The problem with using Facebook Connect to store your identity is that one company would control all of your personal information, and use this as a big part of their business model. By managing your personal identity on a blockchain via smart contracts, you can decide how much information you want to share with companies or other people. This is an area of blockchain innovation known as **"self-sovereign identity"** and refers the goal that attributes about you are certified (written) and stored once, but referenced (read) as many times as needed without necessarily sharing any such information publicly. On our Internet today we try to use cookies to track your online behavior as well as IP addresses, but there is no verifiable means for identifying people securely that is digitally portable. Projects like uPort and ERC-725, Civic and Sovrin are working on how to create universal identity protocols for blockchains.

Internet of Things (IoT) Integration

Another area for blockchain use cases describes how machines can be connected via the Internet. The **Internet of Things (IoT)** is how everyday objects become "smart" objects by sharing and consuming data using the Internet. This is another fertile field for blockchain applications. Wearable computing, smart homes, and autonomous vehicles are all booming examples of how connectivity and intelligence are now being built into all kinds of new "smart" objects. The key thing to realize here is that as blockchain technology evolves, smart objects like those mentioned here will eventually be identified on a blockchain and will have their own **wallets** (accounts) and smart contracts. This will enable them to transact with other smart objects based on rules and protocols – the automated business logic that smart contracts can describe; they can potentially even negotiate deals and pay for them. Imagine that you have solar panels on your roof. These particular panels are "smart" and also blockchain-enabled. Your solar power system could contract with the power system of another house or with a decentralized power exchange to sell any extra power that your panels generated. These kinds of energy economies are already being prototyped, for example by LO3 in Brooklyn, New York. Blockchain technology has a lot of potential to connect smart objects in many other industries such as medical devices, agriculture, and manufacturing. Moreover, the mesh and edge networks being built to connect these devices are potentially more reliable than the current broker-based network paradigm that relies on a centralized cloud server.

Decentralized Autonomous Supply Chains

If you continue further with the notion of smart objects that have wallets and smart contracts which they can use to make purchase decisions, it is not much of a leap to consider the possibility of **decentralized autonomous supply chains**. To some extent, the use cases that were discussed up to this point have something to do with a supply chain. This is because a supply chain, by design, connects suppliers with consumers. The vendors and suppliers are designing, making, and delivering the assets that ultimately reach a consumer. Supply chains involve many different machines, entities, and relationships that need to communicate back and forth in a safe and verifiable manner.

Implementing smart objects and smart contracts across a supply chain can lead to a more frictionless and ultimately automated supply chain, where the rules and decisions can be codified. Currently, many companies are experimenting with leveraging blockchain technology throughout supply chain operations, including retailers such as Walmart for track and trace, and shipping giant Maersk for container capacity and freight transactions. A future of "autonomous" supply chains, that almost run themselves is one of the areas of business and everyday life where blockchain can have the most impact. As we have already discussed, blockchain is a good fit for supply chain because it can be used to verify the provenance and identity of an asset, log and execute transactions over time, and ultimately improve both supply chain efficiency and responsiveness.

Enterprise Blockchain Platforms

Now that we have reviewed the basics of blockchain technology, we can start examining some of the fast-moving next-generation platforms that take advantage of blockchain in different ways. A **blockchain platform** is a group of technologies that incorporate tools such as templates and APIs that make it easier to develop and launch blockchain applications. Orb Weaver is one such platform, initiated at Animal Ventures, which gives developers a head-start to launch a blockchain network and build a blockchain application with all the necessary tools embedded in it. As an open-source project, it allows developers to choose which blockchain network to utilize (e.g. Ethereum, Hyperledger, etc.) and spin up nodes quickly and easily. You will get to use Orb Weaver hands-on in later chapters.[4]

Many companies and researchers are improving the core of blockchain by modifying how digital tokens are used, what kinds of consensus mechanisms are implemented, and the functions of different roles in a network. This section gives a brief description of some of the leading platforms that are being used to develop a new generation of blockchain applications. Of course, this list treats Bitcoin as a Blockchain 1.0 platform, and focuses

---

[4] You can access Orb Weaver at https://animalventures.com/

further on the enterprise-based platforms that have since followed. As can be seen from Figure 1-9, some of these platforms are designed to be cross-industry platforms while others are focused on specific functions like financial services. Due to the speedy growth in the number and types of blockchain platforms and their continued evolution, it is becoming increasingly important to address how to link up various blockchain applications for inter-chain transactions. For this reason, in November 2017, the Blockchain Interoperability Alliance was created to explore and research solutions for blockchain interoperability.

Category	Ethereum	Hyperledger Fabric	R3 Corda	Ripple	Quorum
Industry-focus	Cross-industry	Cross-industry	Financial Services	Financial Services	Cross-Industry
Governing Body	Ethereum Foundation / Clients	Linux Foundation	R3 Consortium	Ripple Labs	JP Morgan Chase / Ethereum
Ledger Type	Permissionless	Permissioned	Permissioned	Permissioned	Permissioned
Crypto-asset	Ether (ETH)	None	None	Ripple (XRP)	None / JPM Coin
Consensus Algorithm	Proof of Work (PoW)	Pluggable Framework	Pluggable Framework	XRP Ledger Consensus Protocol (Low-latency Byzantine agreement protocol)	Pluggable (Raft-based, Istanbul BFT, or Clique PoA)
Smart Contract Functionality	Yes	Yes	Yes	No	Yes

Figure 1-8: Features of top blockchain platforms for enterprise

Ethereum

After the initial rise of Bitcoin, **Ethereum** emerged as the leading candidate for Blockchain 2.0. At the ripe old age of 19, Vitalik Buterin, after studying Bitcoin, proposed the idea of Ethereum in a 2013 whitepaper. The core idea was that a distributed ledger could be used not just to store and validate transaction records, but also contracts or instructions and the scripts required to execute the instructions. As a more generalized blockchain, the network Vitalik proposed would use smart contracts to create programmable transactions that represent more than only financial transactions. The Ethereum network was coded and its Frontier implementation was launched in July of 2015 with contributions from the Ethereum Foundation based in

Switzerland. Ethereum is a permissionless and public blockchain where miners obtain "ether" as the digital token for validating transactions and creating new blocks. It is one of the most mature blockchain platforms and has seen widespread adoption among large corporations, academics and vendors. Ether does function as a cryptocurrency and can be traded on altcoin exchanges, but some new private blockchains have started using forks of the Ethereum protocol mainly for its smart contract features.

Corda

Corda was launched in 2015 by R3, a consortium of large corporations in the financial services industry. It was designed to be an open-source permissioned blockchain platform that businesses can use to limit the visibility of participant data. Sharing of data is done through contracts established between the participants, but the entire blockchain is not transparent to the whole network. Corda does not use any digital tokens meaning it does not have a native cryptocurrency, though it does support smart contracts. Even though it was originally designed for the banking industry, other industries such as insurance, healthcare and supply chain/logistics that have strong industry consortia have also been using the Corda platform.

Hyperledger Fabric

Hyperledger is a cross-industry blockchain platform launched in 2016 by 30 founding corporate members. It is promoted as an open-source umbrella for frameworks, code, and support for various business blockchains, and is hosted by the Linux Foundation. Hyperledger Fabric is promoted by IBM as an enterprise blockchain solution that contains more modular blockchain components. New blockchain solutions could be created that allow for easy variations in the consensus algorithms and membership parameters. IBM has aggressively pushed into this area as a key strategic initiative.

Ripple

Since its founding in 2012, **Ripple** has been focused on blockchain infrastructure for the financial services industry. It has become popular with banks because it is designed to make global financial transactions nearly free. Ripple uses a cryptocurrency called "Ripple" or "XRP" and is touted as being much faster and more scalable than Bitcoin or Ethereum. It has become very popular for global currency exchange where XRP functions as a bridge currency between two currencies that may be lightly traded. Since there are no chargebacks, XRP claims to minimize liquidity costs of international exchanges and is popular for cross-border payments. Many banks and financial institutions are experimenting with either RippleNet or XRP.

Quorum

Quorum is an open-source, cross-industry platform built on the Ethereum blockchain in a collaborative effort between JP Morgan and the Ethereum Foundation. It is a permissioned blockchain that does not incorporate any cryptocurrencies. It does not use the Proof of Work Sybil control mechanism of Ethereum, but instead uses a voting algorithm, and can process smart contracts much more quickly than Ethereum.

Ethical and Other Issues with Blockchain

This chapter has outlined many areas where blockchain technology can have a substantial impact on how people live today. However, it would be incomplete if we were to simply ignore some of the potential issues around privacy and ethics that this technology generates.

What does it mean to have a global database (or computer) without a central authority that anyone can leverage to execute transactions? The fact that there is no central authority storing or maintaining the ledger and that control is distributed throughout the blockchain is very threatening to some people and organizations. It also generates questions about when and how blockchains interact with legal systems, regarding everything from jurisdiction to privacy. Many people wonder what might happen if we change the foundations of how our societies work to include blockchain technology and then some unforeseen bug arises? Similarly, when such nascent systems get attacked, as new technologies often are, questions will arise about who should be held responsible (if at all) for loss of funds or errors in code. Standards will need to be developed that address best practices, formalize verification and how to deal with bugs, as well as provide safe harbors for innovation. These are important questions and topics that have largely gone unanswered to date.

Additionally, it is important to address user issues surrounding the establishment of "identity" applications in blockchain and transacting using the technology. Populations with little access to technology or unsophisticated users could be vulnerable to abuse and end up making sensitive data unwittingly public (and permanent) or losing funds. As this technology's use cases blossom, it is important to keep citizens informed and cautious about how to engage safely. Blockchain is certainly very new and we are only now starting to realize its social, political, and economic implications. Its potential impact is evolving rapidly.

Finally, while crime is not a topic of focus in this book, it is important to note that there are ethical concerns around the use of cryptocurrencies to finance what are being called "assassination" or bounty markets. In 2013, one self-proclaimed crypto-anarchist created the first prediction or assassination market that basically took bets on when famous people like former President

Barack Obama or former Chairman of the U.S. Federal Reserve, Ben Bernanke, would die. The fear is that such predictive markets will incentivize assassinations or other adverse outcomes. Because the blockchain can allow pseudonymous transactions (where your account is known but not necessarily your identity), an assassin could collect the bounty without revealing their identity. This concept was actually popularized in a 1994 book by cypherpunk, Tim May, called *The Cyphernomicon*. So while blockchains can trace transactions more transparently, they can also potentially work to shield those involved in unethical activities.

Chapter Summary

This chapter has introduced the prime concepts behind the exciting new world of blockchain. Because it is a unique combination of research in various fields such as cryptography, game theory, consensus, and distributed network technology, it can seem very confusing at first. The concept of distributed ledger technology (DLT) with no centralized authority may even require a certain leap of faith. This is why it is worthwhile to reconsider such basic notions as transactions, value, and trust, in order to understand why blockchain represents such a foundational change to how we work and live today. Just like in the early 1990s with the growth of the Internet, we are at the beginning of a major shift in how technology can be used to support economic and social activity, while also maintaining trust in society. As a technology, blockchain is continuing to evolve, and even though it is not clear exactly where it is going, it has already led to experiments and changes in enterprises around the globe.

Key Terms

Double-entry bookkeeping
Decentralized database
Distributed database
Centralized database
History of transactions
Transaction
Distributed Ledger Technology (DLT)
Peer-to-peer network
Agreed-upon and append-only
Internet of value
Node
Community of verifiers
Full node
Block
Transparency
Public-key identity
Mining
Digital token
Sybil control mechanisms
Proof of Work
Proof of Stake
Secured
51% attack
Resilient
Immutable
Time-stamp
Verifiability
Permissibility
Game theory

Value
Smart contract
Programmable transactions
Decentralized Autonomous Organization
Satoshi Nakamoto
Digital cash
Hash chain
Merkle tree
Double-spend problem
Cryptography
Public blockchain
Private blockchain
Permissionless blockchain
Permissioned blockchain
Dapp
Cyberpunk
Cypherpunk
Crypto-anarchist
Asset tracking
Know Your Customer (KYC)
Self-sovereign identity
Internet of Things (IoT)
Wallet
Decentralized autonomous supply chain
Ethereum
Corda
Hyperledger
Ripple
Quorum

Questions for Further Discussion

1. What is a Dapp? How is it different from a "normal" app? Go to https://www.stateofthedapps.com/ and select one of the Dapps and write a short description of its purpose.

2. What was Napster? What can blockchain Dapp developers learn from its story?

3. Do you think barter transactions could be supported by blockchain? Go to https://www.bartercoin.info/ to research this issue.

4. Should credit card companies be concerned about the potential impact of blockchain applications on their business model?

5. What are the differences between public/private and permissioned/permissionless blockchains? Give an example of each.

6. Describe something you do repeatedly in a typical day or week that could potentially be automated using smart contracts and what the benefits might be.

7. Go to blockchain.info and look up the genesis block created by Satoshi Nakamoto. What is the actual note that he inserted?

8. Are there any ethical or privacy-related issues that concern you about blockchain? Explain.

9. Think of a business that is required to verify the identity of a customer. Could it use a blockchain identity management application to improve its processes? Explain.

10. What is meant by "smart" objects? Give an example of how blockchain technology could be used to connect them.

Chapter 2 – The Technology Behind Blockchain

Learning Objectives
- Gain a deeper understanding of how blockchain technology works
- Learn about the basic components of the blockchain technology stack
- Review how a transaction works on a blockchain from start to finish
- Examine how blockchain wallets work
- Understand how the SHA-256 cryptographic hash algorithm works
- Look at how mining works and the different options for mining digital tokens
- Discuss how blockchain itself can be used to improve the overall IT infrastructure

Blockchain in Action – Are You Ready for a Blockchain Phone?

Just when you thought there might be no more cool things to be done with blockchain, another project emerges. Apparently, HTC, the Taiwanese consumer electronics company is working on a new "blockchain phone." They are calling the phone "Exodus," and the device will fully embrace the security and cryptocurrency features of blockchain technology. Exodus will have a universal wallet and support bitcoin and ether transactions, among other cryptocurrencies. Eventually it is supposed to have its own native "Exodus" cryptocurrency that phone users can use to trade among themselves. As a concept, this is not far from the innovative practice of airtime swapping common in more rural parts of Africa, where obtaining phone minutes is challenging, and the minutes are bought and traded between peers. With Exodus, we will see a product that combines the realm of hardware with blockchain's software capabilities. Can you imagine using a blockchain phone yourself now or in the future?

Review of the Blockchain Technology Stack

In order to get a better understanding of how blockchain works, it is necessary to do a deeper dive into the technology involved in a blockchain network. Similar to an onion, we can think of blockchains (and most technology, really) as being built in layers, all the way down to a central core infrastructure. Combined, these layers drive the overall functionality of a blockchain and the applications that use this technology.

In many ways, the technology stack that we are familiar with for our Internet can help us understand what is being built into blockchain technology. While this is very simplified, our Internet has three major layers:

• Core infrastructure layer: This layer consists of general protocols like TCP/IP (Transmission Control Protocol / Internet Protocol) that helps establish the communication between computers and the network architecture.

• Middleware layer: Middleware refers to a set of tools, dev-tech, and services that make application development faster and easier. They function as a hidden translation layer between an operating system and the applications on top. Content Management Systems (CMS), query languages, web servers, and application servers were developed as early middleware for our Internet in order to enable publishing and managing text and imagery online (e.g. Websites). Other middleware examples are database access services, web-middleware, messaging middleware, or transaction-processing monitors.

• Application layer: Built on top of core infrastructure and middleware live applications. These are the tools and products you are likely used to using such as Gmail or Uber, etc.

Blockchain has a similar stack, though these are constructed somewhat differently and result in alternative monetization mechanisms than our current Internet allows. Figure 2-1 shows a summary of the many different layers that will help ground your understanding of the basics of how blockchain technology actually works.

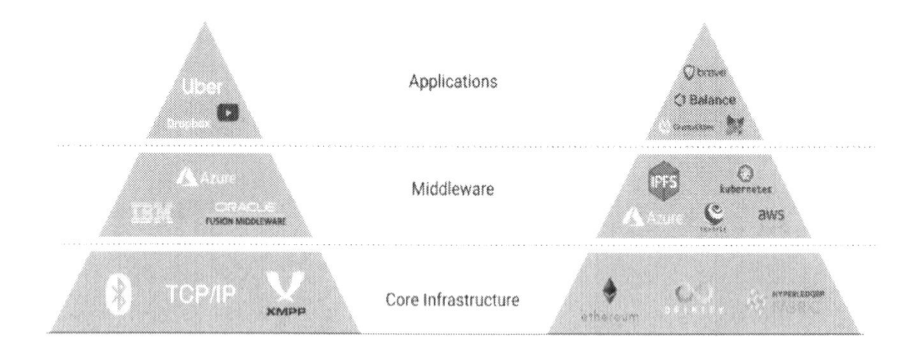

Figure 2-1: Comparing the Internet and blockchain technology stacks

It is useful to start from the bottom of Figure 2-1 and work our way up to the top. The bottom layer, or core infrastructure of a blockchain, is made up of a complex piece of software that is typically programmed in JavaScript, C ++, Python, or Go. It is a mashup of different functions, called **protocols**, which define behaviors for communication and transaction on the network. This includes software that allows for the creation and listing of **nodes** on the network, and their ability to communicate via a peer-to-peer network protocol. Since each node functions as both a client and a server, this means that each node must have the ability to store and retrieve files. A **server** is a connection point for handling client requests such as getting data, while a **client** is software that allows a user to connect to a server and make a request for some kind of service, like retrieving a file. Being able to both store and retrieve files is crucial since core blockchain protocols rely on nodes being able to store a complete copy of the entire blockchain. The software is not an operating system but makes use of GNU (popular free software operating system) capabilities and TCP/IP Internet protocols to allow different types of devices running different operating systems to communicate across the network. Also built into the software are rules for creating new blocks using **consensus** (i.e. Proof of Work and longest chain rule) and rules for how the blocks will be secured via encryption.

Term	Definition	Example
Blockchain Network	A global network of computers using blockchain technology to jointly manage a database of transactions. Similar to simply using "blockchain".	Bitcoin, Ethereum, etc.
Blockchain Protocol	Blockchain protocols are the rules built into a blockchain that determine how it will operate. Some ICOs are built using the protocols from existing blockchain networks like Ethereum.	Consensus protocol, communication protocol, voting protocol, etc.
Dapp	Short for "decentralized application." These are applications that are designed to run on peer-to-peer networks (like blockchain). Dapps are made up of smart contracts.	File sharing, Ethereum voting, etc.
Blockchain / Framework	A collection of blockchain tools and protocols that are customizable and extensible. Usually used to spin up permissioned blockchain applications quickly.	Ethereum, Hyperledger, Corda, OpenZeppelin, etc.

Figure 2-2: Table of blockchain terminology

The most established blockchains are permissionless networks, which means that anyone can participate and install the blockchain software from the open-source community. This is often done from open-source software repositories such as http://sourceforge.net or http://bitcoin.org. By installing the software and downloading the blockchain, you are not necessarily running a "full node" on the blockchain and your node is not yet monetizable (see Figure 2-4). Running a node on a blockchain only becomes monetizable when the node agrees to participate in the contest to actively maintain the security of the blockchain by joining the **"community of verifiers."** In the world of the Ethereum blockchain and its smart contracts, this means that full nodes additionally store and run individual smart contracts. Depending on the way the core blockchain protocols are configured, a full node might be considered to be a "**miner**" and would be rewarded with the native digital token (bitcoin, ether, etc.) for winning the competition to create a block and for verifying the transactions that were collected into the block. Both the smart contract layer as well as the storage and content layer describe platforms for developing blockchain-based applications.

Layer 5: Dapps	Swarm	Storj	Cloud computing	Mesh networking	OpenBazaar	DAOs/DACs
Layer 4: Browsers	Mist	Maelstrom	OmniWallet			
Layer 3: Interop	Exchange	Atomic transactions	Cross-chain message passing			
Layer 2a: Blockchain Services	Timestamping		Smart contract		Layer 2a: Blockchain Services	Reputation / WoT
	Name registry		Decentralized oracle			Messaging
						DHT / file system
Layer 1: Economic	Independent token		Parent's consensus mechanism token		Non-tradeable status	
	Sidechain of external token		Stablecoin + volcoin (exogenous / endogenous)			
Layer 0: Consensus	BTC meta-protocol		Independent chain (PoW / PoS / DPoS)		Data-availability Schelling-vote	
	BTC merge-mine		ETH Contract		Subjective consensus	

Figure 2-3: The many layers of blockchain

Monetizing the Blockchain

Monetizing the Core Infrastructure

Digital tokens are a key component of blockchain technology. In order to motivate people to participate in a blockchain as a full node and help secure the history of transactions, blockchains include tokens as part of an incentive structure. A digital token simply represents value on a blockchain network. Much excitement about blockchain has recently centered on the mining of popular digital tokens such as bitcoin and ether as well as trading these tokens on cryptocurrency exchanges.

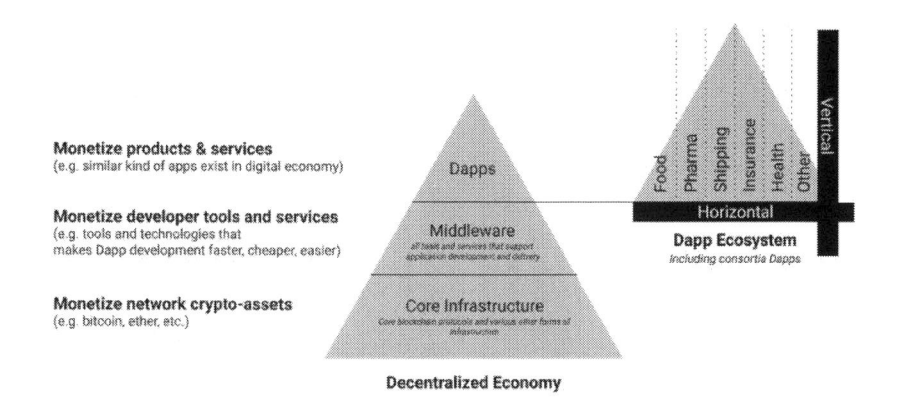

Figure 2-4: Value creation across the blockchain technology stack

The idea of a token is not particularly novel. The tokens used at entertainment establishments like Chuck E. Cheese's, Dave & Buster's, or other arcades, allow kids to play games and move around a facility without having to make new payments at each transaction or interaction with a game. We are also familiar with tokens in the form of loyalty, where we earn miles with airlines, and can use those miles on functions like flights but also trade or sell them at times. In Boston before the T-subway system was modernized, travelers were issued minted "T" coins as the entrance token for using the subway. All of these examples of tokens represent different kinds of "value." Similarly, tokens for blockchain networks come in many shapes and sizes, and people are experimenting with how to codify and incentivize participants in blockchains through token-based economic frameworks.

Bitcoin and ether can be considered examples of "**intrinsic**" or "**native**" digital tokens since each is built into its network. These tokens only exist as entries in a blockchain ledger and must be reached with a user's private key in order to receive any value for them. There are many other types digital tokens and the number grows every day. One example: so-called "**stablecoins**" that are pegged to a fiat currency (like a USD or Euro). Some of the most popular stablecoins today are USD Coin (USDC), Dai (DAI) and Tether (USDT) which are all slightly different in their conception.

The ability to create value at the network core infrastructure through tokens is

Basics of Blockchain

one of the reasons many groups have launched new blockchains with their own digital tokens. The main monetization opportunity at the network core infrastructure layer is tied to the idea that greater usage of a given blockchain (e.g. more transaction volume, more middleware and applications, etc.) will drive greater value of its token underlying token due to network effects.

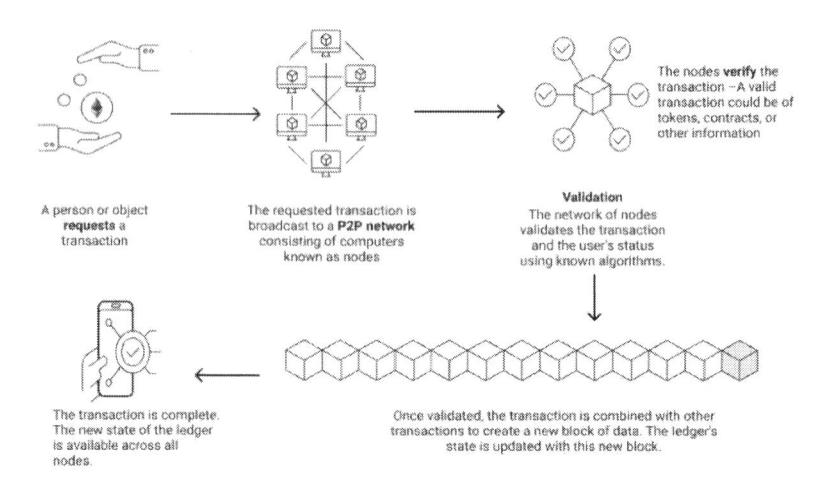

Figure 2-5: Diagram of transactions on a blockchain

Monetizing Middleware

The smart middleware layer in Figure 2-4 represents a logical extension of the original token concept. The goal of achieving a peer-to-peer network for transacting value can go beyond financial value and tokens and include transactions that are basic functions that a computer can perform. The middleware layer of a blockchain technology stack is one of the areas where we are starting to see more experimentation because with the growth of middleware for any core infrastructure comes benefits, such as reduced complexity, improved efficiency, and an increase in application development. For example, the Internet's application layer started to flourish only after both cost and risk of application development diminished because of new middleware solutions. Today's blockchain networks are just starting to see middleware development. For instance, the Truffle suite exists for the Ethereum network, making it easier to build decentralized applications on top of Ethereum. Various middleware solutions are being built with smart contracts and are monetizable products or services. If we compare blockchain middleware tools and services to those of the digital economy, there are similar opportunities: content management and storage, query languages, etc.

Monetizing the Decentralized Economy

The decentralized application layer of the technology stack is where the majority of economic activity will take place. This is where we see use-case solutions: products, application consortia, and services will live at this layer, and will be abundant. Decentralized applications are made up of smart contracts – essentially, software that encodes business logic or governance. Almost any current application that exists in our digital economy can be re-imagined as a product or service in the decentralized economy built on blockchain technology.

Enterprises and startups are already developing various Dapps for their specific industry verticals, and some Dapps will function horizontally across many industries. Consumers can interact with specific Dapps that sit on top of the blockchain stack which take advantage of asset tracking, identity management, and so forth. For instance, one Dapp may check a user's identity to make sure she is over the age of twenty-one and combine this certainty of identity with the ability to buy alcohol over the Internet; since it is generally illegal in the United States for people under twenty-one to purchase alcohol. Monetization of the decentralized application layer of the technology stack is a diverse opportunity for both existing products and entirely new kinds of products enabled by the "Internet of value" functions of this growing decentralized economy. From a timing perspective, while many Dapps already exist, the maturity of core infrastructure and middleware will likely be the catalyst for greater Dapp adoption going forward.

Basics of Blockchain

An Example: KoffeeKoin

The bottom blockchain layer can be viewed as basically containing software. This software describes protocols or rules for participating as nodes, creation of ledgers or databases, verifying transactions through consensus, digital tokens, and how the nodes will communicate and work together on the peer-to-peer network.

To develop these ideas further, we will now explore an example. Let's say that Ava wants to try out a new Mocha-Latte-Frappuccino-Supremo at Barry's local coffee shop. Barry advertises that he accepts a new cryptocurrency called "KoffeeKoin" (KFK) in payment at all of his coffee shops. Ava wants to support Barry's business and decides to try and pay him using KoffeeKoin. In order to do this, she must download the KoffeeKoin Dapp software, which contains all the necessary tools for running a blockchain payment application on her smartphone. Since KoffeeKoin is based on a permissionless blockchain, Ava must first decide how she would like to participate in the KoffeeKoin Dapp. One option would be to download and install a "**wallet**" which would allow her to buy some KoffeeKoin as well as make and receive KoffeeKoin payments. Every computer or smartphone on the KoffeeKoin network must at a minimum have a wallet and be able to process communications from the other nodes via the Internet. A wallet, as suggested by its name, is used to store digital tokens. Using cryptography, the wallet has a unique address which identifies it without revealing the identity of the owner of the wallet. Wallet addresses are public, meaning they are transparent so that all the other nodes on the KoffeeKoin network can see exactly how many digital tokens are in everyone's wallets (without knowing exactly who controls each wallet). If Ava wanted to more actively support the KoffeeKoin application, a second option would be for her to download the version of the software that would allow her to participate as a "node" on the network. If we use the Bitcoin network as a reference point, when you download the Bitcoin Core software you receive four different components: 1) the wallet, 2) the mining and consensus protocols, 3) the full contents of the blockchain, and 4) the peer-to-peer network routing protocols. Everyone at minimum will have the wallet as mentioned earlier, plus the network protocols. But there is the further option to become a full node on the network and be involved in validating transactions and creating new blocks. In order to carry out these functions in our example, Ava would need the full copy of the blockchain and the mining protocols. A third option for Ava is to just join a mining pool and let her computer be used on a shared basis among many other members of the pool to mine KoffeeKoin.

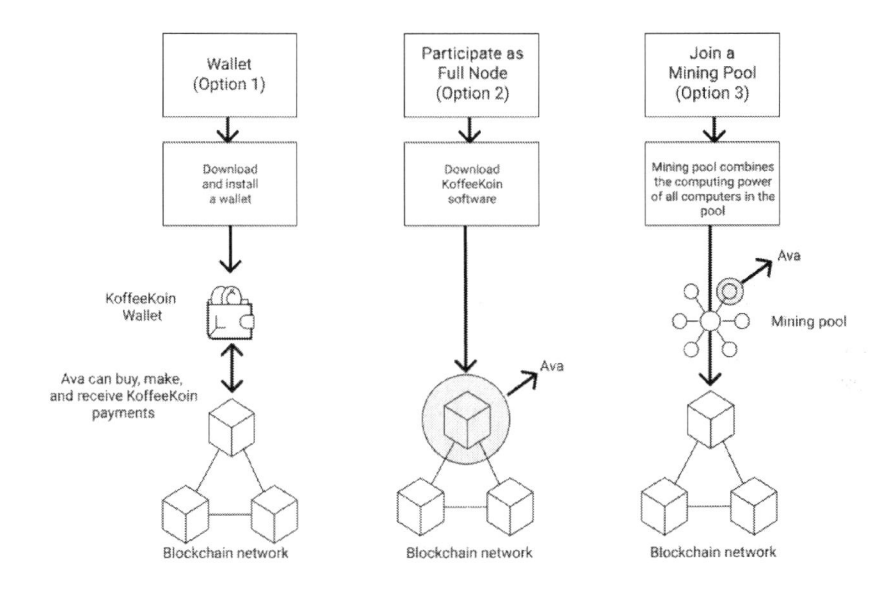

Figure 2-6: Ava's participation options in KoffeeKoin

Now that Ava has installed her KoffeeKoin wallet, she uses the wallet to send a payment to Barry for the Mocha-Latte-Frappuccino-Supremo that Barry has just made for her. Her wallet broadcasts to the KoffeeKoin network via the peer-to-peer protocols in the software that she wants to send some KFK to Barry's wallet. Barry's wallet does not know anything about whether Ava is trustworthy or whether she actually has some KFK in her wallet so the community of KFK verifiers sets to work to validate the proposed transaction. The nodes in the KFK network compete against each other to see how fast they can verify her transaction because she is also offering a very small transaction fee as payment for verifying the transaction. And the way KFK was set up, the first miner to create a whole block of transactions collects all of the transaction fees and also a reward of some extra

KoffeeKoin which gets placed in their wallet.

In order to verify her transaction, a full node on the KoffeeKoin network must examine Ava's wallet to make sure that it is a legitimate wallet and also that the KoffeeKoin in her wallet is legitimate. Every time one of the nodes validates that Ava has a legitimate wallet address and that she has enough unspent digital tokens in her wallet, that node broadcasts the verification to the other nodes. When 51% of the nodes have validated this, the transaction is approved and given a time-stamp and the approved amount of KFK is transferred to Barry's wallet and the transaction is added to the current table or digital ledger. The way that the transaction is validated is determined by the consensus protocol that is built into the KoffeeKoin blockchain. The nodes that participate in consensus-building serve to guarantee that the ledger in its final state is an accurate "system of record."

What is a Blockchain Wallet?

Blockchain wallets provide individual users the ability to transact on a blockchain network directly. To have a wallet essentially means that you have an account on a particular blockchain network. This account provides access to other network participants and the Dapps on top of the network itself. Each account is assigned an immutable account-based identity, (a public key) through which to interact with Dapps and other users. One could almost compare a blockchain wallet to a credit bank account on steroids. By installing a wallet, as Ava did, you gain access to the shared capital of the blockchain network, as you would with a line of credit from a traditional banking institution. The main difference with blockchain wallets, however, is that there is no centralized body determining your credit worthiness or other banking activities – that is done by other network participants.

Blockchain wallets are essential to participation in a blockchain network. Each blockchain network has its own version of a wallet, but the "access" that a wallet provides is much broader than just a financial warehouse as with a bank account. A wallet helps your computer to function as a "virtual machine." Your blockchain **virtual machine** is a higher abstraction than your computer itself. One way of thinking of a "virtual machine" or VM is to think of it as a special area within your computer either on your hard drive or in the cloud, where you can run different operating systems and applications. You may have partitioned your hard drive in the past so you could run both Windows applications and Mac applications on your computer. It is a similar concept for our virtual machine on the blockchain network. It is what allows you to function as a node on a blockchain and run the programs which you need to use to access the functionality of your blockchain. All of this happens separately from other applications running on your computer that might conflict with the global virtual machine running the entire blockchain.

If you were to use a wallet on the Ethereum blockchain network, you can be an account owner of ether (the crypto-asset), you can work as a miner that provides computing power to the underlying network, and you can be a Dapp participant (by making transactions using smart contracts). If you have a specific wallet say, for bitcoin, keep in mind that the wallet doesn't actually store bitcoin in it. What is stored is your **public key,** which is also known as your bitcoin **address**. This is a string of 34 letters and numbers. This address is stored in a table which links up to a complete history of all transactions that are linked to this address. When a miner validates a transaction, all it has to do is look up the public address in order to make sure that there is enough bitcoin in that wallet to complete the transaction and that it hasn't been spent already. Since no one necessarily knows the identity of the person behind any given wallet, it does not matter if the whole network sees a wallet's contents and transactions. You can actually look at Satoshi Nakamoto's wallet and see that he/she has almost a million unspent bitcoin sitting there. Your wallet address/public key has a corresponding "private key" of 64 letters and numbers. Given the encryption, no one can reverse engineer your public key in order to find out your private key. Most cases of hacking involve people being tricked into giving out their private keys or if funds are stored within an exchange (i.e. you do not control your own wallet). When Ava tells her wallet to pay Barry she must "sign" the transaction using the private key stored on her computer or smartphone. The digital signature gets sent to the network where it is validated as corresponding to the public key for the account.

The technology behind wallets has improved greatly over the past few years. Past problems with bitcoin owners losing their private keys or having their keys hacked have centered on issues around wallets. One of the problems with bitcoin is that if one loses their private key, because of the built-in

Basics of Blockchain

anonymity, there is no process for retrieving it as there might be for a more centralized system. When someone decides that they wish to use bitcoin or some other cryptocurrency, the first thing they must do is to choose a wallet. Like physical wallets, there is a wide variety of these available to the consumer. Most cryptocurrency exchanges have their own wallets that the user can download and install from the exchange website. These may be dedicated wallets only for bitcoin, or they may allow storage additional coins. Most of these are web-based wallets and don't require that the user download the entire Bitcoin Core. However, there have been problems with these wallets because hackers can gain remote control of a person's computer and can determine the user's password for their web-based wallets. Mobile wallets which can be used to pay for purchases more easily are similar and can also be hacked if a person loses their phone.

Figure 2-7: Trezor hardware wallet

Some people who buy and sell lots of cryptocurrencies store the bulk of their coins in "**cold storage**." These options are called cold storage because they do not require a continuous connection to a server on the Internet in order to gain access to them. Thus, if someone were to gain access to your wallet, you wouldn't lose all of your digital assets. And cold storage is less susceptible to hacking, too. The simplest form of cold storage is printing out your public and private keys or QR codes in order to create a "paper wallet." Of course, this is only as safe as the place you decide to store the printout! The biggest advancement in wallet technology has come in the form of "**hardware wallets**." These are generally recommended today since they are highly secure for storing private keys and are not continuously connected to the Internet. They are considered to be immune to software viruses and malware. Trezor makes one of the most popular hardware wallets (see Figure 2-7).

The raw hex version ⊕ of the Genesis block looks like:

```
00000000  01 00 00 00 00 00 00 00  00 00 00 00 00 00 00 00  ................
00000010  00 00 00 00 00 00 00 00  00 00 00 00 00 00 00 00  ................
00000020  00 00 00 00 3B A3 ED FD  7A 7B 12 B2 7A C7 2C 3E  ....;£íýz{.²zÇ,>
00000030  67 76 8F 61 7F C8 1B C3  88 8A 51 32 3A 9F B8 AA  gv.a.È.Ã ŠQ2:Ÿ¸ª
00000040  4B 1E 5E 4A 29 AB 5F 49  FF FF 00 1D 1D AC 2B 7C  K.^J)«_Iÿÿ...¬+|
00000050  01 01 00 00 00 01 00 00  00 00 00 00 00 00 00 00  ................
00000060  00 00 00 00 00 00 00 00  00 00 00 00 00 00 00 00  ................
00000070  00 00 00 00 00 00 FF FF  FF FF 4D 04 FF FF 00 1D  ......ÿÿÿÿM.ÿÿ..
00000080  01 04 45 54 68 65 20 54  69 6D 65 73 20 30 33 2F  ..EThe Times 03/
00000090  4A 61 6E 2F 32 30 30 39  20 43 68 61 6E 63 65 6C  Jan/2009 Chancel
000000A0  6C 6F 72 20 6F 6E 20 62  72 69 6E 6B 20 6F 66 20  lor on brink of
000000B0  73 65 63 6F 6E 64 20 62  61 69 6C 6F 75 74 20 66  second bailout f
000000C0  6F 72 20 62 61 6E 6B 73  FF FF FF FF 01 00 F2 05  or banksÿÿÿÿ..ò.
000000D0  2A 01 00 00 00 43 41 04  67 8A FD B0 FE 55 48 27  *....CA.gŠý°þUH'
000000E0  19 67 F1 A6 71 30 B7 10  5C D6 A8 28 E0 39 09 A6  .gñ¦q0·.\Ö¨(à9.¦
000000F0  79 62 E0 EA 1F 61 DE B6  49 F6 BC 3F 4C EF 38 C4  ybàê.aÞ¶Iö¼?Lï8Ä
00000100  F3 55 04 E5 1E C1 12 DE  5C 38 4D F7 BA 0B 8D 57  óU.å.Á.Þ\8M÷º..W
00000110  8A 4C 70 2B 6B F1 1D 5F  AC 00 00 00 00           ŠLp+kñ._¬....
```

Figure 2-8: First bitcoin transaction with Satoshi Nakamoto's note

When you download blockchain software to function as either a simple wallet or as a full node, you have to install all of the network protocols too. One way to imagine this is to think about the old landline telephone networks we used to use. There was a switchboard and operator that could route any originating call to any number, but each household needed its own phone number in order to be reached, and a way to communicate with the rest of the phones (via the network infrastructure). There even used to be a concept called a "party line," which is similar to a mining pool, where different people grouped their infrastructure resources. Blockchains are a more decentralized version of this kind of routing, and do not require operators at switchboards. But the need for shared protocols and basic components (i.e. wallet and network protocols) is relevant. A blockchain's network protocol operates on top of the Internet, in order to communicate with all of the other computers on the network using a peer-to-peer network protocol. All the nodes on a peer-to-peer network are considered to be equally important and they hold an identical copy of the ledger of transactions. This is what enables peer-to-peer value transactions without a middleman using the appropriate consensus rules. Since nodes store data for the whole network, every node on the network is constantly being updated with new blocks of data. One could think of this as similar to a shared spreadsheet application where the spreadsheet is automatically updated among the users.

Sorting Blocks

When a digital ledger gets to a certain size, a protocol in its blockchain software determines that it is time to create a new block. Storing transactions in blocks makes it easier to search and manage the huge number of transactions created and stored on the blockchain. This is equivalent to the shared ledger that is copied to all of the nodes on the peer-to-peer network. The full nodes race to create the new block because they want to collect the transaction fees and also the full reward for creating the block. Keep in mind that every blockchain network (Bitcoin, Ethereum, or our example of KoffeeKoin) or Dapp will operate a completely separate shared ledger.

In creating a new block, a node generates a unique identifier or **block header** for that block which will be used to identify it when it eventually gets chained into the blockchain's history. The block header is a hash of all the transactions in the block. As a reference point, in the case of Bitcoin, a block header is 80 bytes long. In order to ensure that the identifier is unique the nodes participate in a mathematical game that involves using a cryptographic hash algorithm (SHA-256) to generate a unique hash for the entire block. By design, the size of each block in the Bitcoin network is about 1 MB and it will take roughly ten minutes to create a new block. Different blockchains arrive at consensus in different ways. Many use a Proof of Work mechanism for Sybil attack resistance, combined with other protocols, and some new ones are moving to a Proof of Stake technique and even Proof of Elapsed Time.

Say Hello to My Little Friend —SHA-256!

One of the most confusing yet essential aspects of blockchain is the concept of cryptographic hash functions. It is a confusing topic partly because the term "hash" can be used so many different ways and in different contexts in technology circles. We have hash functions, values, and algorithms – we can make a hash out of just about anything! In a basic sense, a **hash function** is a mathematical algorithm that takes input of any size and transforms it into output of a fixed length. So for example, you could transform "Barry's first KFK sale" into a fixed length output of say 20 characters. You could use the same hash function to transform a whole novel into a different output of 20 characters. If you have the output of the hash function, you can recreate the initial input, but the process of transforming the input is very difficult to discern. This hash function output is called a **hash value** or simply a **hash** and they are stored in a **hash table**. Using a hash value makes it easy to search quickly for items and assures that there will be no duplicate values, since a tiny change in the input will yield a complete change in the hash value.

If you have ever used a file compression utility such as Winzip, you may have already experienced how a hash function substitutes shorter values for words in a file. Instead of having common words such as "the" and "and" repeated over and over in a file, the file will be hashed so that common words are replaced with binary values stored in a hash table. The file can be recreated by combining the zip file with the results stored in the hash table. The example below shows how a message was compressed down from 93 characters to 56 using a key to reconstitute the compressed message, saving almost 40% of the space from the original message.

Basics of Blockchain

```
How Much?    40% compressed!
Original:     93 characters
Compressed:   56 characters
Difference:   37 characters (~40%)
```

Original Message   93 characters

Pitter_patter_pitter_patter_listen_to_the_
rain_pitter_patter_pitter_patter_on_the_
window_pane

Compressed   56 characters

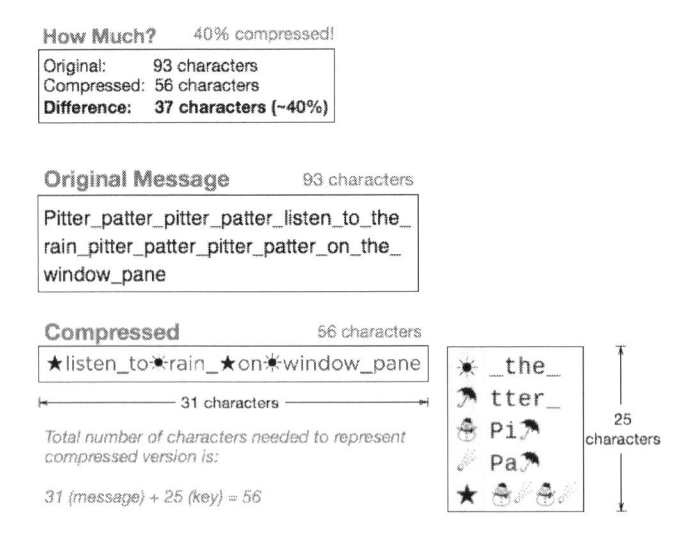

★listen_to✹rain_★on✹window_pane

|← 31 characters →|

Total number of characters needed to represent compressed version is:

31 (message) + 25 (key) = 56

☀	_the_
🎵	tter_
☕	Pi🎵
🖋	Pa🎵
★	☕☕

25 characters

Figure 2-9: How text compression works

A cryptographic hash function is a special type of hash function that is designed to hide the contents of the input values. The goal is to ensure that it is difficult to find any patterns and make it as hard as possible to crack the code without the appropriate key or keys. Cryptographic hash functions have been used for many years to add security to things like Internet passwords. A user's password is hashed with a particular function and the hash value is stored in a hash table for purposes of security.

SHA-256 stands for "simple hash algorithm" and the 256 represents the fact that it is 256 bits long. This algorithm was developed by the National Security Agency in the United States and was declassified by President Clinton in the 1990s. Since then it has become a popular cryptographic hash algorithm because it is virtually impossible to break. Figure 2-10 below shows a demo of the SHA-256 hash algorithm that can be found on the Adesso website. It allows you to set a level of difficulty (in this case, it is set to 4) and then enter in a message in the data window and use this in combination with the given "nonce" to generate the hash value in the top window. Here, we entered "say hello to my little friend" and it generated the hash value shown.

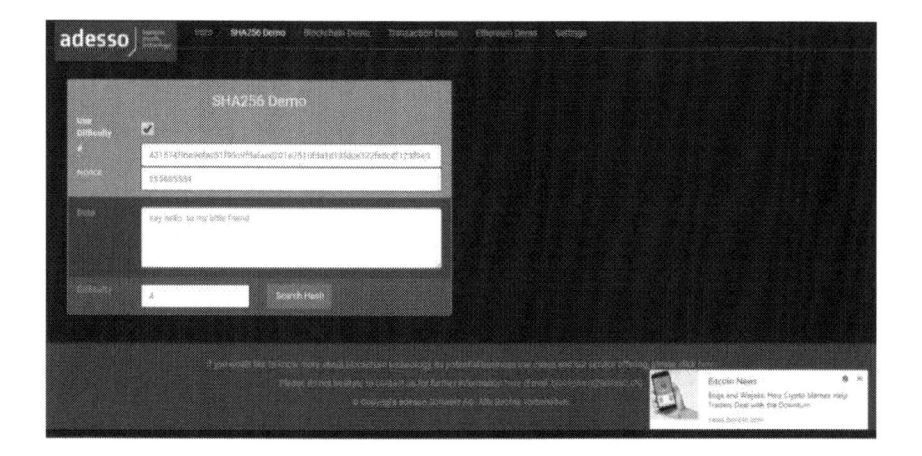

Figure 2-10: SHA-256 demo

Now when we make one tiny change to the input, like capitalizing the "s" in "say", you can see from the screenshot below that this changes the whole hash value. Because of the complexity of the hash function, it is virtually impossible to find a pattern in the changes.

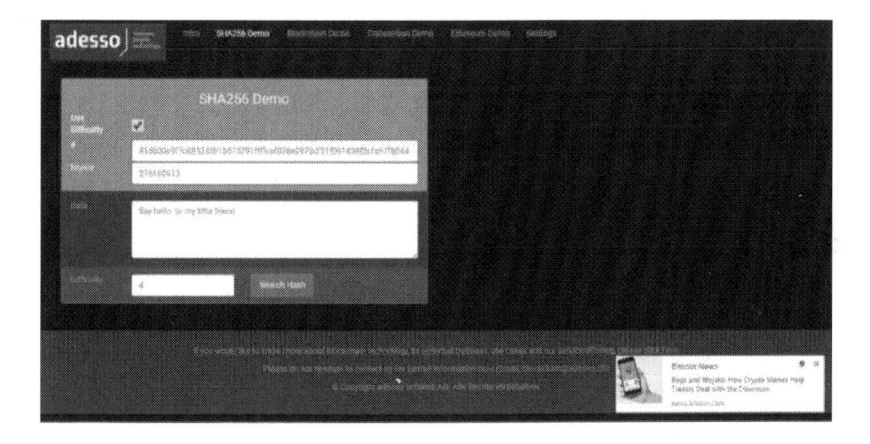

Figure 2-11: SHA-256 demo with change to the data input

Now, in the world of blockchains that use Proof of Work, the contest is to create a hash value that starts with 18 zeros. This is done by changing the **nonce** or "number used once" to adjust the hash value until one is found that matches the desired output protocol. Changing just one digit of the nonce will cause it to generate a completely new hash value. Figure 2-12 below

Basics of Blockchain

shows the effect of changing the nonce value to generate a completely new hash value.

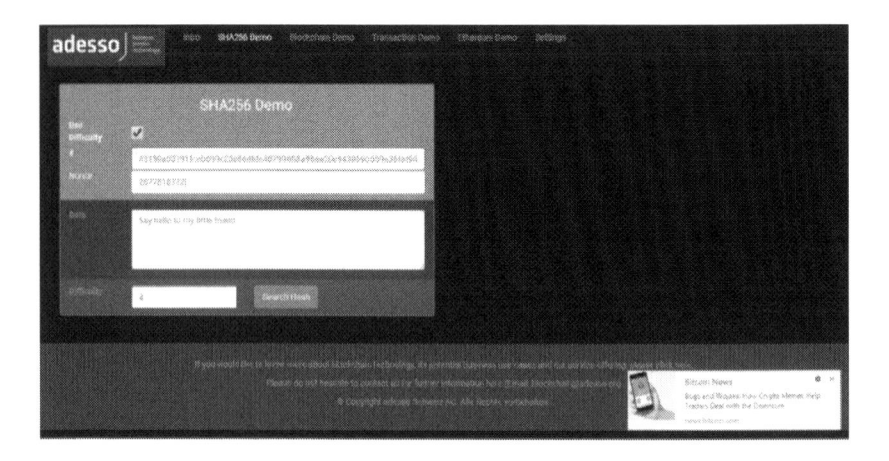

Figure 2-12: SHA-256 demo with changed nonce value

In order to have a higher likelihood of winning – and inputting the correct input that derives the hash – you rely on greater processing power. That is why Proof of Work comes down to raw computing power and the cost of consuming electricity.

An important point about hashing that brings added value to blockchain networks is its ability to make digital items unique. A hash of a PDF document will not compute correctly if the document has been altered. Much like the "Say hello to my little friend" example above, changing one letter makes the input entirely new and therefore the output will not be the same as the original hash. This means you can use hashing to point not just to the *location* of a digital object, but to its *context*.

Most of the questions about how blockchains work center on how miners create blocks and receive awards. Once a miner receives a valid block from another miner it automatically drops the block it was working on and proceeds to start work on another new block. It will take transactions that are queued up waiting to be packaged into a block and generate a new block header. The block header contains metadata which provides certain higher-level information about other data (see Figure 2-13). The first piece of metadata is the link to the previous blockhash. Also included are the difficulty, time-stamp, and nonce data that describe the current block being competed for in mining. The last piece of metadata is the **Merkle tree** root which helps to provide a quick summary of all the transactions contained in the block. Using Merkle trees is an efficient way to encode data from all of the transactions contained in the block into the final hash value.

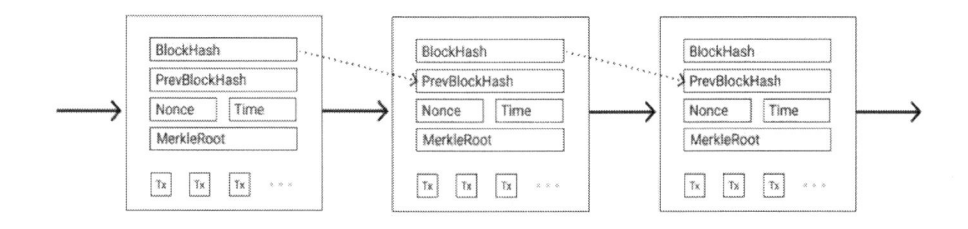

Figure 2-13: Simplified blockchain

There is no set number or ordering of transactions that are included in a new block and some of the more sophisticated miners will try and bundle the transactions that have the highest-paying transaction fees in order to maximize their potential reward. In fact, depending on a miner's geographic location on the network, they will most likely encounter new transactions in a different sequence than miners in other parts of the global network. Transactions with no fees attached may be put aside and processed more slowly. The level of difficulty is the same regardless of how many transactions are included in the block.

Now that we know how the SHA-256 hash function works, we can examine the inputs into this Proof of Work process. Some of the misconceptions about mining stem from the fact that miners can work on different subsets of transactions. The hashing contest is always going on and miners can add new transactions and generate a new block header at any time. There is no rule that says all of the miners have to be working on the same set of transactions. The block header itself is 80 bytes long and represents a hash of all the transactions in the block (from the "Merkle root"). As mentioned above, this is one of the inputs into the hash contest which includes the hash value of the previous block or the "blockhash" as it is sometimes called, a random number called a "nonce", and a time-stamp. By using the blockhash from the previous block as an input into the SHA256 hash function, this ensures that any changes made to previous blocks will be easy to find and make it possible to detect any attempts at tampering with the transaction history. As miners increment the nonce to try and find a blockhash with 18 zeros at the beginning, they may have to go through millions of attempts before they come up with a winning hash value that will allow them to "create" a new block.

The resulting blockhash is a unique 256-bit (or 32 byte) value. It is virtually collision-proof too, meaning that it is highly unlikely that two different values will generate the same hash value. So the blockhash performs two valuable services at the same time 1) providing a unique identifier for each block and 2) maintaining the integrity and security of the block itself. In fact, over time, the probability of tampering with the history of blocks gets even lower because with each new block that is added to the chain, any change in an older block would result in a cascading effect where all the later blocks would have to be changed.

Rewarding Miners

To return to our earlier example of KoffeeKoin, after one of the miners or validators has validated Ava's payment transaction and added it to a new valid block, how is that miner rewarded? By finding the valid blockhash for the new block, the miner has provided a "proof of work" that means he/she has invested in the electricity and computing resources needed to find the blockhash. This essentially ties a real monetary cost to the mining process just like in mining for precious metals. As computing power grows, the difficulty can be increased by requiring more zeroes or even letters to be found using the nonce. This can be seen in the "difficulty" parameter in Figure 2-14 where it was set to only four zeroes. When a miner has found a winning blockhash, the miner announces this to the entire network and when 51% of the miners validate the blockhash, a reward is deposited in that miner's wallet. According to the Bitcoin protocol, miners currently receive 12.5 bitcoin in addition to the total value of the transaction fees for all the transactions contained in that block. Originally, the reward was set at 50 bitcoin, but it has been cut in half every four years; first to twenty-five and now to 12.5 bitcoin. As the reward keeps decreasing, the miners will have to rely more on higher transaction fees in order to pay for the costs of mining.

Consensus

When you download blockchain software and become a full node on a network, this means that you can participate in generating a **consensus** among all of the nodes. In the case of Bitcoin, the consensus rules of the network determine how the participants in the network interact with each other. They define:

• The conditions under which a transaction (i.e. sending tokens from party A to party B) are valid.

• The transaction costs related to sending money from party A to party B.

• The incentive mechanism for validating transactions with a digital token.

• Rules of how to change current consensus rules.

The rules of consensus can vary widely between blockchain networks and can also be changed. This can be extremely difficult to do or relatively simple depending on the blockchain network's governance and core protocols. As people begin to understand the variety of mechanisms for consensus, security parameters, and governance structures that are possible, different blockchain networks are being formed that optimize for key qualities like privacy, throughput, and scalability. This is one of the reasons that blockchain is evolving in so many different directions today.

Basics of Blockchain

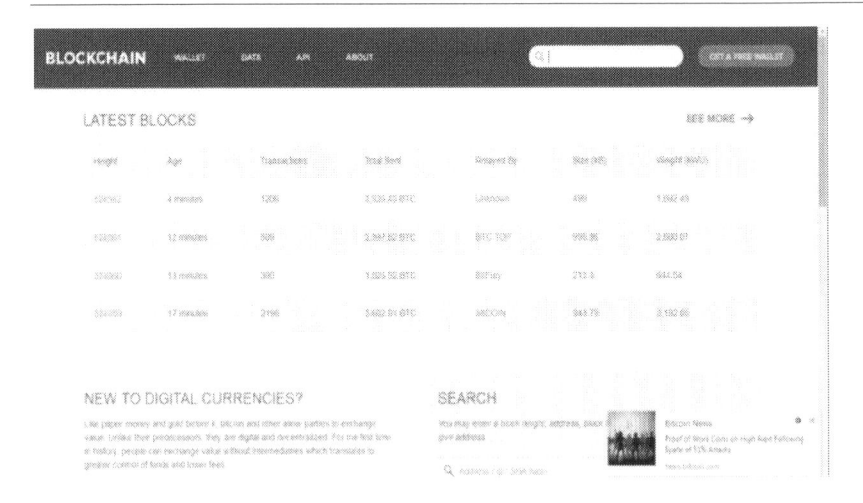

Figure 2-14: Block creation data

As shown in Figure 2-14, the data on the Bitcoin blocks is readily available for anyone to see. This figure shows the current block being created along with the data on the last three blocks that were created. The time (age) it took to mine these three blocks varies quite a bit as does the number of transactions contained in the block. This is because it is not possible to predict how long it will take to generate the winning hash value or the final block content of the winning block. It also shows here the amount of bitcoin sent in each of the transactions and who was the successful miner of each block, displayed in the "relayed by" field. Most of the blocks are close to 1 MB of data, but this can vary too. The height of the block refers to the number of blocks that came before the current block. If you looked at the genesis block mined by Satoshi (see Figure 2-16), you can see that it has a height of "0" since it was the first block. The block "weight" refers to the size in terms of the amount of memory that the block takes up. The kWU stands for thousands of weight units or roughly equivalent to megabytes of memory. The weight varies quite a bit too, though the maximum was raised to 4 kWU or about 4 MB in order to try and increase the volume of transactions processed in each block.

Figure 2-15: Block details

We can also view the details around a specific block that has already been created. Figure 2-15 shows the number of transactions contained in the block, the amount of bitcoin involved in the transactions along with the transaction fees collected by the successful miner, in this case, BitFury. The time-stamp is a crucial piece of metadata because it shows when the block was created and validated. This may be important since other miners are competing to be the first to solve the cryptographic hashing problem and create the new block. With the time-stamp, BitFury can prove that they solved the problem first and therefore are entitled to the reward and the transaction fees. You can also see the hash value of this block and the previous block, along with the Merkle root, difficulty, height and weight.

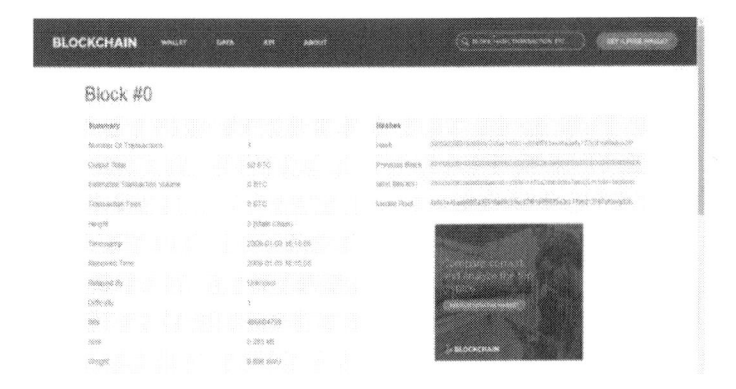

Figure 2-16: Bitcoin genesis block

So, You Want to Be a Miner...

You may have heard stories about people becoming billionaires by mining bitcoin or other cryptocurrencies with their laptop computer in their garage, dorm room, or basement! Now that you know how blockchain works, you might want to start mining cryptocurrencies on your own. But you may wonder if these sorts of gains are still possible today and what you need to get started?

As you know from the previous discussion, miners play a crucial role in blockchain networks. They are the ones who validate transactions and generate new blocks of records to store on the blockchain. While the terminology of mining crypto-assets came from the analogy of mining precious metals for physical coins, it has also been compared to the process of textile weaving. This may be a more intuitive analogy of performing value-adding work that contributes to the overall strength of the fabric, in this case the strength of a decentralized computing network.[5]

It is crucial for the success of a permissionless blockchain network to attract miners to participate. This is why there is always a reward system built into blockchain design. In the past, many users served as miners just out of their altruistic desire to support the blockchain community. As the value of the rewards like bitcoin grew, more and more people got into the mining process in order to make money. Now, large corporations with vast computing resources have taken over the bitcoin mining world, making it virtually impossible to compete and mine bitcoin on a personal computer. In fact, in late 2017, it was estimated that it would take 2.7 million years for a person mining bitcoin on a standard laptop computer to mine a single block.[6]

---

[5] Orban, David. "Weaving Is A Better Metaphor for Bitcoin, Instead of Mining," Bitcoin Magazine, April 15, 2014, https://bitcoinmagazine.com/articles/weaving-better-metaphor-bitcoin-instead-mining-1397609654/

[6] "Bitcoin mining: Can I make money doing it?" Finder.com, October 30, 2018, https://www.finder.com/bitcoin-mining

Evolution of Mining Technology

Back in 2009, when bitcoin wasn't worth much, it was mostly just cryptogeeks and cypherpunks mining out of pure interest. The level of difficulty and competition was such that they could use a standard multi-core CPU from a decent desktop computer to create a new block. Back then, the block creation reward was 50 bitcoin but each coin was only worth a few cents. At current prices, those same 50 bitcoin could be worth hundreds of thousands of dollars, depending on the market. In one of the first bitcoin transactions, an early miner paid 10,000 bitcoin to have two pizzas delivered to his house!

As the value of bitcoin increased, the technology behind mining also improved. By 2010, miners figured out how to connect multiple high-powered gaming cards or GPUs (Graphics Processing Units) to mine bitcoin more efficiently. These graphics cards were meant to lighten the load on the CPU so that users could play more high-end video games. So for a few hundred dollars, anyone could set up a simple mining rig and earn bitcoin.

With the continued rise in the price of bitcoin, more miners joined the bitcoin network and so the difficulty of mining increased. The bitcoin **mining difficulty** is a measure of how much time and effort it takes to mine and create a new block. Using the SHA-256 cryptographic hash algorithm, this just means that more zeroes are added to the beginning of the target hash value. Currently, a miner must find a hash value with eighteen zeros at the beginning of the value. After every 2,016 blocks, the difficulty level is re-evaluated in order to keep the average block creation time as close to ten minutes as possible. Since the computer power increases so rapidly, this means that difficulty increases too as the hardware gets more efficient at solving the cryptographic SHA-256 puzzle. But, as the difficulty increases, so do the power consumption needs for the high-powered machines. This is one of the reasons for the introduction of **FPGAs** (Field Programmable Gate Arrays) in 2011. These required about one third the power to run as GPUs and were also faster. The only issue was that FPGAs required special programming in order to make them mine bitcoin. The special programming and higher cost essentially put individual miners out of business and ushered in corporate bitcoin miners.

The final nail in the coffin of the individual miners came with the introduction of the **ASIC** or Application Specific Integrated Circuits. ASIC systems are designed to perform one computing task and they do it with the least amount of power. ASICs have been around for a long time and have been developed for very specific applications such as smartphones. In 2013, the first Bitcoin ASIC machine came out and changed the whole economics of bitcoin mining. They are more expensive, too, so this was a further obstacle for small scale miners. In 2018, the cost of the top ASIC machine for mining bitcoin was $12,000. There are also specific ASIC chips designed for mining Ethereum, Monero, and other altcoins. This development was especially concerning for the mining community because Ethereum and Monero's Proof of Work algorithms were specifically designed to be "ASIC resistant" in order to prevent the centralization of mining power.

The high expense of mining has sparked significant controversy within the cryptocurrency community. Since mining became very lucrative, it's become increasingly centralized in the hands of fewer and fewer mining companies. The recent drop in the value of bitcoin has led to further consolidation among the mining companies. The main companies are Bitmain in China and BitFury in the U.S.

Approximately 75% of the hash rate is divided among five big mining firms. Critics worry that this makes the Bitcoin network much more vulnerable to a 51% attack. In fact, the Chinese mining firm Bitmain did exert a huge influence in the decision to make a hard fork of Bitcoin in 2017 that resulted in the creation of Bitcoin Cash and Bitcoin Gold.[7]

Mining Pools

As the difficulty of creating new blocks has kept increasing, one way for slower individual miners to improve their odds of winning a block reward has become to pool their computing resources. Pooling meant that if one member were to solve the puzzle, then all of the pool members would get a

---

[7] Oberhaus, Daniel. "What Is an ASIC Miner and Is It the Future of Cryptocurrency?" Motherboard, April 9, 2018, https://motherboard.vice.com/en_us/article/3kj5dw/what-is-an-asic-miner-bitmain-monero-ethereum

share of the reward depending on the amount of computing resources they contributed.

There are a wide variety of **mining pools** that you can join with servers around the world. Some of them are less reputable than others. They vary quite a bit in terms of how they calculate payouts and the fees that they charge. The first pooled mining company was SlushPool. It was founded in 2010 and is located in the Czech Republic. It controls about 10.5% of the hash rate for mining pools and is the fourth largest mining pool. SlushPool seems to be well-run and have regular audits from reputable audit firms. They do charge a 2% pool fee which is on the high end for mining pools.

The second largest mining pool in the world in 2018 is the China-based Antpool. They are owned by the Chinese firm, Bitmain. They are also famous for manufacturing some of the best new ASIC mining machines. They control a little over 13.4% of the hash rate and offer a variety of payout options. Bitmain was involved in a scandal where their ASIC mining hardware came with malware pre-loaded onto it. This malware allowed them to remotely shut down the machine, bringing on complaints from customers that Bitmain could shut down competitors to make more money.

The most popular mining pool with about 29% of the hash rate at the time of writing is BTC.com. They started their pool in 2016 but were already famous for their crypto exchange and their wallet technology. They have one of the better payouts because unlike other pools, they share a portion of the transaction fees as well as the actual mining rewards. Like Antpool, they are based in China but have an office in Germany as well. They have focused their mining efforts on mining Bitcoin and Bitcoin Cash and don't support any other altcoins. Eight of the top ten mining pools are based in China and altogether Chinese mining pools control almost 90% of the total hash rate.

Unfortunately, ASIC machines may still ultimately render mining pools completely obsolete. Since more miners are using ASIC machines, there is the potential for difficulty to increase to a point where even hundreds of thousands of individual miners on standard machines can't compete.

> **My Computer Has Become a Zombie Crypto Miner!**
>
> With the rise in the price of bitcoin and other altcoins like ether and Monero, hacker gangs and developers of malware became more interested in hijacking the mining process. Coinhive came up with a clever way of embedding a JavaScript program onto the machines of visitors to their website, allowing them to use the visitor's CPU to mine Monero. They targeted Monero because it is designed to disguise the parties involved in any transactions on its network. Coinhive encouraged website owners to embed this code on their own websites so that they could in turn earn money by employing the CPU of website visitors to mine Monero. Hackers have gone further and managed to embed this program in such popular sites as Politifact, The Los Angeles Times, Blackberry and Showtime.[8] Their code was sophisticated enough to make sure that they received thirty percent of all money generated by each website; whether they agreed to use it or not. A special cryptographic key determines which site receives the other 70%. Coinhive's meteoric rise made its malware program the sixth most common malware in the world in 2017 and spawned a whole new industry around "cryptojacking."[9] Japan, India and Taiwan have seen the highest rate of infection to date. As fast as counter measures are developed for this, new versions seem to be sprouting up.

Cloud Mining

Some people have no hardware or software resources but still want to get involved in mining crypto-assets. For these individuals, there is the option called "**cloud mining**," where you can simply purchase hardware mining resources which operate solely in the cloud. Since all the mining is done in the cloud, participants don't have to worry about maintaining the hardware and software, the electricity, heat from the machines, and many other issues. Of course, all of these costs can lower the profits significantly. Since these companies operate in the cloud, it is virtually impossible to monitor their

---

8 Krebs, Brian. "Who and What is Coinhive?," Krebs on Security, March 26, 2018, https://krebsonsecurity.com/2018/03/who-and-what-is-coinhive/

9 Osena, Menard. "Cryptocurrency-Mining Malware, 2018's New Menace?," Trend Micro Security Intelligence Blog, February 28, 2018, https://blog.trendmicro.com/trendlabs-security-intelligence/cryptocurrency-mining-malware-2018-new-menace/

operations and their methods for calculating payouts. If they have a string of bad mining luck, such companies may need to have saved bitcoin in order to make any scheduled payouts. This type of mining has been totally unregulated and is a breeding ground for fraud. One such company, Mining Max, was run by a group of Koreans out of Las Vegas. After collecting about $250 million for their Ethereum cloud mining pool, they disappeared with most of the money having spent only $70 million on their operations.[10]

Economics of Mining

The process of mining cryptocurrencies has evolved significantly since the first days of the Bitcoin network, in 2009. No longer the domain of individual hobbyists, it is instead now filled with large corporations running cut-throat operations. Besides the price of the currency being mined, the main determinants of the profitability of mining are the cost of the hardware used and the electricity required to run the mining rigs and also the fans that are needed to cool them down. For this reason, many mining firms have chosen to locate their operations in regions where electrical costs are the lowest. Because of their low-cost state-subsidized electrical power, mining firms in China have a built-in advantage over their competitors. This has led to a majority of miners being located in China. Other mining firms have located their operations near cheap hydroelectric power stations in Kazakhstan and other areas of the world.

Mining firms have reinvigorated a town in rural Washington state because of its cheap power from a dam on the Columbia River. Some firms are starting up in deserts where they can set up solar power plants and use this to cheaply power their mining operations. The increasing demands of cryptocurrency mining operations for electricity is a major criticism of some of the older cryptocurrencies. The idea is that too much electricity is being consumed by an activity that may not help the average person. Currently, the global energy consumption of mining bitcoin is equivalent to the needs of a small country

---

[10] O'Driscoll, Aimee. "20+ Bitcoin scams and how to spot and avoid them," Comparitech, March 8, 2018, https://www.comparitech.com/crypto/avoid-bitcoin-scams/

like Ireland (roughly 2.6GW), and potentially growing to 7.7GW at the end of 2018.[11] This is why some of the newer cryptocurrencies are focused on other ways to decrease or eliminate the need for mining, or are using something like Proof of Stake as part of their consensus protocol.

With the fluctuating price of bitcoin, there has been a renewed focus on the economics of cryptocurrency mining. A recent study found that because of the differences in electric power costs, the cost of mining bitcoin (assuming an ASIC mining rig was used), varied between $531 in Venezuela to $26,170 in South Korea.[12] The United States ranked 41st among the countries studied with an average cost of $4758. Of course, this can vary widely too, from state to state. It turns out that Hawaii is the highest power cost at over $9,000 and Louisiana the lowest at around $3,200. The Bitcoin Mining Calculator shown below in Figure 2-21 can help users determine whether they can make money mining with different pools. It allows users to enter the hash rate, pool fees, along with the cost of hardware and power to find out if it is worthwhile to mine cryptocurrencies with a particular pool. Of course, miners should focus their analysis on reputable mining pools since much of the mining process and rewards are out of their control.

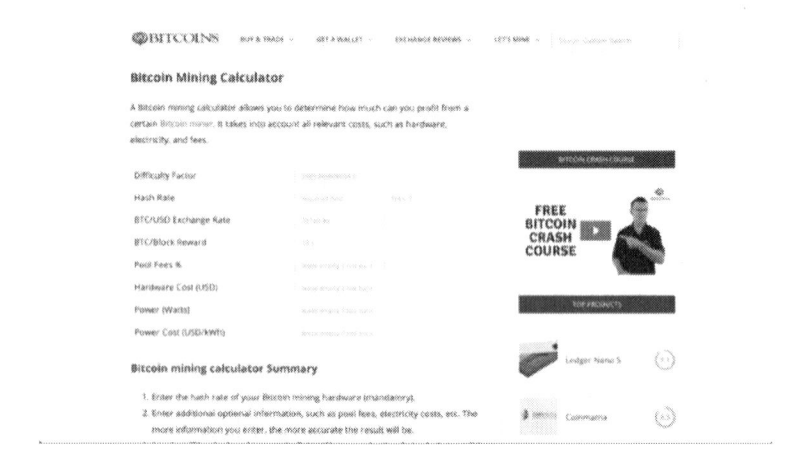

---

[11] Lee, Timothy B. "New study quantifies Bitcoin's ludicrous energy consumption," Ars Technica, May 17, 2018, https://arstechnica.com/tech-policy/2018/05/new-study-quantifies-bitcoins-ludicrous-energy-consumption/

[12] Hankin, Aaron. "Here's how much it costs to mine a single bitcoin in your country," Market Watch, May 11, 2018, https://www.marketwatch.com/story/heres-how-much-it-costs-to-mine-a-single-bitcoin-in-your-country-2018-03-06

Figure 2-17: Bitcoin mining calculator

Can You Still Make Money with a Low-end Machine?

Even if you were to spend a few thousand dollars on a high-end ASIC mining rig and your electric costs were below 14 cent/kilowatt, it would probably only generate a few dollars per day. In an effort to protect and promote small miners who only have access to consumer-grade computers, a number of altcoins have opted for strategies that would make them **ASIC-resistant**. ASIC machines as we already know are programmed to only do one thing; solve the SHA-256 Proof of Work puzzle. And they can do this thousands of times faster than the earlier generation of GPU mining rigs. So to prevent all the mining power from being centralized on a few dominant mining firms, new altcoins are adopting other algorithms besides the SHA-256 cryptographic hashing algorithm for their proof of work. One such algorithm is called "**X11**" which combines eleven different hashing algorithms into one. Since miners using GPU rigs can switch between algorithms by installing different software, they would be able to keep mining under the new hashing algorithm. Keep in mind that no cryptocurrency would be considered to be "ASIC proof" since a new ASIC can be developed that would target the ASIC-resistant altcoin. This has already occurred in respect to Monero and also ether, with new ASIC machines having been released for both of them. But it takes millions of dollars of investment and 3-6 months for new ASIC machines to be developed and released.[13] This timeframe can be even longer given the global shortage of high-end computer chips and the increased difficulty in sourcing them. Some altcoins have gone so far as to do a hard fork in order to change the Proof of Work algorithm to make their coins more ASIC resistant. VertCoin and Monero are some of the most ASIC-resistant coins. Others include Litecoin, Bytecoin, and the lesser-known RavenCoin. Some, like IOTA, are working to move away from mining altogether. This is a highly volatile area with a lot of change coming.

---

[13] Hsue, Derek. "Is The War Against ASICs Worth Fighting?" Token Economy, April 4, 2018, https://tokeneconomy.co/is-the-war-against-asics-worth-fighting-b12c6a714bed

Blockchain as a Service (BaaS)

Earlier we noted that some individual miners were using cloud-based tools to compete with corporate operations, and blockchain technology has begun to collide with the world of cloud computing in other ways now. Enter the concept of **Blockchain as a Service (BaaS)**. Because of the intense hype around blockchain, many large software firms are racing to deploy a version of blockchain that would take advantage of the cloud to create "on demand" blockchain networks. These companies include IBM, Microsoft, SAP, Amazon Web Services, projects like BlockApps, and even the Chinese retail giant Baidu. Animal Ventures is launching an open source platform called Orb Weaver, which allows users to launch a blockchain network on the cloud and provide other services to ease the development of blockchain applications.[14] The basic idea for all these services is that by hosting the blockchain network in the cloud, software companies can help smaller outfits get up and running on a blockchain quickly without the extreme cost of hiring hard-to-find blockchain developers.

If you think about the technology stack of a blockchain, the core layer is very time intensive to develop and requires expertise in kernel development as well as many other disciplines that come together to define blockchain protocols (economics or game theory, mathematics, cryptography, and computer science, to name a few). While there is a growing diversity of protocol technology that gives us greater options for how blockchain core infrastructure is designed and implemented, it is a layer of the stack that involves overcoming significant security and talent constraints. Rather than every company trying to prototype or build their own blockchain, BaaS begins to move the prototyping process up into higher parts of the technology stack. This means that companies, especially those whose business is not as technology-heavy, can develop use cases and prototypes for solving specific business pain points through applications of blockchain higher in the stack. Oftentimes, BaaS providers will combine an enterprise blockchain solution with a systems integration solution.

---

14 Access Orb Weaver at https://animalventures.com/

The upside of spinning up a blockchain using a BaaS implementation includes lowered needs for talent in development and security at the core layer, decreased time to experimentation, and potentially greater customer support. However, outsourcing this work has its downsides as well, including a recentralization of certain functionality, systems lock-in with the chosen provider, as well as the costs of renting the resources to run a hosted blockchain instance.

Information Technology Use Cases for Blockchain

One area where the impact of blockchain technology could be profound is in information technology (IT) itself. This section describes some of the major use cases within the IT world for blockchain.

Storage

In the early days of the Internet, a program came along called SETI that sought to leverage all the computers that were connected to the Net but not being used. When users downloaded SETI they were volunteering their computing power to run software that would search reams of planetary data for scientific discoveries during the hours that users weren't on their computers. We see this kind of model in many places today, through car-sharing apps or even Airbnb: how can we monetize underutilized resources or incentivize their utilization in new ways? For blockchains, the storage and computing question is an opportunity space that Dapps like Storj, Sia, Filecoin and Maidsafe are attempting to build into leading **decentralized storage systems**. Each of these projects is pushing to improve upon existing storage provider services by reducing costs, improving security, or boosting functionality. These Dapps run on the premise that network users can offer their unused storage capacity across desktops, servers, and storage devices in exchange for tokens. This turns storage into a marketplace, where the nodes that store data receive a reward in return for their service. Companies providing decentralized storage Dapps suggest these services will cost a fraction of what centralized storage platforms are offering and can reinvent everything from consumer tools (e.g Dropbox) to enterprise cloud storage (e.g. Box) on alternate infrastructure.

The claim that decentralized storage and file management will reduce costs hinges mostly on the potential to reduce inefficiencies such as the hypertext transfer protocol (HTTP) practice of downloading a file from a single computer, rather than many simultaneously. The InterPlanetary File System (IPFS) estimates that a peer-to-peer approach to video delivery would reduce bandwidth costs by 60%.[15] Decentralized storage could also challenge traditional, more centralized data storage through its differentiated security model. By decentralizing where and how data is stored, these platforms potentially offer censorship resistance and greater network resiliency. No central provider could "take down" your data or alter it, and similarly, you could avoid downtime if your business experienced some kind of network failure or cyber-attack, by relying on many independent nodes that store your data. If privacy is a concern, these solutions suggest the data itself can be split up into small pieces and replicated across the network in a way where no single node or user holds a complete data set. This is similar in concept to how health data is split up today to comply with HIPAA regulations.

IPFS

As with many open-source movements, many projects in blockchain technology are not startups, but rather services for all to use and grow the ecosystem. The InterPlanetary File System (IPFS) is self-described as a "peer-to-peer distributed file system that seeks to connect all computing devices with the same system of files. In some ways, IPFS is similar to the Web, but IPFS could be seen as a single BitTorrent swarm, exchanging objects within one Git repository."[16] The approach is focused on tackling some of the challenges for data distribution, such as computing on large datasets across

---

15 "Why" InterPlanetary File System Website, https://ipfs.io/#why, accessed June 11, 2018.
16 Benet, Juan. "IPFS – Content Addressed, Versioned, P2P File System (Draft 3)" Cornell University Library, July 14, 2014, https://arxiv.org/abs/1407.3561

organizations, hosting and distributing huge datasets, and managing versioning as well as preventing file disappearance. If you look to the future, you can imagine such services someday creating the content-addressing for a permanent Web. Content addressing is an important departure from the way our Web functions today: hyperlinks currently point to addresses not the context of the content. Some examples of using IPFS for websites include inserting videos, pinning, and graphic objects.

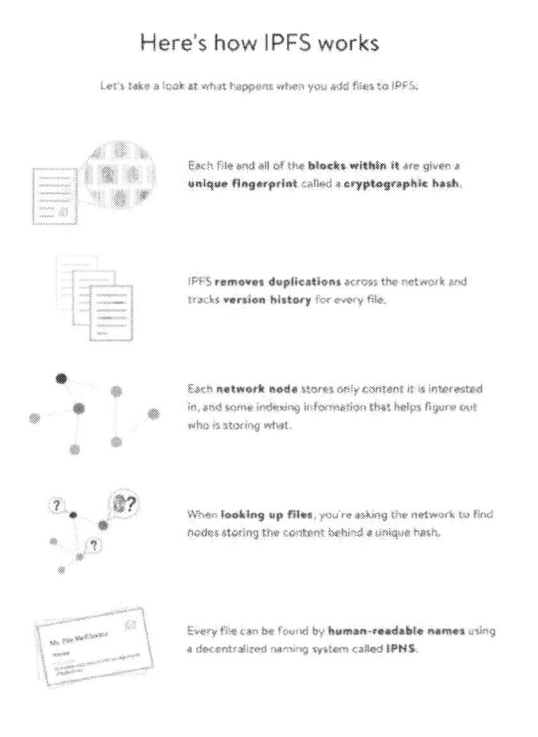

Here's how IPFS works

Let's take a look at what happens when you add files to IPFS:

Each file and all of the **blocks within it** are given a **unique fingerprint** called a **cryptographic hash**.

IPFS **removes duplications** across the network and tracks **version history** for every file.

Each **network node** stores only content it is interested in, and some indexing information that helps figure out who is storing what.

When **looking up files**, you're asking the network to find nodes storing the content behind a unique hash.

Every file can be found by **human-readable names** using a decentralized naming system called **IPNS**.

Figure 2-18: How IPFS works

Edge Computing

The trajectory of IT development has often been tied to **Moore's Law**: the notion that our computing power doubles roughly every 12-18 months. And as our computing power has increased, we have been able to move where and how computing is accomplished. We now have supercomputers in our pockets instead of slow computers that take up a whole room! Contemporary computational power at the edges of networks and the leveraging of large cloud servers makes information technology much more robust. Recent suites of devices that are coming to market allow for computation to be performed locally and then transmitted to the cloud for reference or dissemination across a network.

This is one of the most interesting aspects of blockchain technology as well, since it is similarly designed to work on decentralized networks. We are seeing blockchain computers, like the early version of the 21 Bitcoin Computer, and blockchain phones built by HTC. These are part of a larger story around how local hardware-computing intersects with mesh networks, clouds, and decentralized databases like blockchains to compute and record transactions with data. The work done by devices at the edges is most relevant to the growing Internet of Things – autonomous vehicles or robots that will need real-time data to make decisions or log transactions and which cannot wait for computation to be performed in the cloud and returned with latency.

Web 3.0 and Blockchain

Tim Berners-Lee, founder of the World Wide Web has been looking into blockchain as a part of the next iteration of the Internet, or what most are calling **Web 3.0**. If you look back at the origin story of the first World Wide Web, Berners-Lee has said, "In those days, there was different information on different computers, but you had to log on to different computers to get at it. Also, sometimes you had to learn a different program on each computer. Often it was just easier to go and ask people when they were having coffee..."[17] While we have much greater digital functionality today – using our phones, tablets, desktops, and even watches as devices to connect to one another and communicate – the idea that we need a shared reality (e.g. a moment to sync together over coffee) is as resonant today as ever. Blockchain is part of the early steps toward Web 3.0 and offers novel ways to create shared realities not just for humans but also for machines. Can you imagine

---

[17] "History of the Web," World Wide Web Foundation, https://webfoundation.org/about/vision/history-of-the-web/

what a machine-version of a water-cooler moment or coffee break is like?

Several groups are trying to move the agenda forward in developing a Web 3.0. For instance, the Web3 Foundation advocates for a shift to a server-less Internet, or as their site describes, "An internet where users are in control of their own data, identity and destiny."[18] Other organizations, like the Internet of Blockchain Foundation based in the Netherlands, are trying to foster the adoption of Web 3.0 through user-friendly decentralized frameworks such as Essentia.one. One key aim of Web 3.0 technology is to make encounters opt-in rather than opt-out, and provide greater control for users over their own data as well as digital assets. The services that are being built on top of Web 3.0 infrastructure include file distribution and storage (e.g. Storj, Siacoin, Filecoin, IPFS), decentralized versions of communication platforms like Skype (e.g. Experty.io) and WhatsApp (e.g. Status), and social networks that offer micro-transactions instead of Facebook (e.g. Steemit), as well as freelance networks that function like Upwork (e.g. Ethlance). There's even a competitor to the already crowd-sourced dictionary Wikipedia that is blockchain-based, called Everipedia. These services are still in their infancy but much of the excitement around blockchain technology lies in its relationship to a greater vision for a decentralized economic infrastructure to underpin our digital world.

Obstacles in Blockchain Technology

Blockchains, while offering new frameworks for securing and transacting virtual assets, also come with risks. Below we review some of the most notable security questions facing blockchains.

Sybil Attacks

These are attacks where a peer-to-peer system is subverted when a node in

---

18 Web3 Foundation Website, https://web3.foundation/

the network forges multiple identities and wields undue influence. The main Sybil attack concern in the Bitcoin network is a 51% attack, wherein a majority of the network computing power gets controlled by one actor. Proof of Work requires substantial computing resources, making this kind of attack very expensive. An attacker would need to pay to control many nodes at the same time and for long enough to alter transaction history.

Key Management

You have likely lost your house keys or your smartphone at some point in your lifetime. Imagine losing the keys to your funds and not being able to go to the bank to request a new set. This is the problem of managing cryptographic keys for blockchain users: they are highly sensitive and need to be kept safe but are also relatively easy to lose for most people.

Scalability

There have been many arguments made in blockchain's short lifespan about the problem of scale. This argument typically takes shape around whether block size is capable of accommodating all the transactions in the network over time, about the amount of storage and memory needed to download and validate the entire blockchain as it grows, and even about the volume of transaction throughput that is possible. Scalability questions remain about replicating applications across every node, and about using Proof of Work consensus which requires large amounts of computing power, and thus consumes real-world energy at a growing rate as the network expands. There are many developments underway to tackle different elements of these scalability debates. Some are focusing on "layer-2 scaling," or off-chain solutions that move transaction volume off-chain, and use blockchains as a settlement layer. Other approaches like "sharding" seek to split the entire state of the chain into partitions, or "shards," that have independent pieces of the state.[19]

Dispute Resolution

That you can execute transactions using a blockchain and know that they have been performed is a great tool for removing disputes. But it also opens up questions about the legal responses when a transaction was made in error or circumstances change. There are no clear solutions yet on how smart contracts or other kinds of transactions using blockchains will be seen by legal jurisdictions. While they create execution guarantees that are not inherent to legal contracts, which can require enforcement by courts or authorities, they are hard to undo or dispute within network architecture.

Updating and Governance

There are some concerns for permissionless blockchains in particular over who controls the updating, maintenance, and directional influence for these networks. In theory, there are core developers, client developers, miners, and users, who all have checks and balances based on the ability to propose changes openly on forums as well as update or fork their software in response to code changes. The Ethereum Foundation, which updates the Ethereum network, has moved to streaming its governance conversations live online in order to improve transparency in how its network is governed.

---

19 Jordan, Raul. "How To Scale Ethereum: Sharding Explained," Medium, January 10, 2018,
https://medium.com/prysmatic-labs/how-to-scale-ethereum-sharding-explained-ba2e283b7fce

Ethical and Other Issues with Blockchain

Some of the positive potential impacts of blockchain take advantage of its ability to improve efficiency and lower cost to track things like sustainability or fair trade. Tom Serres and Bettina Warburg proposed in their paper on the future of blockchain-based supply chains, that "Quantitative metrics or reputation scores assigned to identities operating in a marketplace or supply chain will be a key factor in achieving autonomous one- to-one business operations at scale."[20] A study by Deloitte on supply chain talent describes a shift in supply chains where "longstanding industries are blurring into ecosystems – dynamic and co-evolving communities of diverse actors who create new value through increasingly productive and sophisticated models of both collaboration and competition."[21] In such a future, where transparent records help document transactions over time, bad actors may be represented on a blockchain in a way that allows consumers and businesses to make more informed and granular choices. This could be in the form of a product recall, or even new types of certification. For instance, a supply chain application on blockchain could be used to "certify" the origins of goods, allowing conflict items or potentially corrupt transactions to be excluded from the supply chain more easily. The Everledger blockchain application is already doing this by certifying and tracking the origin of diamonds in order to try and keep so-called "blood diamonds" that are being used to fuel wars and terrorism in conflict zones from entering the global supply chain.

---

[20] Tom Serres and Bettina Warburg, "Introducing Asset Chains: The Cognitive, Friction-free, and Blockchain-enabled Future of Supply Chains," foreword by Don Tapscott, Blockchain Research Institute, 28 Nov. 2017, page 50.

[21] Kelly Marchese and Ben Dollar, "Supply Chain Talent of the Future," Deloitte Development LLC, 2015: 6. www2.deloitte.com/content/dam/Deloitte/global/Documents/Process-and-Operations/ gx-operations-supply-chain-talent-of-the-future-042815.pdf, accessed 10 Aug. 2017.

Chapter Summary

This chapter examined the technology that makes blockchains work in more depth. In order to understand where blockchain technology is going it is necessary to have a good understanding of how it works. This includes looking at the overall blockchain technology stack, which extends from the blockchain network infrastructure all the way to the development of specific Dapps that take advantage of different features of blockchain.

Understanding the basic technology behind blockchain involves learning about how wallets work and how they store digital tokens. The most complex piece of the blockchain puzzle certainly revolves around how miners validate transactions and come to consensus. For permissionless blockchain networks, in which miners are motivated by a reward system, consensus is usually reached by providing a Proof of Work by solving the cryptographic puzzle supplied by the SHA-256 cryptographic hash algorithm.

The chapter ended with a discussion of how blockchain is impacting the world of information technology itself. We saw that this is apparent in such areas as data storage and distribution. There is even a lot of discussion as to how blockchain will bring about a wholly new version of the Internet which has been called "Web 3.0".

Key Terms

Node
Server
Client
Consensus
Digital token
Intrinsic/native token
Stablecoin
Wallet
Virtual machine
Public key
Address
Cold storage
Hardware wallet
Block header
Hash function
Hash value / hash

SHA-256
Nonce
Merkle tree
Mining difficulty
Field Programmable Gate Arrays (FPGAs)
Application Specific Integrated Circuits (ASIC
Mining pool
Cryptojacking
Cloud mining
ASIC-resistant
X11
Blockchain as a Service (BaaS)
Decentralized storage system
Moore's Law
Web 3.0.

Questions for Further Discussion

1. For a fun exercise, go to https://bitbonkers.com/ and watch the unique way of visualizing how blocks are being created in Bitcoin in real time. What does the size and color of the balls indicate? Why are the balls falling off of the table?

2. Using http://blockchaininfo.net find the block numbered 1603 in the Bitcoin network. How many transactions are bundled in it? What is the height and what does this mean? What is the total amount of bitcoin processed in this block? What is the amount of the largest transaction? Who mined this block?

3. Go to the SHA-256 demo site at https://blockchain.adesso.ch/#/sha256 and enter in the phrase "blockchain rocks" as an input into the hash function with a difficulty of 4. What are the first four digits of the resulting hash value? What happens to the hash value when you change the input to read "BlockChain rocks!"

4. What is a 51% blockchain attack? How likely is this with the Bitcoin network?

5. What is the collision problem for cryptographic hash functions? How many possible values can the SHA-256 have? How likely is the collision problem to happen when using the SHA-256 hash function?

6. What are the inputs into the SHA-256 Proof of Work puzzle? How do miners earn their reward? What makes this so difficult?

7. What is contained in a block header? How does this link up to other blocks?

8. How many transactions must a new block contain? Are all miners working on the same set of transactions? Is it more difficult to create a block with more transactions in it? Why or why not?

9. Describe how the IT industry as a whole may be impacted by blockchain technology. What is your assessment of the likelihood of this happening?

10. What is meant by Blockchain as a Service (BaaS)? Why might this approach appeal to some companies when developing a blockchain application?

11. Go to any blockchain explorer such as the one at http://www.blockchain.com. Using this tool, find the famous "pizza" transaction from 2010 where Laszlo Hanyecz paid 10,000 bitcoin for two pizzas. What was the actual date and time of this transaction?

Chapter 3 – Bitcoin and Crypto-assets

Learning Objectives
- Gain a deeper understanding of how the Bitcoin network works
- Examine the differences between top crypto-assets
- Examine the top cryptocurrency exchanges
- Look at different cryptocurrency valuation models
- Discuss the concept of digital tokens and value
- Learn how block explorers can be used to gather data

Blockchain in Action —CryptoKitties?!

Remember the rage for Beanie Babies? People built their retirement and college saving plans around the plush, little collectible stuffed animals in the late 1990s. Prepare yourself for the updated version of Beanie Babies – CryptoKitties! Started in 2017, CryptoKitties was the first game built on blockchain technology. The game involves buying, selling, and breeding digital pictures of cats. Since it is built on blockchain, the cat images can't be destroyed and their provenance and ownership can always be traced. So not only are these images "real," but it is also impossible to counterfeit them as we can trace their records through the blockchain. Similar to Beanie Babies, these assets could be traded and sold, even though they are virtual cat images, not physical stuffed animal collectibles. In fact, some people have created whole businesses buying, selling, and breeding new cats. One early generation cat even sold for $140,000 of "real" fiat money at a Christie's auction! Each kitty has its own unique genetic makeup that affects what it looks like but also what its offspring will look like. Certain combinations may even unlock special "ascension" cats; that is, with a previously unknown characteristic! The success of CryptoKitties has spawned a whole bunch of new CryptoCollectibles games and opened up new possibilities for how blockchain can be used in the gaming industry. Players and scenarios may move between games or virtual worlds in the future. While relatively short-lived as a fad, CryptoKitties may point the way forward for other innovations on the blockchain using digital assets.

What Are Crypto-assets?

No doubt you have heard about the asset bitcoin and the rise of cryptocurrencies. You may have heard that they are the domain of drug dealers and assassins, or that they represent a big financial scam. But over the past few years, cryptocurrencies have gone from being a relatively unknown technology only used by geeks to become a darling of the fintech industry. It was just in 2008 that Satoshi Nakamoto published a proposal for the development of a new digital token or currency, which has now come to be known as "bitcoin." Valued today at many billions of dollars in market capitalization, the success of bitcoin has spawned thousands of would-be imitators and competitors, forming a whole new industry in the process. From the outset, the Bitcoin network was created to be a digital peer-to-peer payment system that would allow users to store, send, and receive money without using a financial intermediary such as a credit card company or bank. All the subsequent digital coins after the creation of bitcoin were called "altcoins" and include popular cryptocurrencies such as Ripple, Litecoin, and Ethereum's "ether."

One of the ingenious things about blockchain technology is that it was developed using some elements of game theory and economics. In order to motivate people to participate in a blockchain and help to secure the history of transactions, these systems included an incentive structure that uses "**digital tokens**." A digital token is just a way of representing value on a blockchain network. You may have heard the terms *digital token* and *digital coin* (like bitcoin and altcoins) being used interchangeably. This is in part because many of these assets have overlapping characteristics. Tokens and coins related to blockchains both fall into the more general category of "crypto-assets." Given the often confusing manner in which these terms are employed, it may be best to start off with some definitions.

Crypto-assets are the broadest concept of value on a blockchain. They are purely digital and transacted in the form of coins or tokens, but can represent anything from a store of value to a means of payment (or medium of exchange), to a physical asset. A useful way to think about all crypto-assets is across three broad categories that have some differences: cryptocurrencies, crypto-commodities, and crypto-tokens.

Cryptocurrencies

A **cryptocurrency** is defined as "any form of currency that only exists digitally, that usually has no central issuing or regulating authority but instead uses a decentralized system to record transactions and manage the issuance of new units, and that relies on cryptography to prevent counterfeiting and fraudulent transactions."[22] As a currency it functions as a "digital asset" that can be used as a medium of exchange that works on a blockchain or a distributed ledger to provide a record of financial transactions. These digital assets can also be called "coins" or "currency tokens." Often, cryptocurrencies are issued by a set of protocols that control the addition of any new coins. Bitcoin is considered to be the first successful example of a digital coin. Digital coins that have come after bitcoin and run on their own blockchain are now known as "altcoins." These alternative coins try to position themselves as improvements on the Bitcoin network model.

In addition to running on its own blockchain, a digital coin is designed to function like currency in that it represents a store of "value" and can be used as a medium of exchange (e.g. for payments). In economics, "value" is commonly defined as a measure of the benefit provided by a good or service to an economic agent. This is basically the maximum amount that a specific person will pay for a good or service. Fiat currencies (like the dollar and euro) were invented to facilitate the transfer of value. Cryptocurrencies are, in a similar fashion, digital coins that have their own monetary policies and uses, where value is driven by the market and secured through a blockchain. The most common type of crypto-asset today is certainly the currency token. In fact, twenty-four of the top twenty-five digital tokens are currency tokens. When you pay a transaction fee to use a currency token like bitcoin, you are basically paying for the service of using the digital ledger on bitcoin's blockchain. While the listing of tokens on exchanges is largely a social marker (some exchanges will list some tokens while others will not), the ability to convert a token into fiat currency or other tokens is an important indicator of fungibility.

Crypto-commodities

Commodities are a class of assets that represent raw materials and different goods or things that bring value. **Crypto-commodities** are not that dissimilar

---

[22] "Cryptocurrency," Merriam Webster website, accessed June 3, 2018, https://www.merriam-webster.com/dictionary/cryptocurrency

– they are the digital way to represent commodities or physical assets on a blockchain. These tokens are also secured with the time, computational power and cost of electricity that cryptocurrencies like bitcoin require. Governments are looking at regulating tokens like ether – used to perform transactions on the Ethereum network – under the lens of commodities, in part because the tokens are being used as a way to run smart contracts rather than just store value or make payments. Some critics argue that categorizing certain tokens as commodities is just a way to get around industry regulations, while others suggest this classification of tokens could be seen as a way for holders of traditional assets to tap into the huge global liquidity pool that is pouring into ICOs.

A subset of crypto-commodities includes "asset-backed tokens," which are designed to be digital representations of tangible assets – such as precious stones or real estate – as well as intangible assets, such as intellectual property. Everledger is a company that tokenizes diamonds, linking the physical asset with a digital twin. Representing and tracking assets that are unique (non-fungible) has been a challenge for many businesses dealing with existing assets (think land titles, diamonds, or art) and is a growing opportunity space for new digital assets. In many ways, the innovation at work is the additional ability to fractionalize ownership of an asset digitally and trade that unique value over time securely. For instance, what if you could "ICO" a Picasso painting and manage the ownership via tokens? While these types of tokens have not been as popular as the others, there is additional mounting interest in tokenizing assets across global supply chains as a means of tracking high-value or highly-regulated products such as diamonds, pharmaceuticals, agricultural products, and military defense products. As for other intangible crypto-commodities, we are even seeing approaches that focus on attention economics, which argue that since our attention is a scarce commodity, it can also be tokenized and traded. Enter the "Basic Attention Token," which allows for a blockchain-based model for digital advertising using the Ethereum blockchain and Brave platform to offer services that can be obtained with the token. Generally, crypto-commodities enable us to make the value of an asset digitally-divisible and unique, enabling new value exchange and liquidity.

Other Crypto-tokens

Crypto-tokens represent a smattering of other tokenized assets or purposes in a blockchain environment that fall outside the categories of cryptocurrency and commodity. If we look to the traditional world of finance as a reference point, there are usually four classes of assets: cash, commodities, fixed income, and stocks. We have covered the blockchain-equivalent of cash and commodities, but there are benefits that people receive from the functions of stocks and fixed-income assets that can also be conferred in the blockchain space. Stocks offer rights such as governance and ownership, as well as dividends; we can see similar functionalities in the blockchain space. The ability to use tokens to confer voting and governance rights in a network is an important element of using a blockchain. Conferring dividends and interest is also possible, depending on how a blockchain or token is implemented.

Besides cryptocurrencies, today we have terms like network tokens, security tokens, utility tokens, stable coins/tokens, and reputation/reward tokens. While these classification systems are not all mutually exclusive, it is helpful to think of how a token is being used. Below are some of the ways people are thinking of broader crypto-tokens (or assets) beyond the basic distinction between cryptocurrencies and crypto-commodities.

Category	Crypto-currency	Crypto-commodity	Network Token	Utility Token	Security Token	Stable Coin
Description	Volatile store of value with an (approximately) fixed supply	Digital way to represent commodities or physical assets on a blockchain	Needed to participate in an open network	Needed to participate in an open service	Token as call on assets held / custodied by a company	Token with value stabilized by algorithms and collateral
Creation	Created by network protocol	Created by Dapp software	Created by network protocol	Created by Dapp software	Created by Dapp software	Created by Dapp software
Example	Bitcoin	Everledger	Dfinity	Numeral	Digix	Maker DAI
Sample Purpose	Frictionless secured payment / transactions	Rpresenting an asset, but not necessarily collateralized by a company / entity	Usage or participation fees of a network	Dapp usage / participation	Linking real-world and digital asset value	Decreased volatility for transactions using digital token

Figure 3-1: Simple taxonomy of token classification and usage

Network Tokens

Network tokens are a broad category that encapsulates tokens created by their network, rather than by a Dapp. Usually you need these tokens to install software, run software, store data, pay for computation, or participate in governance on a given blockchain network. An example is the Dfinity network, where you would need to buy or possess Dfinity tokens (DFN) in order to perform these functions. Network tokens are similar to utility tokens, in that they are utilized for actions on a network, with the significant exception that they are not created by Dapp software but rather by the network protocols. Another example might be if a social network issued its own token. As long as you are on their platform, you could use their token to execute transactions. In effect, this is what the platform Steemit has done: it's a social media platform that integrates STEEM as a token for posting, searching, or commenting on their platform. Ether, the token that powers the Ethereum network can be classified as both a cryptocurrency token and a network token: you can trade it's value on an exchange or you can use it to manage transactions on the Ethereum platform itself. You might be using ether to pay for transactions or alternatively to pay for the computer power needed to execute a smart contract.

Utility Tokens

Utility tokens are sometimes called "app coins" because they are usually linked to a specific company or project's blockchain application. There are many tokens that are built on top of existing blockchain platforms like Ethereum. These tokens are often created at the beginning of a new Decentralized Application (Dapp) and are given to investors as part of their Initial Coin Offering (ICO). These tokens make it easier to buy and sell services. One example is Numerai, which is an application built on the Ethereum network that aims to crowdsource trading algorithms for hedgefunds, and requires Nuermaire (NMR) tokens to participate. Utility tokens are growing in popularity.

Security Tokens

As one can imagine, **security tokens** represent an investment in an asset. Like a security, they are backed by the tradable resources of the issuing entity. For example, Digix and Goldmint are asset-backed tokens that make it easier to own gold assets. This type of token is seen as a possible movement in the blockchain world and the Security and Exchange Commission (SEC) in the U.S. has taken note, moving to regulate these tokens just as they would securities. This is why all the companies that rushed to launch an ICO are now trying to avoid having their token listed as a security token. If classified as a security token, this will put restrictions on who can invest in the tokens and how they can be used. Until now, utility tokens have been much more popular since they are much easier to launch and are still in a regulatory gray area. A number of platforms such as The Elephant have been set up to assist companies in launching their own tokenized securities. Other groups like the Swarm Fund are working to become the "blockchain for private equity," where partial ownership in collateralized investments is tradeable via tokens. These assets could be anything from buildings to businesses to hedge funds. Swarm Fund is using the SRC-20 protocol, which is an extension to the popular ERC-20 protocol for Ethereum-based tokens, but additionally carries properties "that describe real world assets, such as their location, purpose, legal rights and obligations, and transfer restrictions."[23]

Some analysts predict that this will be the next big wave in tokens. However, there remains little clarity from regulators globally about how to classify tokens, and whether some tokens are exempt from the Howey Test traditionally relied upon to determine whether an asset is a security in the U.S. This "test" was a precedent set in 1946 to determine whether transactions were investment contracts. Amidst the gray area of token regulation, some attempts have been made to self-regulate through projects like the **SAFT** (Simple Agreements for Future Tokens) framework to help those projects raising funds through an ICO to register with the SEC in order to be as compliant as possible. SAFTs essentially define investment contracts that allow investors to fund the technical development of token-based projects. No tokens are received in exchange for funds when using a SAFT, but they

---

[23] "Swarm Basics," Swarm Fund website, accessed September 10, 2018, https://swarm.fund/swarm-basics/

can be created later once a network is developed. One way to conceptualize the difference between a utility token and a security token is to think of utility tokens more like "coupons" for services by a specific company, rather than partial ownership of assets. Utility tokens are more like going to an arcade and winning tickets which can only be redeemed at the arcade prize counter. Outside of the arcade, the tickets lose their value, but inside the arcade, they continue to be useful.

What Are ICOs?

In the rush to get into cryptocurrencies many Initial Coin Offerings (**ICO**s) have been created. Similar to an Initial Public Offering (IPO), this is when a project opens up for investment by individuals and institutions. In return for sending cryptocurrencies like bitcoin or ether to a project, investors receive some amount of tokens related to the project that either exist already or will be dispersed upon technical development of the project. Billions of dollars have been raised using ICOs already. However, because of the ease in launching these fundraising efforts – crowdfunding campaigns on steroids – a large percentage of recent ICOs have used the ERC-20 Ethereum standard. This particular standard describes basic functions and events that a token contract built on Ethereum must have. In fact, it has been shown that it only takes 30 minutes to launch a utility token on Ethereum's platform with this standard. All you need is a couple hundred lines of open source token code, some ether, an Ethereum wallet, and a platform on which to deploy it.

Unfortunately, the ease of raising these funds has meant that many ICOs are poorly thought out, if not outright scams. *The Wall Street Journal* did an intensive study of 1,450 ICOs and found that 271 of them appeared to be fraudulent. The prime indicators were things like plagiarized prospectuses or white papers and promises of risk-free, huge profits. Some ICOs were guaranteeing returns of over 40% per month. Many of these ICOs used stock photographs of people to create fictitious boards and celebrity endorsements. Still, the 271 fraudulent ICOs generated about $1 billion in investment money between them. Overall investment in ICOs has topped $12 billion since the SEC started tracking them in 2017.

While crypto-assets, and especially cryptocurrencies have seen many highs and lows in the last decade, many are concerned that the ICO fundraising route has grown too large and is impeding the growth of more innovative mechanisms in the larger decentralized economy. As with stocks, real estate, gold, a collectible, or any asset you might buy, if you are considering purchasing a crypto-asset be sure to think about whether the token you are buying can have long-term value.

Top Ten Cryptocurrencies by Market Capitalization

While the overall value of each cryptocurrency does fluctuate quite wildly, these were the top ten cryptocurrencies in terms of their total market capitalization as of summer 2018. One important note: market capitalization is not necessarily a sound way to measure the value of cryptocurrencies. Similar to how market cap is calculated for the stock market, you multiply the number of coins in circulation by the price per coin. Price and market cap can be manipulated by off-market trades. Nvidia software engineer John Ratcliff once described how you could launch the biggest cryptocurrency on the market if you created a total supply of one trillion tokens and sold just one token to an external party for $1. In this scenario, your coin would technically have a market capitalization of $1 trillion USD. Another criticism of using market cap is that often many of the coins for a given network are still held in reserve by the network's founders. A more sound market cap calculation would therefore include the crypto-equivalent of "shares outstanding," or the coins that are not in circulation but are part of the total number. Inflation rates for cryptocurrencies are codified and therefore should also play a part in any valuation model. With these caveats in mind, we will now examine these top cryptocurrencies to ascertain the niche they each are attempting to fill.

Figure 3-2: Top ten tokens by market capitalization Summer 2018

Bitcoin

As has been previously discussed, bitcoin was the first successful cryptocurrency. All the other cryptocurrencies created after this are called "altcoins" since they represent alternatives to bitcoin that attempt to make improvements to the Bitcoin network model in some capacity. The origin of bitcoin goes back to the enigmatic Satoshi Nakamoto, who coded its first implementation in 2009. Since then, bitcoin has experienced many ups and downs, but remains by far the leading and longest-functioning cryptocurrency currently in existence. For many people, the Bitcoin network is synonymous with illicit activity. The infamous WannaCry malware virus tried to extort payments from victims of $300 in bitcoin. Because of the transparency of the Bitcoin wallets, authorities have been able to track the WannaCry ransom and it appears that this malware program only generated about $100,000 worth of bitcoin, which was withdrawn in 2017.

Actions such as these have certainly increased the controversy surrounding bitcoin. However, bitcoin is important because it has proven that a digital asset running on a decentralized network was feasible. Combined with the use of consensus and cryptography, it was the first successful decentralized application running on blockchain technology. Some of the controversy (and also excitement) surrounding the Bitcoin network is the fact that it is not controlled by any government or banking institution. Millions of dollars-worth of tokens can move freely between digital wallets without any need for a middleman to validate the transactions. Though the wallets are transparent, police cannot freeze the contents as they could with a typical account at a bank. All of this happens alongside consensus and cryptography protocols which reduce concerns about fraudulent transactions or issues with counterfeiting. Some of the potential benefits of the Bitcoin network include:

• Maintaining a permanent and transparent record of transactions on the blockchain

• Faster payment processing

• Cutting down on transaction fees from third parties

• Supporting international payment processing

• Simplifying processing of high-value payments

• Reducing the paperwork associated with banking accounts by using wallets

• Domestic and international transactions confirmed within an hour regardless of size

• First truly global (and non-national) currency

Bitcoin is not without its challenges, despite these benefits. The fact that there is no centralized control means that there is no arbiter if issues arise. For instance, if a wallet owner loses his/her private key, that user is out of luck and has no other recourse. Also, even though the blockchain itself may be very challenging to hack, attackers have become very creative with respect to how they can steal from wallets. The growth in cryptocurrencies has also spawned many fraudulent tokens which continue to attract investors.

There are also technical issues to consider in the Bitcoin network. In particular, how to get the overall Bitcoin community to upgrade its software and protocols. One of the biggest controversies is with respect to changing the size of the blocks that are mined. Currently, the standard protocol is that they are about 1 MB in size and it takes roughly ten minutes to mine a new block. However, the more transactions that use bitcoin, the longer it may take for those transactions with low or no transaction fees to get verified and included in a new block. This is because transaction fees are incentives for miners. This means that only three or four transactions are processed per second as compared to a credit card company like Visa which can process over 20,000 transactions a second. Those unprocessed transactions will sit longer in a queue and possibly lead to disaffected users. This issue is what is termed a "scaling" problem and reflects concerns as to how BTC might grow to become a feasible global currency. One solution that has been hotly debated among Bitcoin Core developers is the idea of increasing the block size to 2 MB instead of 1 MB. This would double the number of transactions that could be bundled into a block. This change has not been incorporated into the BTC protocols since some were concerned that it would put smaller miners at a disadvantage. For now, increasing transaction fees is being employed as a more natural way to manage the growth of BTC.

Of course, Bitcoin continues to evolve and change. One crucial way that it has changed in the past is through the use of **forks**. A fork is a mechanism for adding new features to the blockchain or for dealing with the effects of hacking or some kind of disastrous bug in the system. In order for a change to the protocol to occur, there must be a consensus of the users of the network. A **hard fork** is when a majority of the nodes agree to change the protocol in a way that is incompatible with the old rules. For example, a hard fork would be required if a consensus of BTC miners decided to increase the size of blocks to 2 MB. Some of the original miners could decide to continue on with the old protocols for creating new blocks. This would precipitate a major split in the blockchain. This is exactly what happened when there was a hard fork in the Ethereum blockchain which created the new Ethereum Classic blockchain (that maintained the old code base) and an updated Ethereum blockchain (that contained a change). Each of these chains had their own coin after the fork.

Basics of Blockchain

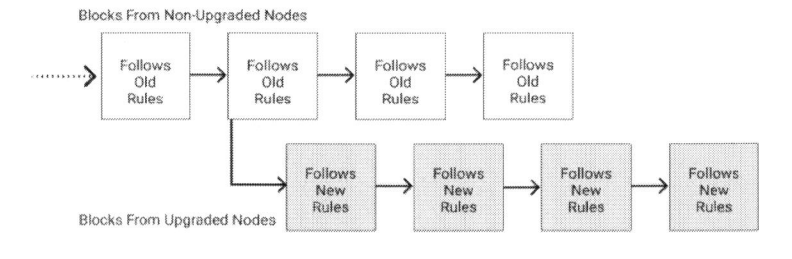

A Hard Fork: Chain Diverges And Non-Upgraded Nodes Continue With Old Rules

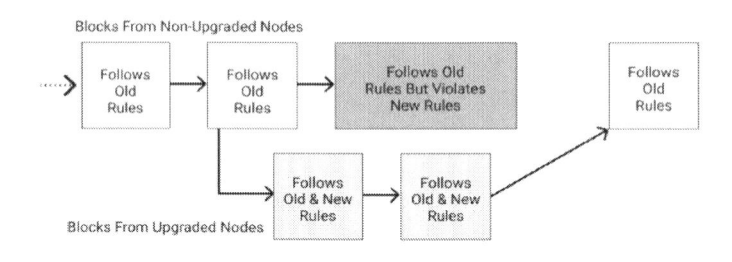

A Soft Fork: Blocks Violating New Rules Are Made Stale By The Upgraded Mining Majority

Figure 3-3: Hard fork diagram

A **soft fork** is different in that the change in the protocol is backwardly compatible with the old protocol. This might be the case if the mining protocol were changed so that block size was limited to 500 KB instead of 1 MB. New blocks that were only 500 KB would still fit the old protocol and so they would be allowed under both the old and new rules. Those miners that do not upgrade to the new protocol will have a problem since when they attempt to mine 1 MB-sized blocks they will be rejected by the updated miners. This can lead to a hard fork if they decide not to update their software to the new protocol and keep mining under the old one. The soft fork has been the most commonly used method for making minor upgrades to the BTC rules in the past.

Colored Coins

In 2013, a project to develop something called "colored coins" began as a way to add more functionality to the whole Bitcoin blockchain. Colored coins are supposed to represent real assets such as cars, real estate, precious metals, and stocks and bonds. They are very easy to issue using the existing Bitcoin blockchain technology. A change in the Bitcoin program was made in 2014, which made it possible to "color" a bitcoin by adding notes such as "this represents an ounce of gold" or "this represents a thousand euros." Transferring ownership of these assets then became almost free. The problem was that Ethereum came along with its support for smart contracts and smart objects and this replicated much of the functionality of the colored coins. Colored coins have not yet been used much and in 2018, Coinprism, one of the leading colored coin wallets shut down. Time will tell if they become generally accepted.

Implications of Forks for Cryptocurrencies

There is a lot of debate about the value of forks for cryptocurrencies. In many senses, forks serve as a governance tool – a way to create checks and balances in the progression of a blockchain – because they allow software and protocol updates to be proposed by core developers or community members but do not require everyone to accept them. Forks are a way to evolve a codebase through the consent of its users. Acceptance of updates is often incentivized since miners and users want to be a part of the longest chain, which will have the most continued transactions, and thus, profit. There are also times when updates deal with critical existential or security questions for how a specific blockchain will continue, and the community of users and miners decide to refrain from updating, preferring to maintain an older version of the software (such as with Ethereum Classic or Bitcoin Cash).

Some argue that forks weaken the cryptocurrency overall and should be avoided. They suggest this is especially true when forks represent some kind of corrective measure to refund coins that were siphoned off due to buggy smart contract code, rather than bugs in the blockchain protocols. There are additional criticisms that forks are influenced by powerful leaders in the crypto community, who can sway users by commenting on proposals or using social media to tell certain narratives. But others argue that forks are necessary for cryptocurrencies to evolve and grow and that they will be more stable in the long run. As with any codebase, a blockchain's protocols need maintenance and upkeep as new attack vectors are discovered and the economics of the platform shift over time. Keep in mind that when you own a cryptocurrency or coins, all you really own are a pair of private and public keys that give you access to your records on the blockchain ledger. So if the software changes there is some concern that your keys will no longer work.

These issues came to a head in 2017, when the Bitcoin network experienced two hard forks. In August, Bitcoin Cash was launched and then Bitcoin Gold followed in October. The rationale for creating Bitcoin Cash was that part of the Bitcoin community wanted to increase the speed of transactions and forked to change the block size on their chain to 8 MB. Bitcoin Gold, on the other hand, wanted to discourage the corporatization of mining and so created an algorithm that limited the use of specialized mining hardware as part of its fork. Both of these new cryptocurrencies have had initial success and Bitcoin itself has continued to grow in usage. However, an earlier attempt to create a fork with a larger block size failed (Bitcoin Classic) and another one was suspended (Segwit2x) before it could take effect.

Cryptocurrency traders love it when a cryptocurrency forks, partly because of the volatility that could ensue. In the case of the Bitcoin Cash fork, bitcoin holders were offered an equivalent amount of the new Bitcoin Cash currency after the fork took effect. This was in anticipation that the value of the original bitcoin would go down. However, the price of bitcoin went up substantially after the fork and holders of both got a large bonus. One potential reason for the spike was that the controversy around the fork had been holding bitcoin back and once resolved, the market felt there was less uncertainty about its future.

Where Did All the bitcoin Go?

When you own bitcoin all you own is a pair of keys that unlock your record on the Bitcoin ledger. If you lose your private key then you have no recourse, and you have lost your access to your digital currency forever. It has been estimated that as much as $30 billion dollars-worth of bitcoin has been lost or misplaced by bitcoin owners. A study done by forensic analytics firm, Chainalysis, concluded that somewhere between 2.78 million and 3.79 million bitcoin have been lost or misplaced.[24] This figure includes the one million bitcoin that Satoshi Nakamoto has left untouched in his/her original wallet. Given that it is only possible to mine 21 million bitcoin due to the protocol's structure, and over 16-million of those have been mined, we have already reached a very large percentage of all bitcoin in circulation.

Stories of hard-drives that were thrown away with hundreds of bitcoin abound from early adopters. One computer enthusiast and early miner in Melbourne claims to have stored "several thousand" bitcoin on a cheap flash drive. When he saw the price go up he tried to reclaim it off the drive but was unable to retrieve it; missing out on tens of millions of dollars of a potential windfall. He insisted on anonymity since if his wife found out he said, "I'm dead." In many cases, these kinds of losses occurred because bitcoin was almost worthless in its early days. Early miners didn't put much effort into taking care of their bitcoin.

When the price of James Howell's 7,500 bitcoin rose to be valued at $127 million, he petitioned his local landfill in Wales to let him try and dig it up. Apparently, he had been an early miner and accumulated 7,500 bitcoin which he stored on the hard drive from his old computer. One day, tired of seeing it laying around, he decided to throw it away. Now it sits in the local landfill with four years of accumulated waste lying on top of it. The local council has denied Howell's access to the landfill, saying that it will stir up all kinds of toxic waste and create an environmental nightmare. If the price of bitcoin keeps rising, we'll see if they soften their position given that the township might receive a healthy portion of the windfall. While "losing" one's bitcoin is a real possibility without effective key management, some consider the non-physicality and tamperproof qualities of bitcoin and other altcoins to be a primary benefit, making them harder to attack than traditional assets like cash or even banked money. Given that people lose or misplace hundreds of millions of dollars of coins and paper currency each year this amount of lost bitcoin might actually be an improvement.[25]

---

[24] Roberts, Jeff John and Nicolas Rapp. "Exclusive: Nearly 4 Million Bitcoins Lost Forever, New Study Says," Fortune, November 25, 2017, http://fortune.com/2017/11/25/lost-bitcoins/

[25] Kiger, Patrick J. "How much money do people accidentally throw away every year?" How Stuff Works,

Altcoins

One way to track some of the most interesting new variations in blockchain is by studying altcoins. Instead of creating a fork to add new features or updates, some developers have simply left bitcoin and started fresh by creating whole new digital tokens. Most of these are trying out new protocols and models to solve some of the scalability and speed problems being encountered with the Bitcoin network. Some are offering more support for developing Dapps or making it easier and cheaper to attract new users. Many are moving to get rid of the problems with miners by shifting from a Proof of Work protocol to a Proof of Stake or some other modification to the standard. Below are some of the top altcoins today:

Ethereum (ETH)

Ethereum's daily trading volume actually surpassed Bitcoin's volume in May of 2017 and generally has remained on the rise. As a result, Ethereum is the leading candidate for Blockchain 2.0. At the ripe old age of 19, Vitalik Buterin, after studying Bitcoin, first proposed the idea of Ethereum in a 2013 whitepaper. The core idea was that a distributed ledger could be used not just to store and validate transaction records but also contracts or instructions and the scripts required to execute the instructions. As a more generalized blockchain, the network Buterin proposed would use smart contracts to create programmable transactions that represented more than financial transactions between accounts.

The Ethereum network was coded and its Frontier implementation was launched in July of 2015, with contributions from the Ethereum Foundation based in Switzerland. Ethereum is a permissionless and public blockchain where miners obtain "ether" as the digital token for validating transactions and creating new blocks. It is one of the most mature blockchain platforms and has seen widespread adoption among large corporations, academics, and vendors. Ether does function as a cryptocurrency and can be traded on

https://money.howstuffworks.com/how-much-money-accidentally-throw-away2.htm

altcoin exchanges, but it should also be thought of as a token that allows for the management of a finite resource, namely computing power. If you think about the role of ether, anyone wishing to execute a smart contract must spend a certain amount of token to pay for the computing power necessary to run the scripts. If no token were required, the network could be spammed by contracts that execute on an infinite loop and hog up all the computing resources. Many new private blockchains have started using forks of the Ethereum protocol mainly for its smart contract features.

In 2016, Ethereum was the subject of an attack where a large quantity of ether was siphoned off to a separate "child DAO" account by using a recursive call exploit. This became known as "The DAO attack." A huge debate ensued among the Ethereum community about how to respond to this attack. Some thought that the response should be to do a soft fork and upgrade the software. However, there was concern that this upgrade would open the platform up to DDOS (Denial of Service) attacks. Others wanted to roll back the fraudulent transactions and make it up to those who lost their funds in the buggy DAO project's smart contract. In the end, it was decided by the community that a hard fork was in order, and so Ethereum Classic (ETC) was the name given to the original version of the Ethereum network that wanted to maintain its code and disagreed with the update that rolled back funds.

Ripple (XRP)

Ripple (XRP) was started in 2012 as a payment processing network. It is really quite different from the Bitcoin network in a number of ways. While it does make use of distributed ledger technology on a peer-to-peer network of servers, and the servers also perform the function of validating transactions, that is where the similarity ends. Most argue that it's not even really a blockchain network. Ripple's main purpose is to move large quantities of money around the world in the most efficient manner – almost a payment rails for banks. Tokens are not mined as they are in Bitcoin, and the XRP tokens function more like security tokens and an arbitrary quantity (100 billion) of them were issued at the start of Ripple.

The basic strength of Ripple is that it is designed to help banks move any kind of asset around the world more quickly and cheaply. Assets could be gold, currencies, or other cryptocurrencies. And Ripple is claiming that they can scale the network to process 50,000 transactions/second; much faster than Bitcoin or Ethereum's speed. But by maintaining its own list of approved validating servers, Ripple has been criticized for going back to a centralized model of control. Additionally, XRP has been the subject of ongoing SEC investigations into whether it is an asset or a security. This has had a dampening effect on them in general.

Bitcoin Cash (BCH)

Bitcoin Cash (BCH) is a cryptocurrency born out of the hard fork of Bitcoin in August 2017. The big issue that caused the fork in the Bitcoin mainnet was that of scalability. As the popularity of bitcoin increased, so did the volume of transactions that the network was tasked to handle. As the Bitcoin network grew, its "latency" or time lag, for transactions went from one second to fourteen seconds. For merchants using bitcoin for small Point-of-Sale transactions this became unacceptable. If you paid the absolute minimum transaction fees the median wait time for validating a transaction was thirteen minutes!

After a long and tedious debate about how to solve this problem, those miners that wanted to increase the block-size of Bitcoin in order to process more transactions more quickly voted to do a hard fork and create Bitcoin Cash. The new token has a block size limit of 8 MB as opposed to the original 1 MB limit of Bitcoin. Owners of bitcoin were given an equivalent number of BCH at the time of the fork. This gave a big boost to owners's overall cryptocurrency holdings. In order to attract the all-important miners to BCH, the network lowered the difficulty level for mining new blocks. This attracted so many miners over from BTC that there was a significant drop in the BTC hashrate.[26]

---

[26] "What is Bitcoin Cash? A Basic Beginners Guide," Blockgeeks Inc, https://blockgeeks.com/guides/what-is-bitcoin-cash/

EOS (EOS)

Even though Bitcoin and Ethereum have dominated the cryptocurrency market, EOS (EOS) is a new digital coin that has grown rapidly since its launch in July of 2017. EOS is a complete Dapp development platform like Ethereum, with the capability to customize user interfaces and build smart contracts. EOS's founder, Dan Larimar, was involved in other successful cryptocurrency startups and has gathered a group of developers to try and build a platform for building better Dapps and DAOs. They developed the EOS blockchain to process over 50,000 transactions/second. The network does not require the use of miners, but instead uses a **Delegated Proof of Stake (DPoS)** protocol. This consensus protocol uses elected delegates to fine-tune such issues as block-size, fees, and transaction size. The goal is to speed up the process of confirming transactions. New blocks are currently generated every three seconds. However, there are many criticisms of EOS, in particular that it is developing a constitutional protocol that is essentially re-centralizing power in the hands of people rather than code. As the researcher and Cornell academic Emin Gün Sirer noted in a recent tweet, "If you like EOS' governance, you can achieve the exact same effect in Ethereum or Tezos by pumping all payments through a contract that delays payments until approved by 15 out of 21 arbiters. EOS' entire value proposition can be simulated elsewhere."[27]

Litecoin (LTC)

Litecoin is the brainchild of ex-Google employee Charlie Lee. In 2011 he wanted to create a version of Bitcoin that everyone could afford and use. If Bitcoin were the cryptocurrency equivalent of gold, Litecoin was built to be the new "silver": a version of Bitcoin that was cheaper and suitable for everyday use. It is an open-source clone of Bitcoin with a few modifications. First, instead of every ten minutes, new blocks are mined every 2.5 minutes. That way merchants who need to do a lot of small transactions each day can get these processed much more quickly than they could on the Bitcoin

---

[27] @el33th4xor, June 28, 2018, https://twitter.com/el33th4xor/status/1012383632999239680?s=11

network. It does use miners to perform a Proof of Work task, but it is a simplified version of the SHA-256 algorithm and does not require as much computing power. Theoretically, anyone with a computer could compete for the rewards of creating new blocks in Litecoin. Recently, one company has begun producing ASIC chips that are specifically designed for mining Litecoin and this is upsetting the community of miners. In 2017, Litecoin was one of the first cryptocurrencies to implement a new feature called "Segregated Witness" or **SegWit**. Simply stated, this helped decrease the load on their blockchain by moving the signature data for all transactions off of the main chain and onto a sidechain. The sidechain runs parallel to the main chain and allows access to the signature data while not slowing down the block creation and maintenance process. Litecoin continues to be one of the most popular cryptocurrencies.

Cardano (ADA)

Cardano (ADA) is another up-and-coming digital token. Charles Hoskinson, one of the co-founders of Ethereum, founded Cardano to be a Blockchain 3.0 platform. According to him, the Blockchain 1.0 was Bitcoin and digital tokens, 2.0 was Ethereum and smart contracts, and Cardano is evolving to be Blockchain 3.0. As such, Cardano takes the best features from the first two generations and attempts to solve the issues of scalability, interoperability, and sustainability. They have developed a new version of the Proof of Stake consensus protocol called Ouroboros, that tries to find a happy medium between processing speed and fairness to miners.

To increase interoperability between blockchains, Cardano is trying to eliminate the need for cryptocurrency exchanges through the use of "**sidechains**." These sidechains will run in parallel to the main chain and will contain a compressed version of the other blockchains that are to be linked. This will allow for checking the transactions stored on other chains and linking them to the transactions on the main chain. In order to improve the network's long-term sustainability, including support for future growth and research in Cardano, a certain portion of each block reward is set aside in a "treasury." Developers can apply to the treasury for a grant which gets voted on by Cardano stakeholders. Some of these features are still being worked out, but the Cardano developers are particularly proud of the fact that they are basing their development on sound design principles taken from academic research.

Stellar / Chain (XLM)

Stellar (XLM) is similar to Ripple in some ways. In fact, Jed McCaleb the founder of Stellar was also a co-founder of Ripple. Their native token was originally called "Stellar" but now goes by the name "lumens" or "XLM." Both of these altcoins have focused on improving the overall efficiency of cross-border payments and transfers. Currently this is done in our financial system by having a domestic bank maintain its own account in a corresponding bank in another country. Funds that are transferred must go through a somewhat tedious process of reconciliation between the two accounts, which can take several days at best. Using a cryptocurrency for these transactions instead can increase liquidity and speed up cross-border payments. Stellar has partnered with IBM to focus on improving cross-border transfers especially for the countries in the South Pacific region. They are aiming at processing 60% of the cross-border transfers from this region with their digital currency. Additionally, they have partnered with Deloitte to develop payment applications. Thirty banks signed onto their platform already and they are looking at partnering with other high-profile payment processors. In order to gain some highly coveted developers, Stellar recently announced they were purchasing Chain for $500 million.[28] This type of acqui-hire transaction is likely to become more common as cryptocurrency firms jockey for key talent.

IOTA (MIOTA)

One of the most unique altcoins is the IOTA (MIOTA) coin. IOTA attempts

---

[28] Muhn, Julie. "Stellar to Acquire Chain.com," Finovate Blog, June 25, 2018, http://finovate.com/stellar-to-acquire-chain-com/

to take all the benefits of having a distributed, trustless network while resolving some of the issues around scaling, mining, and validation. This altcoin does not use blockchain technology to create a distributed ledger the way the Bitcoin network does. Instead, it makes use of an alternative tool called "**Directed Acyclic Graphs**" or DAGs in order to remove the need for miners and even a blockchain. DAGs are not a new tool, and have been popular subjects of mathematicians's research for years. IOTA is a complete platform that was originally developed to make micro-payments between devices in the Internet of Things (IoT). There is no separate set of mining nodes in the IOTA network. Any user who makes a transaction must consequently participate in validating two other transactions, almost a round-robin of validation.

It is widely acknowledged that at some point traditional blockchain networks like Bitcoin will be susceptible to brute-force attacks from high-powered quantum computers. IOTA attempts to forestall this and was designed with quantum computing resisting cryptography in mind.[29] Instead of a blockchain, IOTA creates something called the "**tangle**." This involves complex math in order to link up transactions. The tangle also removes the necessity of paying mining fees, meaning it can process micropayments as well as large transfers of value. Interestingly, unlike Bitcoin or Ethereum which use the traditional blockchain approach where the more users it has the slower it gets, the more users IOTA has on the tangle, the faster it works. The IOTA group continues to sign up an impressive set of partners across the global business landscape. However, it has also come under scrutiny by leading researchers, such as Neha Narula at MIT's Digital Currency Initiative, for various cryptographic vulnerabilities.[30]

---

[29] Popov, Serguei. "The Tangle" Version 1.4.3, April 30, 2018, page 26,

https://assets.ctfassets.net/r1dr6vzfxhev/2t4uxvs1qk0EUau6g2sw0g/45eac33637ca92f85dd9f4a3a218e1ec/iota1_4_3.pdf

[30] Narula, Neha. "Cryptographic vulnerabilities in IOTA," Medium, September 7, 2017,

https://medium.com/@neha/cryptographic-vulnerabilities-in-iota-9a6a9ddc4367

Tronix (TRX)

In 2017, the 27-year-old Justin Sun, launched Tronix. The focus of Tronix was to develop a platform for sharing media on a decentralized network; thereby basically disintermediating other popular app-sharing platforms such as the Apple Store and Google Play Store. Using the Tronix platform, users pay developers directly for sharing their apps and media content without paying the typical 30% fees taken by the other platforms.

Justin Sun is no newbie to the world of cryptocurrencies. He's a graduate of the University of Pennsylvania and was a founder of China's version of Snapchat before becoming an executive overseeing the growth of Ripple in China's markets. Tronix has already launched its own smart contracts and has its own Tron Foundation. Tron's value recently took a nose dive when it was discovered that they had plagiarized some of the content in their whitepaper. Other concerns have arisen about the huge number of its Tron (TRX) coins – one billion – they minted.

> **Dogecoin**
>
> In 2013 a meme featuring pictures of a Shiba Inu dog with its inner monologue, usually in a broken English, typed over the picture in Comic Sans typeface made the rounds across the Internet. The meme spawned the creation of "Dogecoin," a cryptocurrency that took the image as its inspiration and logo. While originally a bit of a joke, created by Jackson Palmer and Billy Markus, it became more legitimate once a community started trading it and its market cap reached $60 million in 2014. Today, Dogecoin is used somewhat for online tipping.

Figure 3-4: "Doge" meme that influenced dogecoin

Up-and-Coming Cryptos to Watch

Since there are so many new cryptocurrencies competing for our attention today, it is important to focus on the logic of the use case behind each one, as well as the key differentiating technology traits. Here are a few emerging cryptos that present interesting arguments for their new tokens.

Zcash (ZEC)

Zcash is a cryptocurrency that is designed to improve on the privacy of permissionless blockchains. It is a fork of the Bitcoin protocol. Bitcoin transactions are totally transparent by design, which can present issues for certain transactions. For example, if a big public business event results in an expected bitcoin transaction, this could reveal the owner of the bitcoin wallet. Zcash is pioneering the use of "**zero-knowledge proofs**," which is a cryptography mechanism for proving properties about encrypted data without revealing the data itself. The bank JPMorgan Chase has incorporated some of the Zcash privacy technology into its Quorum blockchain.

Monero (XMR)

Since its debut in 2014, Monero has been one of the fastest growing cryptocurrencies out there. Its claim to fame is that it is supposed to be untraceable and anonymous, unlike the Bitcoin network, where everyone can see anyone else's wallet and trace individual transaction histories. This means that authorities can know the addresses of some of the wallets where illicit transactions occur in bitcoin, although they can't necessarily tell who owns them. Monero (from the Esperanto word for "money") is open-source like Bitcoin but utilizes a combination of cryptographic elements (ring signatures and stealth addresses) that randomizes addresses even further so that Monero transactions are totally untraceable. One might think that this functionality is meant to further illicit Dark Web activity, but in fact, one of the criticisms of

Bitcoin is that it lacks **fungibility.**[31] This is a tricky, but important concept in the crypto world. Simply put, fungibility refers to how interchangeable one asset is for another asset of the type or class. We all know that you could exchange a 20 Euro bill for two 10 Euro bills, and this would mean that Euros are a highly fungible asset. But if someone borrowed your blue Bianchi road bike and gave you back a different blue Bianchi road bike, you might not be too happy; meaning that bikes are not a very fungible asset.

Because all the transactions that a bitcoin has been involved in can be traced, this leads to the idea that some of the money could be "tainted" by having been used in illegal transactions. And so, if you receive some of this tainted bitcoin, you yourself might become a suspect to the authorities. If this line of reasoning holds, then not all bitcoin are perfectly interchangeable. The untraceability of Monero means that there is no concept of tainted or clean money, and thus it is also perfectly fungible. Monero is also designed to be ASIC-resistant to prevent dominance by corporate miners and remain conducive to small mining operations.

Dfinity (DFN)

Dfinity is a protocol that seeks to become an "Internet Computer." It was founded by longtime crypto-entrepreneur Dominic Williams in order to address some of the scalability issues around running smart contracts on the Ethereum platform. While improving the execution speed of smart contracts, the network also added more functionality so that longer Dapps could be run on its platform. One of the major innovations to Dfinity's technology is its use of **Threshold Relay** as part of its consensus mechanism. Rather than use Proof of Work or Proof of Stake, Threshold Relay creates a random group of validators on the network derived from a cryptographic beacon instead of **crypto-economics** (like staking). This changes some of the security threats that crypto-economic frameworks engender (e.g. relying on incentives built on the idea that participants won't want to see their holdings decrease in value). Dfinity is also quite different from the other tokens in that it has

---

[31] "What is Monero? Most Comprehensive Guide," Blockgeeks Inc, https://blockgeeks.com/guides/what-is-monero/

created governance features of the network to enable voting to undo fraudulent transactions rather than relying on hard forks. This can make it less appealing to attempt to hack than some of the other "immutable" Dapps like Bitcoin.

> **A New Way to Fund Your Local Police**
>
> In 2017 Germany's Cyber Crime unit shut down an e-book and audio piracy platform Lul.to. They moved quickly to shut down the site and arrested its operators. In the process, they found a whole basket of cryptocurrencies that the site's users had accumulated. In total, the police found 1,312 bitcoins, 1,399 bitcoin cash, 1,312 Bitcoin Gold and 220 ether.[32] When these cryptocurrencies were sold off over the span of two months, the sale netted the government almost 12 million Euro, which was to be used to help support further criminal investigations. Given the rise in this type of crime, government authorities are learning quickly to include these types of crypto-assets in seizures in the future.

Popular Cryptocurrency Scams

One of the reasons that cryptocurrencies get so much negative press is because as fast as new ICOs are launched, new ways are found to scam people out of their money. Some of these are discussed in the following section.

FOMO-based ICOs

As mentioned earlier, despite the extreme security used, bitcoin and cryptocurrencies in general, are now infamous for all of the fraud and scams

---

[32] Voss, Oliver. "Bayern verkauft Bitcoin für 12 Millionen Euro," Der Tagesspiegel, May 28, 2018, https://www.tagesspiegel.de/wirtschaft/internetkriminalitaet-bayern-verkauft-bitcoin-fuer-12-millionen-euro/22611878.html

surrounding them. One of the benefits of cryptocurrencies is that they are unregulated and semi-private, but this also makes them prime targets for criminals. One of the biggest scandals is simply raising funds without ever intending to deliver value, relying on people's Fear of Missing Out (FOMO) to do the heavy lifting. *The Wall Street Journal* study mentioned earlier in the chapter found that a high percentage of cryptocurrencies examined were totally fraudulent, but had nonetheless raked in over a billion dollars from investors.[33] All that was needed to launch an ICO was to modify some open source code and slap together a fake website with phony pictures and bios of the team members. Promises of sky-high profits and even commissions for signing up new investors were some of the other tip-offs that an ICO was a fraud. A new coin called "My Big Coin" shut down after taking in $6 million in deposits that went straight into the accounts of its "Directors." The South Korean markets have been especially susceptible to these kinds of schemes.

Fake Exchanges

Another large-scale fraud related to cryptocurrencies has to do with fake exchanges. Exchanges such as Coinbase perform a very important service in that they provide an easy on and off ramp into bitcoin or other popular cryptocurrencies. This is where owners can convert their bitcoin to dollars or vice versa. The exchanges normally take a fee for providing this service. In the early days of bitcoin, the infamous Mt. Gox exchange shut down and bitcoin valued at a half billion dollars (at that time) just disappeared. This certainly slowed the adoption of cryptocurrencies and gave bitcoin a bad reputation. However, fake exchanges are still popping up. The best way to avoid these scams is to stick with reputable known exchanges and do research before using one.

---

[33] Shifflett, Shane and Coulter Jones. "Buyer Beware: Hundreds of Bitcoin Wannabes Show Hallmarks of Fraud," The Wall Street Journal, May 17, 2018, https://www.wsj.com/articles/buyer-beware-hundreds-of-bitcoin-wannabes-show-hallmarks-of-fraud-1526573115

Mining Pools

One of the most successful strategies for Bitcoin miners has been to pool computing resources with thousands of other members of a "**mining pool**." The problem is that the human organizers of the pool are the ones who decide how to split up the proceeds from the mining operations. These pool organizers can not only skim profits, they can also shut down suddenly and take all of the proceeds. Hackers have also broken into some mining pools and tricked members into revealing their private keys and emptying their wallets. One mining pool called AntPool, was found to be selling mining hardware that included malware that would allow them to remotely shut down equipment of customers or competitors and make themselves more profitable. There have even been cases of malware that installs itself on individual's computers, turning them into zombie mining machines; mining bitcoin for the malware's creators without the knowledge of the computer owners.

Several clever bitcoin Ponzi schemes have sprouted in recent years too. They function much like Bernie Madoff's famous Ponzi scheme, where they promise huge returns on investments and use later investments to actually make some payments to the early investors. Many high-profile investors like Jamie Dimon of JPMorgan Chase and Warren Buffett of Berkshire Hathaway have claimed that all cryptocurrencies are just one big Ponzi scheme that will come crashing down at some point. One Texas man launched an investment service in 2013 called Bitcoin Savings and Trust and was sentenced to prison in 2016 for creating a Ponzi scheme. Another example is the Mining Max operation, a Korean cryptocurrency mining company where members were forced to become "affiliates" and were rewarded for signing up new investors. Executives at Mining Max appear to have embezzled $250 million from 18,000 investors and are now on the run from Interpol.[34]

---

[34] Goenka, Himanshu. "Multimillion Dollar Cryptocurrency Scam By Mining Max Busted In South Korea," International Business Times, December 20, 2017, http://www.ibtimes.com/multimillion-dollar-cryptocurrency-scam-mining-max-busted-south-korea-2630744

Cybercrime and Cryptocurrencies

Since the beginning of the Bitcoin network, cryptocurrencies have had a dark side to them. The average person probably views the mystery around the anonymous founder of Bitcoin, Satoshi Nakamoto, as highly suspicious. In 2011, Silk Road was founded as the "eBay for drugs" and 97% of the transactions handled on this site were conducted using bitcoin. Cryptocurrencies are ideal for criminal activity because of the highly secure, yet pseudonymous wallet feature. The fact that it supports international payments is even better. The FBI estimates that Silk Road helped generate $1.2 billion in bitcoin-based sales.[35] When it was shut down in 2013, and the founder jailed for life, dozens of new darknet marketplaces sprang up to replace it. One of the leaders, AlphaBay, was also shut down in 2017. Even though bitcoin transactions are pseudonymous, law enforcement authorities are able to monitor suspicious wallets and track their activities. Patterns in transaction activity revealed many of the owners of these wallets to be engaged in criminal activities such as the hackers who created the WannaCry ransomware virus.

It was also significant that when authorities shut down Silk Road and AlphaBay, the assets of thousands of users who stored their cryptocurrencies on the markets, were also seized. On Silk Road alone, 26,000 bitcoin were seized that were worth hundreds of millions of dollars. AlphaBay was estimated to be ten times larger than Silk Road when it was finally shut down.[36] Taking down these markets involved a high degree of coordination among multiple countries, which is a growing trend in enforcement. Advances for everyday users are of course also advances for criminals. Recently, the development of new cryptocurrencies such as Monero and ZCash has allowed the actual ownership of specific wallets to be hidden from view, making it difficult to track activity and find patterns of regular users but also criminal activity. With the history of cryptocurrencies on the darknet and these new coins, it's clear that criminal activities have definitely contributed to

---

[35] Caffyn, Grace. Bitcoin on the Dark Web: The Facts," CoinDesk, September 23, 2015,

https://www.coindesk.com/bitcoin-on-the-dark-web-the-facts/

[36] C.M. "Silk Road Vs. AlphaBay: Before, During, & After Seizure," Darwebnews.com, January 10, 2018,

https://darkwebnews.com/darknet-markets/silk-road-vs-alphabay-before-during-after-seizure/

the popularity of cryptocurrencies.

What Makes a Good Token Project?

We have just taken a brief look at some of the many different cryptocurrencies out there. From this discussion you should see that the whole idea of digital tokens and decentralized applications is evolving in interesting ways that attempt to solve some of the foundational limitations of blockchain and Bitcoin. Below are some considerations to keep in mind when considering investments in cryptocurrencies or blockchain networks.

Leadership

One of the most important things to evaluate is the leadership team. Do they have experience in the blockchain world? Are they actively participating in the project's development? Do they hold any specific technical expertise? What is their track record for technology development, startup management, or innovation?

Community

Is there a wider community of developers working on the platform? What is the project's plan for community engagement? How do participants behave on social media and across peer networks relevant to their technology? Is the project open-source? Does the project host meetups or participate in any industry-relevant conferences?

Mission

Is the project committed to doing something to benefit the world? Is it focused on addressing a known industry challenge? Can the project participants explain the mission and how it differs from existing projects clearly? Is there a whitepaper or other form of documentation around the product roadmap and technology?

Security and Law

What is the project's approach to securing its technology? How does the leadership team view security for personal information, privacy, and jurisdictional differences? What is the project's approach toward "decentralization"? Is the project abiding by best practices in cryptography? What is the project's stance on complying with regulations and engaging with regulators?

Exert Caution

Some of the worst tokens out there are nothing more than MLM schemes, where the early investors make money and the later ones are left high and dry. If a project claims to be the next Bitcoin, promises huge returns, or asks you to recruit people into the network, this is generally a bad sign. Other indicators to evaluate are the market capitalization by total token supply, the inflation factor coded into the coin, the usability of a token, the number of active users (if any), the security track record of a project (and of its leadership), and the level of censorship resistance used in the model.

How Decentralized are Blockchains?

Many of the top cryptocurrencies are not actually very decentralized in terms of the ownership of their coins. For instance, the site https://arewedecentralizedyet.com (see Figure 3-5) shows the percentage of money supply held by the top 100 accounts for many cryptocurrencies, (see Ripple, Stellar, and IOTA at over 60% of the coins in each of those networks). Of course, most importantly, good tokens have a use case that makes sense and are not based on fuzzy technical advantages. As always, do your homework before diving into any of these.

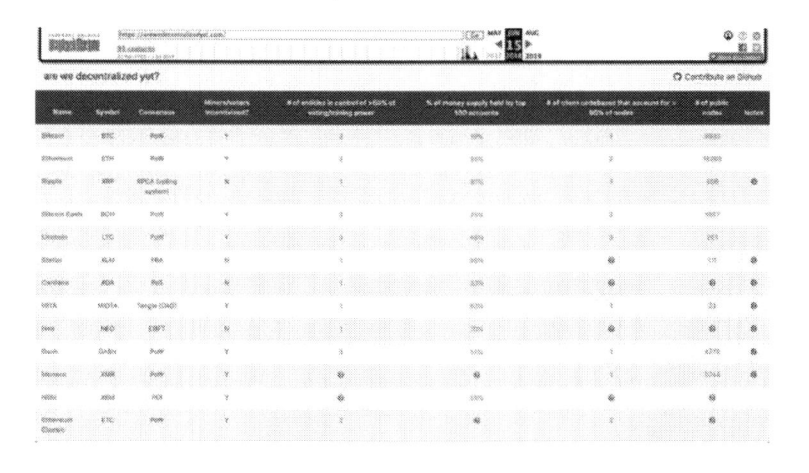

Figure 3-5: Analysis of decentralization of top tokens

Digital Token Exchanges

In the early days of cryptocurrencies and digital tokens it was much more difficult to buy and sell coins. There was special software to install and difficult financial transfers to set up. This could also vary widely depending on your geographic location. The hurdles for adoption were annoying to many potential investors and turned many of them against cryptocurrencies. But the emergence of digital token or **cryptocurrency exchanges** has made this much more straightforward. Cryptocurrency exchanges are similar to the exchanges we understand in our financial markets today, such as the New York Stock Exchange, where stocks are traded.

However, cryptocurrency exchanges can be confusing because they differ from country to country, they are limited with respect to which cryptocurrencies they exchange, and new ones are popping up regularly while old ones sometimes disappear. One study showed that since 2016, 80% of the top exchanges were either gone or had dropped well out of the top standings.[37] An exchange or "digital currency exchange" (DCE) might be

---

[37] Sedgwick, Kai. "80% of the Top Cryptocurrency Exchanges from 2016 Have Been Replaced," Bitcoin.com, https://news.bitcoin.com/80-of-the-top-cryptocurrency-exchanges-from-2016-have-been-

considered as an entry and exit ramp into the world of cryptocurrencies. DCEs are set up as online platforms to allow users to trade their digital currencies and tokens for other digital currencies or for traditional fiat money like dollars and euros.

Much governmental regulation lately has focused on controlling exchanges and the cryptocurrencies that they are allowed to handle. This makes sense because regulatory bodies often pay most attention to places where an asset is exchanged for fiat value (traditional money), since that is where fraud, money-laundering, and investment regulations can come into play. Exchanges make money by charging fees for each transaction, but these can vary widely from a flat fee to a certain percentage. Also, cryptocurrency exchanges may be quite different in terms of what payment options they accept. Some accept credit cards like Visa or PayPal but charge a relatively higher fee. Many banks and exchanges have disallowed this practice, since banks do not want to have to protect against fraud in cryptocurrency transactions. If you wish to link your bank account and pay directly, this may take longer as this is a red flag for many banks who frown on customers getting involved with cryptocurrencies. Some are limited to customers in the country where they are located and others like Kraken, can handle customers worldwide. Generally speaking, exchanges can serve as:

• Trading Platforms – basic websites that connect buyers to sellers and take a transaction fee. May provide access to sophisticated trading tools and require an account to be set up.

• Brokers – similar to currency trading dealers, they allow anyone to buy and sell but at the prices which they determine.

• Direct Trading Platforms – function to connect individual traders to each other to buy and sell at the prices which the individual sellers determine. Popular in global trading settings.

replaced/?utm_source=OneSignal%20Push&utm_medium=notification&utm_campaign=Push%20Notifications

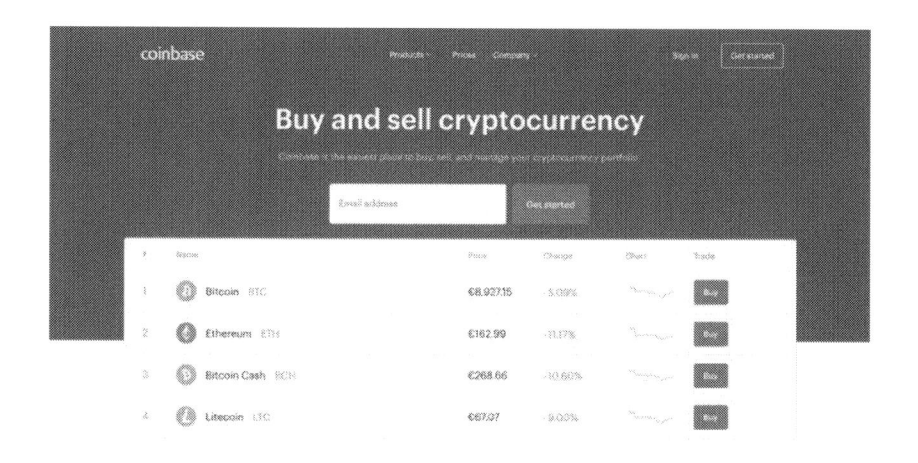

Figure 3-6: Coinbase exchange

The growth of cryptocurrency exchanges has fueled interest in safely buying cryptocurrencies. Some traditional financial investment advisors are now even advising that a portion of a typical portfolio should include some of the best of the cryptocurrencies. Exchanges come and go so quickly that it is virtually impossible to keep track of them. They have been the source of much of the worst fraudulent activity in the cryptocurrency space. The industry is still trying to shake off the bad image left by the failure of the Mt. Gox Bitcoin exchange in 2014, which lost 850,000 bitcoin. The owner has been arrested and charged but almost half a billion dollars' worth of bitcoin is still unaccounted for. For this reason, some have set up shop in countries where there is little regulation of their activities. A few of the most stable exchanges today are listed below.

Coinbase

This is one of the most reputable and reliable exchanges out there today. It is especially popular in the U.S. but can be accessed in 32 countries and counting. It claims to be one of the most popular exchanges in the world and support bitcoin, Bitcoin Cash, ether and Litecoin. Coinbase functions as both a trading platform and a broker and recently started a Coinbase Index fund that tracks these four digital assets. Founded in 2012, Coinbase is based in San Francisco and claims to have over 20 million users. It has attracted over $210 million in startup funding from well-known venture capital funds such as Andreesen-Horowitiz.

Coinbase has used these funds to aggressively acquire other cryptocurrency firms and develop new tools for its platform. It charges a 1.5% fee for purchasing tokens which can vary depending on the amount purchased and the method. Users were angered recently because it was discovered that a bug had caused Coinbase to double charge their 1.5% for some customers. Some users complain that they are too similar to a normal bank and require lots of documentation in order to set up an account. Coinbase claims that it is the first exchange to be approved by U.S. regulators and has instituted Anti-Money Laundering (AML) and Know Your Customer (KYC) protocols just like any other American bank. This means that if the company suspects your account is being used for criminal purposes they can go ahead and shut it down or freeze it without much notice. Attempts at patenting things like "exchanges" and "hot wallets" has further riled some of the early blockchain developers, who designed these tools as part of an open-source system.

For first-time cryptocurrency buyers, Coinbase is often recommended since the company has made its platform very easy to understand and use. To set up an account, customers simply need to link their Coinbase account to a bank account and initiate an ACH automatic transfer for buying bitcoin. This is because Coinbase does not hold dollars in customer accounts. Transferring funds can take the usual 3-5 working days and then the customer can purchase bitcoin or other cryptocurrencies. This is another reason why cryptocurrency day-traders do not use this platform.

Bitstamp

This exchange has been around since 2011 and is based in Slovenia. The founders have had the system audited regularly and have gained a reputation for having a reputable exchange. In the beginning, Bitstamp launched to avoid the hassle of trying to buy on the Mt. Gox exchange which took days to transfer funds from Europe. After the collapse of Mt. Gox it became a popular exchange among Europeans and grew rapidly. Currently, Bitstamp trades bitcoin, Bitcoin Cash, ether, Litecoin and Ripple. Traders like it because it allows instant deposits even with credit and debit cards and because it has reasonable fees and fast execution. Bitstamp has since moved its main office to Luxembourg and has been approved by the EU's regulatory agency to sell to buyers in over 50 countries.

Kraken

Kraken ranks second behind Coinbase in terms of total sales volume. It was started in 2011 and is based in San Francisco. It services customers from North America (except New York), Europe, and Japan and is designed more as a platform for the intermediate and professional trader. It supports trading of fifteen different digital tokens including Dogecoin, EOS, and Monero. Kraken is especially oriented towards mobile devices and claims to be the top mobile trading platform among the top five exchanges. Fees can vary depending on account size but are reasonably competitive with the rest of the industry. Traders like the fact that they can set up a margin account to trade on margin. Kraken has had issues with customer service and review of blogs reveals some complaints about setting up accounts and accessing funds.

Decentralized Exchanges

One thing to keep in mind with the exchanges listed above is that they are essentially third parties or intermediaries helping you exchange your tokens. In a sense, by using an exchange, you are re-intermediating the direct transactions that blockchains enable. Several groups are working on creating **decentralized exchanges** – or simply, protocols that allow you to exchange across tokens with others without using a company in the middle. The centralized exchanges we know today are more readily targeted by attackers since they hold many accounts worth of tokens at any given time. Currently there exist several projects to try to decentralize the way that tokens can be exchanged. These include but are not limited to OmiseGo, 0x Protocol, and

Airswap.[38] The functionality of decentralized exchanges is being built, but does not yet rival the centralized versions. They are harder to use and lack the liquidity of the larger, centralized exchanges. In the long run however, they should grow since they are designed to have less down-time, more privacy, and less censorship potential.

OTC Crypto Exchanges

On the wilder side, there has been a huge growth in what are called OTC ("over the counter") exchanges for cryptocurrencies. These exchanges attempt to skirt some of the regulatory restrictions against cryptocurrency exchanges found in countries such as China, South Korea, and India. The idea of OTC token trading is that they can handle large blocks of tokens by negotiating more directly with brokers. Trades are not on a typical exchange and so are considered to be "off the books" and just involve transfers to and from individual wallets. Messaging between buyers and sellers is handled by texting or by tools like Skype. Genesis Trading is an example of this type of firm. Based in New York City, they began connecting institutional investors to buy/sell large blocks of bitcoin in 2015. They have since expanded to include ether, Litecoin, and Ripple in their stable of cryptocurrencies. Their minimum transaction size is $25,000, so they are generally not focused on the consumer market.

Adoption Rate of Bitcoin

One of the true tests of an emerging technology such as blockchain is to examine the adoption rate. Despite all the ups and downs of the most successful blockchain Dapp, Bitcoin, how many consumers and businesses are actually using bitcoin? Will you be paying your student loans and mortgages with bitcoin in the future? What are the trends for bitcoin usage

---

38 Glazer, Phil. "Decentralized Cryptocurrency Exchanges," Hackernoon, March 6, 2018,

https://hackernoon.com/decentralized-cryptocurrency-exchanges-93039613eeb7?gi=53caccb37577 looking like today? Since we can actually see all of the wallets on the Bitcoin network, a Cambridge University study showed that there were between 2.9 - 5.8 million active user wallets in March of 2017.[39] Given the current growth rate, this number is expected to grow to 200 million by 2024. The number of active users does not include all of the hot wallets or bitcoin addresses on popular regional exchanges such as Bithumb in South Korea and Bitflyer in Japan, which both have about one million users on their platforms. If these are included in the calculation, the total is probably closer to 10 million unique Bitcoin users. As the price of bitcoin spiked, Coinbase, the most popular digital currency exchange saw huge growth in its user base in 2017.

Late in 2017, bitcoin futures began to be traded on the CME and CBOE markets. This makes it easier for institutional investors to engage in this market, which could further stabilize bitcoin and improve its liquidity. The high volatility of bitcoin pricing makes it more difficult for retailers to accept it as a payment method, though a growing number of banks such as Goldman Sachs and major retailers such as Newegg, Microsoft, and Expedia are now accepting bitcoin. If the cryptocurrency becomes more mainstream, this should further help to stabilize its price.

---

[39] Hileman, Dr. Garrick and Michael Rauchs. Global Cryptocurrency Benchmarking Study, University of Cambridge, 2017, page 8, https://www.jbs.cam.ac.uk/fileadmin/user_upload/research/centres/alternative-finance/downloads/2017-04-20-global-cryptocurrency-benchmarking-study.pdf

> **Cold Storage**
>
> **Cold storage** is the term used to talk about keeping your tokens offline, and is often a necessary security protocol for storing large amounts of crypto-assets. When your crypto-assets are not present on a web server or computer they are much less susceptible to attacks. Several key methods for keeping assets in cold storage include:
>
> A USB stick containing an encrypted wallet file (often kept in a safety deposit box or safe)
>
> A "paper wallet" or your private key written on paper (and often kept in a safety deposit box or safe)
>
> An offline hardware wallet (such as Trezor or Ledger)

Interestingly enough, the rise of crypto-assets might signal a rise in demand for physical safes and safety deposit boxes in traditional banks – who knew! Coinbase has been offering a cold storage service to institutional customers for a handsome price ($100,000 initial setup fee), and others will likely enter this service industry.

Financial Modeling for Cryptocurrencies

The goal of financial modeling in general is to try and predict a firm's financial performance. Mathematical models are built to make use of historical data, often coming from three key financial statements: the income statement, balance sheet, and cash flow statement. This Three-Statement Model is part of the basic education of all business students. More advanced financial models are used to analyze mergers and acquisitions, discounted cash-flows (using NPV), IPO valuation models for pricing initial public offerings, forecasting, and also options pricing models.

All of these financial models involve some attempt at valuing different assets under different circumstances. Valuing an IPO usually involves coming up with an "IPO discount." Pricing options and other financial securities involve making economic models and valuing companies as a whole. Because of the extreme volatility of cryptocurrencies and our historical lack of experience with how they work, it is difficult to apply these financial models to effectively value them.

Part of the difficulty in valuing crypto-assets, and digital tokens in particular, is that they don't have any dividends or cash flows in the traditional sense, and they vary quite widely in terms of what kind of asset is represented. There are some **relative valuation models** that attempt to value cryptocurrencies relative to others. One such model is called the Equation of Exchange Monetary Model which attempts to put a value on the network, supply, and velocity of a cryptocurrency.[40] On-chain transactions are used here as a measure of the value of the network itself. Other metrics that are used to value cryptocurrencies include:

- **Network Value to Transactions Ratio** (NVT) – this measures the currencies market cap relative to daily transaction volume

- **Transactions Per Second** – this is an especially important ratio for those digital tokens aspiring to reach the consumer market

- **User Characteristics** – namely, how is the ownership of a token distributed throughout the wallets

- **Mining Profitability** – measuring the number of big and small miners and their profitability

- **Exchange Trading** – Looking at how many exchanges are supporting a token, and how trading is dispersed among them

If we look at the price history of bitcoin, for example, since its inception in 2009 there have been many price "bursts." In December of 2011, the price went from $31 to $2 per bitcoin. Two years later, the price dropped from $1,242 to around $600.

---

[40] Glazer, Phil. "Valuation Models for Cryptocurrencies," Hackernoon, February 22, 2018, https://hackernoon.com/valuation-models-for-cryptocurrencies-f03e9437786e

Basics of Blockchain

Figure 3-7: Bitcoin price history

The price of bitcoin continued to fluctuate from announcement to announcement as the cryptocurrency evolved. The crash of the Mt. Gox exchange in 2014 sent the price back down to near its lows. More and more adoptions by companies, banks and countries in 2016 and 2017 kept the price moving upwards. Much of the negative news affecting bitcoin in 2017 and 2018 came from China, as the government announced more crackdowns on bitcoin exchanges and trading. However, after most of these declines, the price continued to reach new highs.

As seen by Figure 3-12, the volatility of bitcoin's price has decreased since 2010, although it remains highly volatile in comparison to fiat currencies, which generally have volatility ranges between 0.5 and 1.0 %. One difference from other asset bubbles is that after every major dip, bitcoin itself doesn't disappear. People continue to hold (sometimes called HODL as a meme in the crypto-community) and use it for transactions. Some experts predict that the price will continue to stabilize further in the next few years, in part because of the mechanics of the Bitcoin network itself. Since over 16 out of 21 million possible bitcoin have already been mined, and given the rates of block creation and the fact that the mining reward will be halved every four years, the estimate is that the last bitcoin will be mined in the year 2040. As the reward for creating new blocks continues to decrease, miners will transition to a different payment system where more and more of their revenue will come from transaction fees.

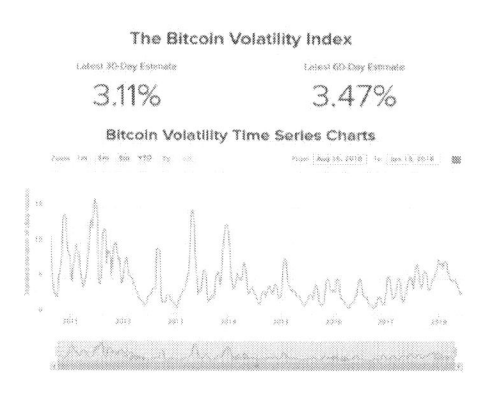

Figure 3-8: Volatility of bitcoin over time

Digital Cash or Digital Gold?

There are several narratives that circulate regularly about what kind of asset bitcoin (and other altcoins) represent. Essentially, they boil down to whether these tokens more closely resemble cash or gold. The difference relies to a large degree on what you think money is. By digital gold, we can think of two scenarios: bitcoin as an asset that almost is never used to make payments but is used by speculators to hedge against macroeconomic scenarios in the global economy, or global money where it acts as a decent standard of value for payments (think 19th Century use of gold).

As Vitalik Buterin, the founder of Ethereum, has touched on over Twitter: "The whole 'collectibles, then gold, then fiat, then bitcoin' narrative is only one way of understanding the history of money, and in many significant ways an incorrect way. See: David Graeber's 'Debt, The First 5000 Years.' ... Money always evolves in the following four stages, collectible -> SoV -> MoE -> UoA" - no, no, no!"[41] The acronyms here stand for **"Store of Value**,**" "Medium of Exchange**,**"** and **"Unit of Account**.**"** And the main criticism that Buterin (and others) make of this thinking is that Medium of Exchange arguably preceded Store of Value when we think about money as a historical method to keep records and allow the exchange of gifts and the ability to clear debt. People have used bitcoin as a store of value and also as a medium of exchange (sometimes buying pizza or coffee with bitcoin!).

---

[41] @VitalikButerin, Twitter, April 3, 2018, https://twitter.com/vitalikbuterin/status/981071033548488704

Basics of Blockchain

Blockchain Analytics

If you wanted to analyze data from a blockchain network like Bitcoin, how would you go about it and what kind of questions would you ask?

Since the size of the Bitcoin blockchain is currently about 210 GB, this would be a perfect candidate for a Big Data analytics application. Because of blockchain's emphasis on identity and trust, the actual data on the blockchain will be much cleaner. Though there will still be opportunities to look for patterns among the transactions. This should be true for both public and private blockchains. On public blockchains such as Bitcoin, one could identify which wallets are receiving funds of a certain frequency and type. It would therefore be possible to identify which wallet was receiving the ransomware payments from the WannaCry malware attack.

This is a very new area of research and the implications are not really known at this point. A number of startups have started to focus on blockchain analytics. These include Chainalysis, Elliptic, and Skry. Chainalysis is the leader and has created special software for tracking transactions and wallets. Their analytics have been used in investigations around the world. There are also groups like Amberdata that offer blockchain health and intelligence to be able to understand maintenance. Amberdata has some of the most sophisticated tools for analyzing blockchain performance (see Figure 3-9 below).

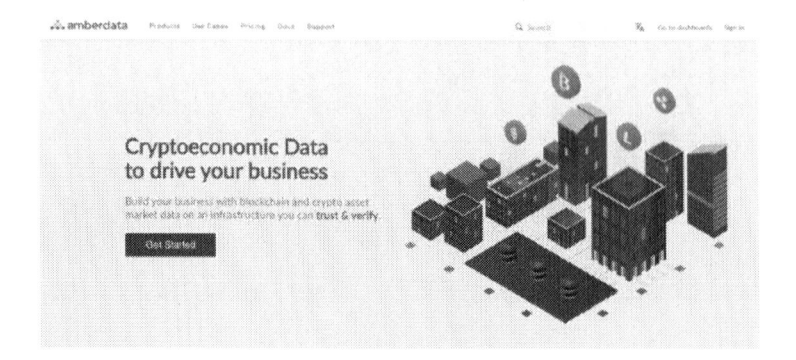

Figure 3-9: Amberdata analytics

Access to data from the Bitcoin, Bitcoin Cash, and Ethereum networks can be found at http://blockchair.com. This highly interactive site lets users filter and sort the block data for each of these platforms. Data sets under one million records in size can even be exported for free as .csv files for further analysis.

The Layers of Bitcoin and Ethereum

If you pay attention to some of the innovations in the blockchain space, from Lightning Network's growth to scalability attempts in Ethereum, you will notice that the conversation often revolves around "layers." These layers describe some of the different functionalities as well as where and how to innovate for scalability. For instance, you can think of the Bitcoin public blockchain as a global settlement layer which represents Layer 1. Similarly, for Ethereum, the base consensus protocol represents Layer 1. There are many ideas circulating about how best to scale blockchains, increasing the throughput of transactions without compromising the decentralization of the network. Sharding is a way to split the transactions collected by nodes into sections, so that not every node processes every transaction; making it a scalability idea that works at Layer 1 of Ethereum.

But most ideas for making blockchains more scalable surround Layer 2, or "off-chain" solutions. For Bitcoin, the Lightning Network offers a Layer 2 approach for increasing transactions. For Ethereum, Layer 2 scaling solutions include off-chain solutions such as state channels, Plasma, and Truebit. Layer 2 approaches try to do more with the existing capacity of the network, rather than trying to increase the base consensus protocol's capacity. These approaches live "on top of" Layer 1, and are implemented as software that interacts with Layer 1 through smart contracts. Basically, Layer 2 solutions extend the utility of blockchains (bringing lower transaction costs and greater speed) by referring back to the security and finality of operations on Layer 1.[42] Using state channels (similar to payment channels) is one way of limiting the number of transactions that need to get processed on Layer 1, by collecting a bunch of transactions and their order off-chain over the Internet and then settling those transactions on-chain. You can think of this as similar to the way Apple bundles your purchases from iTunes into a monthly bill, or how you might use an application that allows you and your roommates to pay different household costs and only settle once with each other at the end of the month, still accounting for all the changes in between. Plasma is an alternative scalability solution at Layer 2, where you can create "child" or sub-chains to the main Ethereum network that allow you to perform thousands of transactions at lower cost and higher speed without having all the computation performed on the mainnet, but still able to reference it. These scalability approaches differ in their purpose and security assumptions, and we will continue to see innovation at different layers of blockchains in the future.

---

42 Stark, Josh. "Making Sense of Ethereum's Layer 2 Scaling Solutions: State Channels, Plasma, and Truebit," Medium, February 12, 2018, https://medium.com/l4-media/making-sense-of-ethereums-layer-2-scaling-solutions-state-channels-plasma-and-truebit-22cb40dcc2f4

Regulatory Considerations

Regulators across the globe are looking at blockchains and crypto-assets in a variety of ways. There have been outright bans on crypto-trading (i.e. South Korea, Venezuela, Argentina) and also attempts to attract startup founders through crypto-friendly regulations (i.e. Estonia, Switzerland, Japan, Malta). But the landscape is still shifting in terms of how crypto-assets will be regulated and if blockchain technology will receive different treatment, avoiding being lumped into the regulation of securities.

The events that have unfolded in Venezuela are a particular example that both regulators and blockchain innovators are paying great attention to. The economic depression and massive hyper-inflation occurring in Venezuela, as well as the larger humanitarian crisis, have led both citizens and the state to become much more interested in cryptocurrencies. A cup of coffee has cost upwards of one million bolivars, and the national currency has lost an estimated 99.9% of its value since 2016.[43] Many families have set up crypto-mining operations in their homes to help make ends meet. Mining in Venezuela is basically an act of arbitrage, since electricity is so cheap, citizens are paying for an underpriced commodity and then selling the bitcoin they convert it into for a profit. One Venezuelan who works at Purse.io, a blockchain company, tweeted in May 2018: "Venezuelans no longer able to buy or import computer parts, especially GPUs. The government is confiscating everything to mine cryptocurrencies themselves."[44] As crypto-assets and their regulation continue to evolve, we may see more approaches that use such assets as an alternative to the nation-state backed fiat currencies.

---

43 "Why are Venezuelans mining so much bitcoin?" The Economist, April 3, 2018, https://www.economist.com/the-economist-explains/2018/04/03/why-are-venezuelans-mining-so-much-bitcoin

44 @Codiox, Twitter, May 30, 2018, https://twitter.com/codiox/status/1001929759343960065?s=11 and http://www.noticierodigital.com/2018/05/especial-nd-gobierno-prohibe-importacion-de-equipos-para-minar-criptomonedas/

Ethical and Other Issues with Blockchain

Like any kind of investing or gambling, trading crypto-assets, especially cryptocurrencies, with their wild swings for fast profits can really get the adrenaline pumping. A rehab clinic and treatment center in Scotland recently announced that they would offer treatment for "cryptocurrency addiction." One of the downsides of having easy access to digital tokens around the world is that people with little experience or knowledge can get caught up in the trading frenzy around them. Stories abound on discussion boards about people who have lost all their savings and gone into debt in order to continue buying them. There are stories of people even jumping out of tall buildings when they discovered they lost everything. At present, this kind of trading addiction is much more common in men and teenage boys, even some as young as 13 and 14. Like any form of gambling, the symptoms of cryptocurrency addiction include:[45]

- Spending too much time thinking about cryptocurrencies
- Spending a high percentage of your income on cryptocurrencies
- Getting angry if you have to limit your time on a computer
- Disrupting relationships with friends and family
- Lying to friends and family about how much you have invested and/or lost
- Missing work in order to trade cryptocurrencies
- Continuing to trade after losing money in order to win it all back

Although not officially recognized yet by the counseling profession as a specific type of addiction, some larger cities already have support groups for cryptocurrency addiction. At any rate, if you answered yes to two or more of the above questions, help is available. And you can find help by talking with an addiction counselor or therapist.

---

[45] "A Guide to Cryptocurrency Addiction," Castle Craig Hospital,

https://castlecraig.co.uk/resources/gambling/cryptocurrency-addiction/crypto-addiction-guide/

Chapter Summary

This chapter has taken us on a tour of Bitcoin and the world of crypto-assets. At the highest level we can talk about crypto-assets which include all the different types of cryptocurrencies, commodities and other digital tokens. The biggest debate currently among regulators surrounds whether digital tokens function as a security, currency, or something else, because this will determine how to approach regulation in the future. One important takeaway from this discussion is that these digital assets are evolving quickly and are attempting to meet some perceived deficiencies with respect to privacy, governance, scaling, and mining protocols. This has given rise to literally thousands of new ICOs with all the potential scams associated with them. We examined how some of these scams are propagated both amongst the ICOs and the exchanges. Details on the top ten cryptocurrencies by market capitalization were discussed along with some of the up-and-coming digital tokens. We also outlined how digital tokens try to adapt using hard and soft forks and what these mean for the future of crypto-assets. We then examined the role of digital currency exchanges and looked at some of the top exchanges like Coinbase and Kraken. This led to a discussion of some of the increasingly important tools for financial modelling and blockchain analysis, both areas of considerable interest at the moment.

Key Terms

Crypto-asset
Cryptocurrency
Crypto-commodity
Crypto-token
Network token
Utility token
Security token
Simple Agreements for Future Tokens (SAFT)
Initial Coin Offering (ICO)
Fork
Hard fork
Soft fork
Colored coin
Delegated Proof of Stake (DPoS)
Segregated Witness (SegWit)
Sidechain
Directed Acyclic Graph (DAG)
Tangle
Zero-knowledge proof

Threshold Relay
Crypto-economics
Mining pool
Cryptocurrency exchange
Decentralized exchange
Cold storage
Relative valuation models
Network Value to Transactions Ratio (NVT)
Transactions Per Second
User Characteristics
Mining Profitability
Exchange Trading
Store of Value
Medium of Exchange
Unit of Account
Layer 1
Sharding
Layer 2

Questions for Further Discussion

1. Check out this map of coins at http://mapofcoins.com/bitcoin
2. What are a hard and a soft fork? How might a hard fork affect the value of a digital token?
3. Why does the Bitcoin network have an issue with scaling? What are some of the proposed solutions?
4. How can you analyze the quality of a crypto-asset project? Give examples of each.
5. What is an OTC crypto exchange? How does it differ from typical exchanges?
6. There has been much discussion recently about how to identify "fake news." Imagine what a Dapp built on blockchain for identifying fake news might look. What type of blockchain design would it use? How would the fake news be validated? How would the community of validators be motivated? Find an example of a blockchain app being built for this purpose.
7. Go to http://blockchair.com. Use the block explorer to answer the following questions:
a. When was the BTC block with the most transactions mined? How many transactions did it have?
b. What was the highest total amount paid for mining a BTC block (including fees) in U.S. dollars? Which miner mined it?
c. Export all of the BTC block data for the month of May in 2018 as a .csv file. Import this into Excel and create a report showing the average number of blocks mined by each miner.
8. Imagine you were considering investing in crypto-assets. What kind of data and ratios would you look at in order to decide? Which factor would be the most important for you?
9. What has made the price of bitcoin so volatile since its inception in 2009? Do you think it will stabilize in the next few years? Why or why not?
10. Go to http://cryptocompare.com. Find a digital token that is not in the top ten and research its value proposition. What is the overall purpose of the token? Does it make sense? What does the community supporting it look like? Do you think this token will be around in five or ten years? Why or why not?

Chapter 4 – Ethereum and Smart Contracts

Learning Objectives
- Explain the different components of the Ethereum platform
- Gain a deeper understanding of how Ethereum works
- Understand the concept of smart contracts
- Learn about other Ethereum-based frameworks
- Learn the basic tools for programming with Solidity
- See how smart contracts are created in Remix
- Use Remix and MetaMask to edit, run, and compile a token contract

Blockchain in Action – Ethereum in Space

In Spring 2018, NASA announced funding for research on how to use Ethereum blockchain technology to develop autonomous spacecraft.[46] It is well-known that there is a huge amount of space debris floating around the Earth today and even danger from small asteroids. Currently, it takes a lot of time for engineers to see the debris and steer satellites around it. This is impractical for deep space probes since too much time elapses between acquiring the data about debris location and making the necessary course adjustments. A potential solution is to use smart contract technology from the Ethereum blockchain to automate the navigation process. The new project, known as the Resilient Networking and Computing Paradigm is part of NASA's new emphasis on developing more efficient and agile deep space probes. Ethereum-based smart contracts will help spacecraft to recognize debris and react without any human intervention. Automating the labor-intensive process of gathering and analyzing this data will free up valuable time for space engineers, allowing them to focus on more interesting problems of space exploration. This shows again that blockchain technology is being tested on many more problems than just launching more cryptocurrencies!

Basics of Ethereum

Fueled by his understanding of the limitations of Bitcoin, a 19-year-old named Vitalik Buterin wrote a white paper in 2013 that envisioned a new, open-source blockchain platform called Ethereum. Buterin is one of the most recognizable people in the blockchain community. While still a teenager, he became fascinated with the idea of cryptocurrencies and co-founded and wrote articles for *Bitcoin Magazine*. He was also awarded a prestigious Thiel Fellowship, which gives young people $100,000 to drop out of college for two years and dream up something new and innovative. The result of Buterin's

---

[46] Riley, Zachary. "NASA Wants To Use The Ethereum Blockchain To Automate Spacecraft," Value Walk, April 17, 2018, https://www.valuewalk.com/2018/04/nasa-ethereum-blockchain/

research on the limitations of Bitcoin became the white paper describing Ethereum: he imagined a blockchain that could do more generalized, *programmable* transactions.

The Bitcoin network solved the double-spend problem, making it possible to transact online with much greater certainty, but was fundamentally only designed to transact the crypto-currency bitcoin. It is not really a network architecture that supports diverse applications. Ethereum, by contrast, is designed to support more complex financial and programmable transactions. It too makes use of a digital token – called "ether" (ETH) – for processing transactions, but can also store and execute programs. Ethereum has grown to be the second largest digital token by market capitalization. More importantly, it has the largest community of developers. This cohort is committed to improving the Ethereum ecosystem through applications, use cases, and startups. The main attraction of Ethereum is that it allows developers to create and deploy **decentralized applications** (Dapps) on its platform. Dapps can be thought of as decentralized software – code that gets executed across all the nodes in a given blockchain architecture. Code that is programmed to execute using the Ethereum network is written and stored in the form of smart contracts. Ethereum is flexible enough that transactions can be permissioned or permissionless, and avoids some of the issues with miners by not paying a block creation reward, but just a transaction fee.

The creativity of developers in the Ethereum community is leading to many new kinds of blockchain applications. The Ethereum platform forms the backbone for new applications by making sure they are free from censorship (if you pay to execute a transaction it will execute), have no downtime, and have no third-party interference. It is also the platform that has spurred the huge increase in Initial Coin Offerings (ICOs), since it is easy to launch a new digital token on Ethereum. Most of these tokens are meant to fund the development of Dapps.

Ethereum Foundation

After the release of Buterin's initial white paper, a Swiss-based company called Ethereum Switzerland began formal development of the platform in

2014. Other early developers working on the project included Mihai Alisie, Anthony DiIorio, Gavin Wood, and Charles Hoskinsin. They are all regarded as co-founders of Ethereum. This initial company eventually became the non-profit organization called the Ethereum Foundation. In July-August of 2014, the Ethereum Foundation took the unusual step of crowdfunding their development project through the public sale of 60 million pre-mined "ether." Participants could purchase ether with bitcoin, and the success of this public sale generated over $18 million worth of bitcoin. The money was intended to fund the ongoing development of the Ethereum platform through annual grants from the Foundation. This was one of the largest crowdfunded projects at the time. Although its coffers shrank initially as the value of bitcoin dipped, today the Foundation is one of the best-funded blockchain organizations in the world, holding almost $200 million in assets.[47]

With the invention of the global virtual computing platform called the Ethereum Virtual Machine (EVM) and the use of smart contracts, the idea was that Ethereum could be used to create a more egalitarian society. With greater access, transparency, and accountability, people would be able to participate in the global economy on their own terms, relying less on banks and government institutions. This emphasis also helped attract partners at the outset and made the project attractive to developers. So far, the Ethereum Foundation has proved itself capable of evolving and responding to serious threats to the ecosystem and staying true to its mission. This has instilled confidence in the platform and led Coinbase, one of the more prominent cryptocurrency exchanges to list ether on its exchange in 2016, which helped to open ether to the broader U.S. market. Given that the Foundation has a large stake invested in ether and the original founders own hundreds of millions of dollars's worth of ether, public ownership of ether is an important diversification that ensures the continued development and use of the Ethereum platform. The long-term success of the Ethereum network will likely depend on governance of the Foundation, incentives for development projects, and corporate adoption of the technology. The Foundation funds research that help build out the broader Ethereum ecosystem and has a

---

[47] "The Ethereum Foundation is Now the Richest Blockchain Company with Assets at Nearly $200 Millions," Trust Nodes, May 25, 2017, https://www.trustnodes.com/2017/05/25/ethereum-foundation-now-richest-blockchain-company-assets-nearly-200-millions

roadmap that includes research focused on issues of scalability and the movement from Proof of Work to Proof of Stake.

Ethereum Virtual Machine (EVM)

The Ethereum platform possesses its own programming language, called **Solidity**, which is similar to C++ or JavaScript. To really understand Ethereum it is important to examine one of its key protocols called the **Ethereum Virtual Machine or EVM**. What is really clever about the EVM is that it enables the computers on the Ethereum network to function as a kind of global computing resource. Computer owners on the network are rewarded with ether for their role in executing smart contracts and verifying transactions. So instead of being rewarded for winning a cryptographic puzzle, as in Bitcoin, they are rewarded for committing a valued resource (i.e. computing power) to participate in the Ethereum community. It is a "virtual" machine in that it doesn't really exist except as a loose confederation of nodes on the Ethereum network.

The EVM is the powerhouse that executes smart contracts. Each participant in the network adds computing power to the network, and all decentralized apps (also known as Dapps) can purchase use of this power by spending ether. These decentralized apps are bundles of smart contracts that dictate the appropriate ether spend for network participation. This differs from bitcoin predominantly as ether is the method in which computing power is valued as a resource, referred to as "gas," and not treated simply as a digital currency.

Ethereum currently has two different types of accounts; **externally-owned accounts** (EOAs) and **contract accounts**. Both types come with an ether balance attached. The main difference is that a contract account can have program code stored with it. This contract code is executed by the nodes in the network which also serve to validate the code. All of the accounts and transaction fees are measured in terms of "**wei**." A unit of ether is equivalent to 1e18 unit of wei, so wei are incredibly small increments and are often referred to in "gwei," or billions of wei.

What is Ether? What is Gas?

Sometimes one will see the terms "ether" and "Ethereum" used interchangeably. However, this is a slight error in terminology. Ethereum refers to the entire open-source platform for developing distributed applications, while "**ether**" is the actual digital token that is used to fuel the platform. Buterin came across the term "ether" in his readings and liked the fact that according to ancient Greek natural philosophy, ether, like air, could be thought of as an omnipresent, yet invisible material existing above the "terrestrial sphere."[48]

Figure 4-1: Ethereum Foundation logo

Similarly, the Ethereum Foundation prefers to think of ether as being the "fuel" for running decentralized applications on the Ethereum network. The way the EVM is set up, network users have access to a global network of computers that is fast, efficient, and always available. However, running applications on the EVM is not free and so ether can be used to transfer value to the computer owners on the network. You can think of ether as a tool for resource management of the computing power of the network. Just as your own computer has an activity monitor that allows you to toggle between applications and use CPUs effectively, a global decentralized computer also needs to manage who uses the computing power. Payment for computing power allows effective management of a scarce resource because

---

[48] "Aether," Wikipedia, accessed November 6, 2018, https://en.wikipedia.org/wiki/Aether_(classical_element)

there is very little incentive to spam the network or run an infinite loop of code if you are required to pay for all that computing. If you run out of fuel, your program stops!

One can acquire ether by purchasing it on an exchange, by creating blocks for the Ethereum network, or by running and validating transactions on the Ethereum network. Since the movement away from Proof of Work to Proof of Stake, mining of ether has diverged greatly from mining bitcoin. The reward for creating a new block is capped at five ether coins. The Ethereum Foundation sold off 60 million pre-mined ether to crowdfund the research on Ethereum and gave 12 million more ether as seed money to the Foundation. Ether is also different from bitcoin in that as the power and time needed to process a smart contract go up, so does the fee paid. It is also different with respect to the number of possible ether in circulation. Bitcoin is capped at 21 million coins, whereas there is no firm limit on the number of ether, although only 18 million ether can be mined in a year, given that a new block is created every 14-15 seconds.

A cursory survey of Ethereum applications will illustrate the importance of another Ethereum network concept: **gas**. Gas is used by developers of Ethereum as the fuel for running their applications. As you already know, Ethereum is unique in that it is designed to host Dapps. Each of these programs varies considerably in terms of size and complexity. As a result, the amount that is charged to run these programs on the EVM must also vary. Costs are broken down by line of code and can be tiny fractions of one ether coin. Gas became a way to aid developers in accounting for the cost of running their programs as they were building. The basic idea was to decouple the price of running Ethereum transactions from the more volatile price of ether. In order to run your transaction on the EVM, you must specify how much you are willing to pay as the "gas limit" and you must actually have enough gas in your Ethereum wallet to afford to run the proposed transaction. If you run out of gas, your transaction will fail and the nodes on the EVM will refuse to execute it. For example, it might cost 3 gas units to add two numbers together, whereas the standard cost for creating a new contract is 100 gas units. Gas can be further subdivided into the lowest unit of currency in Ethereum which is the wei. By going to the Ethereum Gas Station https://ethgasstation.info/ we can find out that the current cost of gas is 1.4 Gwei (billion wei), which equates to billionths or tiny fractions of ether. This means at current prices, a standard transaction on Ethereum costs about $0.012. It is important to estimate the costs of programs since the costs of storing data on the EVM can accrue very quickly.

What Is a Smart Contract?

Ethereum is the most popular platform for developing, storing and executing smart contracts. **Smart contracts** can be thought of as computer programs that encode the rules for just about any kind of contract using programming languages such as Solidity, which has similarities to C and JavaScript, or Vyper, which looks more like Python. Solidity is considered to be a **Turing-complete** programming language, meaning it supports all of the programming structures of a full feature language like C. Typical contract logic might look like an Aristotelian syllogism: if event X happens, then do Y. The contract logic can be used for simple contracts that just transfer tokens or more complex contracts, like qualifying a home buyer for a loan. The basic idea of how a smart contract works is as follows:[49]

1. Logic is encoded into smart contract program language

2. Nodes on the EVM compile, validate, store, and replicate the smart contract across the network

3. When the triggering event(s) occur, the contract is executed by the nodes on the network

4. Changes are made to the appropriate accounts on the network as a result of successfully executing the contract

Simple smart contracts could be written just to transfer digital tokens between wallets, store information, or perform calculations. More complex smart contracts are being developed for banking, healthcare, insurance, real estate, digital rights management, and much more. You name an industry or service

---

[49] Desjardins, Jeff. "The Power of Smart Contracts on the Blockchain," Visual Capitalist, October 24, 2017, http://www.visualcapitalist.com/smart-contracts-blockchain/

and there are applications being developed to support or advance it (see Chapter 5). Smart contracts are also key to expanding the functionality of the Internet of Things (IoT). Some of the attributes of smart contracts include:

• Security – smart contracts are encrypted and have a high degree of security

• Redundancy – copying a smart contract across all of the nodes on the network ensures redundancy (though lowers efficiency of the network)

• Accuracy – contracts are validated by many nodes on the network

• Autonomous – there is no need for a third party to be involved in the execution of a contract, lessening the potential for bias or mistakes; additionally, smart contracts are a tool for automating business logic, and allowing machines to transact without intervention

• Efficiency – by eliminating middlemen, the cost of transactions is minimized

• Transparency – on a permissionless blockchain, all parties have access to the shared ledger; transactions can be audited

---

ERC-20

ERC-20 (Ethereum Request for Comments, #20) is a protocol used by token contracts. It lays out a set of rules for the functions a contract must have and what they do. For example, an ERC-20 token must have `function balanceOf(address _owner) view returns (uint256 balance)`, which, for the given address (`_owner`), should return the number of tokens it has (`uint256 balance`). The full list of functions is given here: https://github.com/ethereum/EIPs/blob/master/EIPS/eip-20.md.

ERC-20 is important because it allows other people's Dapps to interact with your token contract. For example, if we wanted to list our token on an exchange and we followed the ERC-20 standard, the exchange's software would "just know" how to move our tokens from one person to another. As of July 2018, there were over 100,000 ERC-20 token contracts on the Ethereum blockchain.

History of Smart Contracts

The term "smart contracts," was coined by the computer scientist and legal scholar Nick Szabo in 1996. One question Szabo was trying to answer was: how should principles found in our legal history or common law be applied to the new realm of digital relationships?

As he then wrote, "The basic idea of smart contracts is that many kinds of contractual clauses (such as liens, bonding, delineation of property rights, etc.) can be embedded in the hardware and software we deal with, in such a way as to make breach of contract expensive (if desired, sometimes prohibitively so) for the breacher."[50] Szabo saw the possibility early on of combining network transmission, more sophisticated messages, and existing norms around business relationships. As he elaborates, "I call these new contracts "smart", because they are far more functional than their inanimate paper-based ancestors. No use of artificial intelligence is implied. A smart contract is a set of promises, specified in digital form, including protocols within which the parties perform on these promises."[51]

The definition of smart contracts has many interpretations. Vitalik Buterin put forward his own as: "a mechanism involving digital assets and two or more parties, where some or all of the parties put assets in and assets are automatically redistributed among those parties according to a formula based on certain data that is not known at the time the contract is initiated."[52] Although smart contracts have caught the attention of many industries as a new digitization lever for their businesses, there are also valid criticisms of how smart contracts navigate the code-to-law relationship. As Patrick Murck of the Harvard Berkman Center has said, "The two things to

---

[50] Szabo, Nick. "Smart Contracts: Building Blocks for Digital Markets, 1996,

http://www.fon.hum.uva.nl/rob/Courses/InformationInSpeech/CDROM/Literature/LOTwinterschool2006/szabo.best.vwh.net/smart_contracts_2.html

[51] Szabo, Nick. "Smart Contracts: Building Blocks for Digital Markets, 1996,

http://www.fon.hum.uva.nl/rob/Courses/InformationInSpeech/CDROM/Literature/LOTwinterschool2006/szabo.best.vwh.net/smart_contracts_2.html

[52] Buterin, Vitalik. "DAOs, DACs, DAs, and More: An Incomplete Terminology Guide," Ethereum Blog, May 6, 2014,

https://blog.ethereum.org/2014/05/06/daos-dacs-das-and-more-an-incomplete-terminology-guide/

know about smart contracts is that they're dumb, and they're not contracts."[53] Even Vitalik Buterin has lamented that he should have adopted something more like "persistent scripts" to describe the automating nature of this code. The criticism of their "smarts" often hangs on the need for smart contracts to have an input or "oracle," that tells a contract a condition has been met in the real world in order to execute the remainder of the digital agreement. Smart contracts that connect physical assets and the digital world are, to some degree, reliant on a source of authority to determine what has transpired in the real world. In this sense, critics like the Bitcoin maximalist Jimmy Song see the "Turing-complete" trait of Ethereum smart contracts as a liability, calling them "Turing-vulnerable," because the ability to create more complicated contracts also makes them more challenging to analyze for security.[54]

The criticism of the "contractual" nature of smart contracts is often about how these agreements will be treated in the courtroom. That said, the usability of smart contracts is being tested today for contracts with complicated conditions as well as for more simple "if-then" kinds of contractual relationships (such as circumscribed back-office automation) that do not have many contingencies. Even LegalZoom is experimenting with smart contracts through a collaboration with the company Clause.[55] As people continue to debate the accuracy of the nomenclature, the idea of using code that executes as written to codify (and automate) business relationships has grown dramatically, and will likely continue as we transition from human interactions to trades made by and between machines.

---

[53] Cawrey, Daniel. "Why Ethereum Needs 'Dumb' Contracts," CoinDesk, June 29, 2016, https://www.coindesk.com/ethereum-dao-dumb-smart-contracts/

[54] Song, Jimmy. "The Truth about Smart Contracts," Medium, June 11, 2018, https://medium.com/@jimmysong/the-truth-about-smart-contracts-ae825271811f

[55] "Legal Zoom to Offer Smart Legal Contracts With Clause," PRNewsWire, September 17, 2018, https://www.prnewswire.com/news-releases/legalzoom-to-offer-smart-legal-contracts-with-clause-300713717.html

Figure 4-2: Meme on smart contracts

Roadmap of Ethereum

While some are predicting that Ethereum will soon overtake Bitcoin as the most well-known blockchain application, it has had its fair share of controversies and obstacles over the last few years. One of the appealing features of Ethereum is the simplicity with which digital tokens can be created and issued. In May 2016, some members of the Ethereum community announced that they were creating a venture capital fund to support projects built on Ethereum and called the fund "**The DAO**," or Decentralized Autonomous Organization. It was designed to be a traditional fund that accepted proposals for projects to be built on Ethereum and grow the ecosystem of innovation for the platform. It's main difference from a traditional fund was that it's "code was law," and the smart contract code governing The DAO enabled owners of DAO-tokens to vote on submitted projects through the blockchain and then automatically appropriate funds to those winners.

The DAO was specifically designed with the crypto-asset and Dapp communities in mind. In order to fund it, these members decided to crowdfund The DAO by offering to exchange ether for their own new digital tokens. It was a huge success and generated 12.7 million ether (worth about

$250 million at the time). Unfortunately, however, a hacker found a security flaw in the smart contract code surrounding a "recursive call" which was then exploited to drain about $50 million worth of ether tokens generated by The DAO. This hack led to a huge split within the Ethereum community as they tried to decide how to handle such a massive loss of funds. Some wanted to do a soft fork that would involve a change in the software to fix the bugs that were exploited. Others wanted to do a hard fork and essentially refund the lost ether by creating a new version of the Ethereum chain. The hacker even got involved in the debate and said they would reward those who voted for the soft fork.

A vote among all the holders of ether resulted in a super majority (89%) voting for the hard fork. This disagreement led to a split of the main blockchain where those who voted against hard fork (and maintained the original Ethereum chain) became Ethereum Classic and the new fork that solved for the attack retained the name "Ethereum." The whole debate was important because it showed that the community could evolve and change to account for major bugs or disruptions in the network. It also brought to the fore many of the social norms and governance issues that surround technology that is supposed to execute as written, sparking debates about whether "code is law." The DAO tokens were eventually delisted from the major exchanges late in 2016. Many point to The DAO incident as the beginning of the U.S. Security and Exchange Commission's interest in how ICOs work.

Casper

Casper consists of two research projects at Ethereum both of which contribute to Ethereum's road-mapped transition from Proof of Work to Proof of Stake. The first project is a hybrid model between Proof of Work and Proof of Stake, called Casper the Friendly Finality Gadget (FFG), meant to ease that transition. This consists of a Proof of Stake protocol overlaid on top of the normal ethash Proof of Work protocol that will use every 50_{th}

block as a finality checkpoint.[56]

The second project is Casper the Friendly Ghost (correct by construction). In layman's terms, CBC sets up a strawman called an "ideal adversary" that puts forward exceptions or faults in the partially-built protocol in order to allow the protocol to be dynamically improved until it is complete. Both of the projects are underway in order to achieve benefits such as increased decentralization, energy efficiency, security, and scalability. Making the move away from Proof of Work will help to ensure the viability of the overall Ethereum platform in the future.

Plasma

One of the distinct limitations of the Ethereum platform is the size or scalability of the programs it can run. Announced in August 2017 by co-authors Joseph Poon and Vitalik Buterin, **Plasma** is the effort to create scalable autonomous smart contracts for Ethereum. The proposed framework uses Ethereum as the blockchain to enforce transactional state transitions, but allows scalability by introducing a "parent and child" set of blockchain relationships. As the white paper abstract states, "By framing one's ledger entry into a child blockchain which is enforced by the parent chain, one can enable incredible scale with minimized trust (presuming root blockchain availability and correctness)."[57]

Governance

How might we go about making changes to Ethereum, and who is responsible for doing this? **Ethereum Improvement Proposals (EIP)** are the standards for protocols across the Ethereum platform and can be found here: https://eips.ethereum.org/. EIPs are the means for people to recommend changes to various parts of the Ethereum platform and receive

---

[56] "What is Ethereum Casper Protocol? Crash Course," BlockGeeks, https://blockgeeks.com/guides/ethereum-casper/

[57] Poon, Joseph and Vitalik Buterin. "Plasma: Scalable Autonomous Smart Contracts," https://plasma.io/

comment as well as a process for adoption or deferment. The repository for improvements is housed on GitHub and open to anyone here: https://github.com/ethereum/EIPs

EIPs can be assessed along the following set of status terms (from GitHub):[58]

- **Draft** - an EIP that is undergoing rapid iteration and changes

- **Last Call** - an EIP that is done with its initial iteration and ready for review by a wide audience

- **Accepted** - a core EIP that has been in Last Call for at least 2 weeks and any technical changes that were requested have been addressed by the author

- **Final (non-Core)** - an EIP that has been in Last Call for at least 2 weeks and any technical changes that were requested have been addressed by the author.

- **Final (Core)** - an EIP that the Core Devs have decide to implement and release in a future hard fork or has already been released in a hard fork

- **Deferred** - an EIP that is not being considered for immediate adoption. May be reconsidered in the future for a subsequent hard fork.

EIPs are also categorized into the following types of improvements: Core, Networking, Interface, ERC, Informational, and Meta. Comments on EIPs is made via Gitter (https://gitter.im/).

Additionally, Ethereum core developers set a publicly available agenda on GitHub and then livestream their meetings via YouTube, meaning anyone who wants to observe or participate in their proceedings can do so.[59]

[58] "The Ethereum Improvement Protocol Repository," GitHub, https://github.com/ethereum/EIPs
[59] See for instance; https://github.com/ethereum/pm/issues/21

On-chain Versus Off-chain Versus Side Chain?

As you get deeper into the weeds with Ethereum, you will likely come across terms such as "**off-chain**," "**on-chain**," or "side chain." These concepts have become especially important in discussions to resolve major issues and bugs in the platform. When developers submitted the proposal of the hard fork for The DAO to the Ethereum community (client developers and users) for comment and voting, this was an example of how governance issues were resolved in an "off-chain" manner. In other words, the solution was not built into the Ethereum protocols. As Vlad Zamfir, one of the key researchers at the Ethereum Foundation puts it, "'On-chain governance' refers to the idea that the blockchain nodes automatically upgrade when an on-chain governance process decides on an upgrade and that it's time to install it. No hard forks required."[60] The deliberation process of hard-forks is part of off-chain governance, as the blockchain platform itself does not have protocols for moving through a decision. A key insight here is that off-chain governance necessitates the participation of node operators, as their decisions help define the outcome.

Newer blockchain platforms such as **Dfinity** are trying to improve on this by putting the rules for governance directly into their protocols so that they can avoid potentially fatal issues such as The DAO hack and the resulting hard fork. Dfinity's protocols allow for making direct changes to the ledger when there is a consensus among all of its coin holders. As these networks continue to grow, one of the biggest debates now in the blockchain community concerns scaling up the platforms to allow for higher processing volume and speed. One solution is to take some of the processing of transactions off-chain to lessen the burden on the main chain. It's similar to when you work on a text document on your local machine and then upload it as a Google document for joint editing. Doing this reduces the amount of processing that the web servers have to do. Several major initiatives are now focusing on off-chain Ethereum processing. One is from Dispatch Labs where they are looking to integrate the storage of large amounts of data off-chain with the

60 Zamfir, Vlad. "Against on-chain governance," Medium, December 1, 2017,
https://medium.com/@Vlad_Zamfir/against-on-chain-governance-a4ceacd040ca

on-chain processing of the smart contracts.[61]

If two banks, A and B, wanted to have thousands of Ethereum transactions between each other every day, it might behoove them to create a special **sidechain**. The sidechain would be much quicker and cheaper to run than it would be to have each transaction on the main Ethereum chain where a transaction fee would be incurred for each one. With a sidechain, all it takes is for the parties to use one transaction at the end of the day to settle their accounts on the main Ethereum chain.

---

[61] Witherspoon, Zane. "Dispatch Protocol: Technical White Paper," September 17, 2018, https://www.dispatchlabs.io/wp-content/uploads/2018/03/Technical-Whitepaper.pdf

> **Time to Pay Rent?**
>
> One of the issues facing the Ethereum network is scaling. Because the volume of data and transactions has grown so rapidly, it has put a huge burden on the nodes doing these operations on the network. Vitalik Buterin, the founder of Ethereum, has proposed that users may need to start paying rent in order for the system to keep storing their data. He reasons that paying rent would generate resources for data storage and reduce the data storage needed for those who decide not to pay the rental fees. The fees would be determined by the length of time the storage was needed.[62] Users have been generally cool to the idea of paying more and this proposal has been very controversial. However, "rent" is essentially subsidized by the platform today, and will likely need to be resolved for future usability.

Mining Ethereum

While there are many similarities between **mining** on the Ethereum network and mining on the Bitcoin network, it might be useful to consider how they differ. As previously mentioned (see Chapters 2 and 3), it takes about ten minutes on average to create a new block on the Bitcoin network, whereas on Ethereum, it takes about fifteen seconds to add a block. Ethereum miners are awarded 3 ETH plus the transaction fees included with the block for each block they create. Keep in mind that a transaction on Ethereum could include processing the program code stored on the network for supporting a smart contract. Mining ether is also designed to be ASIC-resistant so that small, individual miners can compete with the big mining firms using cheaper GPU mining rigs. This is accomplished by using the **ethash** hashing algorithm, which is designed specifically to be solved by GPU machines, as opposed to the SHA-256 algorithm used by Bitcoin.

Just as with bitcoin, as the price of ether rises, more miners compete to create new blocks and the associated hash rate increases. To keep the block creation time at fifteen seconds, the network can adjust the difficulty of the hashing

---

[62] Reiff, Nathan. "Ethereum Founder: Users Should Pay 'Rent' on System," Investopedia, March 29, 2018, https://www.investopedia.com/news/ethereum-founder-buterin-wants-you-pay-slow-down-ethereums-growth/

algorithm to make it harder. Assuming that one has access to cheaper electricity, it may be worthwhile to purchase a GPU machine and install the full Ethereum network protocols that are needed to become a miner. With Ethereum, it may not be as much about making a fortune as it is with the mining of bitcoin. Some people do it because they want to participate more actively in supporting the goals and operation of the Ethereum network. As Ethereum moves away from a Proof of Work mechanism to a Proof of Stake, the role of the miners will continue to evolve.

Ethereum Versus Bitcoin

Much time is currently being spent on debating the merits of Bitcoin versus Ethereum. Will one dominate the world of blockchain as we move forward? Or could both be transplanted as the technology evolves past their limitations? As we know, the Bitcoin network launched the first successful crypto-asset built on blockchain technology and has been around since 2009. Ethereum is a relative newcomer, having launched in 2015. During the intervening years, a number of digital tokens were released that focused on trying to be faster or more scalable than Bitcoin.

However, Ethereum was very different than all of these altcoin projects since it focused on developing a global computing network or platform. While most of the other digital tokens were simply operating as distributed databases or ledgers to track crypto-assets, Ethereum could do this and more. The Ethereum blockchain allows users to easily store and execute program code on the blockchain and these became known as "smart contracts." This innovation has made Ethereum much more flexible and useful as a platform for developing more distributed applications than Bitcoin. The greater versatility in programming is one reason that people have started to refer to Ethereum as "blockchain 2.0" and why ether is currently the second most popular crypto-asset with a market capitalization of $28.7 billion (June 2019). Of course, the next great innovation that will overtake both Bitcoin and Ethereum could be around the corner. The basic differences between Ethereum and Bitcoin as networks are summarized below in Figure 4-3, which lists figures for June 2019.

Aspect	Bitcoin	Ethereum
Inception Date	2009	2015
Market Capitalization	$205.5 B (August 2019)	$ 22.8 B (August 2019)
Digital asset	bitcoin	ether
Expected block generation speed	10 minutes	10 - 19 seconds
Smart contracts	"Light contracts"	Full support of smart contracts
Consensus	Proof of Work	Proof Stake / Proof of Work
Public/private transactions?	Permissionless transactions	Permissioned and permissionless
Quantity of Tokens	Limited to 21 million bitcoin	About 100 million ether (no cap)
Mining hardware	ASIC	ASIC-resistant

Figure 4-3: Comparing Bitcoin and Ethereum (June 2019)

While Ethereum is much quicker than Bitcoin in processing transactions and has the ability to develop and process Dapps, one of the biggest determinants of its value is the size and dedication of its developer community. In most of the IT world, the technology with the biggest developer community usually wins. The tool for developing smart contracts, Truffle has been downloaded more than 250,000 times. The MetaMask browser for Ethereum has over 500,000 users. And the IPFS database tool handles up to 4.5 billion queries a day. All these tools and libraries can be found in one single open source platform known as Orb Weaver. Orb Weaver supports various other blockchain networks and services as well.[63] While Bitcoin is dependent upon mass consumer adoption, Ethereum appeals more to the corporate world because of its greater use of smart contracts. Ultimately, its continued expansion seems assured due to its consistent investment in research projects.

63 Access Orb Weaver at https://animalventures.com/

> **The New Swiss Crypto Valley**
>
> Have you ever heard of the Swiss city of Zug? Before the rise of crypto-assets not many people had heard of it. But now Zug and the nearby city of Zurich are claiming that they are the center of the blockchain universe. With their liberal government and traditions of direct political participation, blockchain has been a good fit for the Swiss, and the government there has largely embraced the technology. As the official location of the Ethereum Foundation is now in Switzerland, many developers and startups have relocated to Zurich. While the SEC and legislators in America debate how to regulate crypto-assets, the liberal Swiss are embracing them. The Swiss government is already fairly decentralized and is becoming a test-bed for blockchain-based applications such as e-voting and their own ICO called "Bitcoin Suisse."[64] Time will tell if the real Silicon Valley can catch up with the Swiss as more blockchain talent heads to Zug.

DAOs and DACs

If we take the concept of smart contracts to its logical extreme, we might imagine a collection of smart contracts that could be used to create a set of interlocking rules for a digital corporation. This is what is termed a **Distributed Autonomous Corporation (DAC)**. Sometimes also called a DAO (Distributed Autonomous Organization). These organizations are designed to run and maintain all their transactions and rules on a blockchain using smart contracts. Individuals participating in a DAC or DAO are essentially participating in automated businesses. Smart contracts grouped together into a DAC or DAO can potentially take over many functions that would usually require a board or other governing body. Some examples of attempts to create DAOs include "The DAO," which we discussed earlier in the chapter, and DASH. DASH is a cryptocurrency started in 2014, which attempts to operate as a self-governing DAO, funding itself by allocating 10% of mining fees associated with its cryptocurrency propagation to the DAO.

---

[64] Wolfson, Rachel. "Swiss Investors on What Silicon Valley Can Learn About Blockchain Adoption From 'Crypto Valley,'" Forbes, July 6, 2018, https://www.forbes.com/sites/rachelwolfson/2018/07/06/swiss-investors-on-what-silicon-valley-can-learn-about-blockchain-adoption-from-crypto-valley/#5d4994f33576

Recent attempts to build DAOs and DACs doesn't necessarily mean that organizations will all disappear or become indistinguishable, but just that there are new models that include more self-executing functions for tasks that lend themselves to automation. The marketplaces we have grown accustomed to already rely heavily on automation through algorithms and may become more templated and decentralized with time. An example might be a DAO that is created to support the buying and selling of used cars. If you have ever tried to buy or sell a used car, you know that there are many potential pitfalls in the process. There are always issues about the history and provenance of the car. Then the car is tested and valued, followed by a negotiation and an exchange of information, possibly an application for a loan, and title transfer and tax paid. By using a series of smart contracts, much of this process could potentially be automated. Companies are already working on this possible application. Auto companies such as Renault are actively researching uses for blockchain technology.

Storing Data on Ethereum

Storing data in the Ethereum blockchain is very costly. As of July 20, 2018, if you wanted to store a gigabyte of data in a bytes variable in a smart contract, it would cost about $882,566 USD![65] Unfortunately, one of the jobs of a web server (maybe even its most important job) is to send a website's users the actual web page code and its content, including hefty images and videos. So how can we get a Dapp to people that want to use it while staying true to our decentralized intentions? One possible solution is IPFS, the Interplanetary Filesystem. IPFS is a decentralized network of nodes, each of which stores data based on its hash. Like Ethereum, users of IPFS run their own nodes: nodes store files that they download from other IPFS nodes, and they send these files to other users that request them. As pointed out in the IPFS whitepaper, it's a lot like the service BitTorrent.

IPFS has no blockchain and no incentive mechanism. Consequently, there are no guarantees that anyone will host your file for free, just like there is no guarantee people will seed large torrents for BitTorrent. Therefore, IPFS users will typically run their own nodes that serve their own files, at least for a while. Due to the IPFS network's decentralized nature, once a file is downloaded by other IPFS users it will be replicated across those users's nodes.[66]

A few projects leverage the blockchain to provide a more stable service. The FileCoin project proposes adding a blockchain to IPFS, allowing nodes to be reimbursed for storing users' files and allowing users to pay to have their files permanently available on a decentralized network. Other projects, including Sia and MaidSafe, also have this goal but different mechanisms for achieving it.

---

65 (Sources for cost: https://ethgasstation.info/, https://www.coingecko.com/en/price_charts/ethereum/usd; https://ethereum.stackexchange.com/questions/872/ 640K gas per kilobyte * 3 GWei/gas * (1/1000000000) ETH/GWei * 1000000 kB/GB * $459.67 USD/ETH)

66 Health, Coral. "Learn to securely share files on the blockchain with IPFS!" Medium, February 20, 2018, https://medium.com/@mycoralhealth/learn-to-securely-share-files-on-the-blockchain-with-ipfs-219ee47df54c

Ethical and Other Issues with Blockchain

This chapter has introduced some innovative ideas such as DAOs and DACs, which could use smart contracts to run much of an organization without human interference. Supporters claim that they will help eliminate manipulation and corruption in certain spheres. However, the implementation of code-based organizations certainly raises other questions. As an autonomous corporate entity do they still have the legal power to enter into legal contracts and negotiations? Can they sue other entities or be sued? What is the liability of their creators? Can the creators be prosecuted if one of their smart contracts breaks a law? Should their information be available to governments; and if so, how?

One of the toughest issues with blockchain overall is the idea of jurisdiction. Even though smart contracts and transactions are designed to be run on global networks of computers, if there is a problem, in which jurisdiction should it be adjudicated? Since contract law can vary substantially between different jurisdictions, this can be an especially thorny issue when creating a smart contract that spans multiple political boundaries. The same can be said for banking and financial regulations, data privacy, and intellectual property laws and regulations. Globally various groups are working on resolving some of these complex legal and regulatory issues.

Chapter Summary

This chapter has provided an in-depth view of the overall Ethereum framework. Ethereum incorporates the blockchain technology discussed in earlier chapters but also represents a major departure from the Bitcoin framework in that it supports the development and execution of distributed applications. To do this, software was developed that gives users access to the global supercomputer called the Ethereum Virtual Machine. The focus on global decentralized computing and decentralized software development is part of why Ethereum is referred to as "blockchain 2.0". The history of Ethereum and how it was founded in response to Bitcoin was reviewed, including its launch through a crowdsale (now called ICO) to bring in its startup capital. The Ethereum Foundation and many in its community have put effort into growing the ecosystem of projects that use Ethereum to promote the survival of the platform and attract developers and users by providing support for research in new tools and giving easy access to them. The DAO hack in 2016 was a crucial moment for the Ethereum community as they learned how to respond to a major crisis. While controversial, the response also inspired further confidence in the Ethereum project overall and in its ability to evolve decision-making alongside its technology.

There is plenty of discussion about how Bitcoin compares to Ethereum. Bitcoin is the first successful decentralized application built using blockchain technology. It has been around the longest, has the largest market capitalization, and is widely recognized and accepted for financial transactions. Vitalik Buterin envisioned a platform that could handle many different types of "transactions" using blockchain technology; when he couldn't get the Bitcoin community to evolve in this direction, he went ahead and founded the Ethereum network. The core difference between Bitcoin and Ethereum is that beyond supporting a cryptocurrency (ether) the Ethereum network also serves as a flexible platform for developing, hosting, and executing decentralized applications (Dapps). In order to do this, some participants lend their computing resources to the network to create the global Ethereum Virtual Machine or EVM. These participants are paid by Ethereum users with ether, which helps fuel overall network processing. Ethereum led to the rapidly growing implementation of smart contracts which contain program logic and are designed to run autonomously without any third-party interference. Smart contracts can be further linked and bundled to create DAOs and DACs which attempt to automate how organizations and companies operate as much as possible. The impact of this technology is predicted to change entire areas of business such as insurance, finance, healthcare, real estate, law, government, and supply chain management. One of the newest areas for smart contract application is across the growing Internet of Things, where blockchain technology is being used to create smart objects.

This chapter also introduced the user to some of the tools that developers use to create Dapps on the Ethereum platform. These include the programming language called Solidity, the Remix interface and the MetaMask tool. By following the instructions given here, users created and modified a basic token contract which was run on a test blockchain network and debugged.

Key Terms

Decentralized application (Dapp)
Solidity
Ethereum Virtual Machine (EVM)
Externally-owned account
Contract account
Wei
Ether
Gas
Smart contract
Turing-complete
The DAO

Casper
Plasma
Ethereum Improvement Proposal
Off-chain
On-chain
Dfinity
Sidechain
Mining
Ethash
Distributed Autonomous Corporation (DAC)

Questions for Further Discussion

1. How is Ethereum different from the Bitcoin network?
2. What is a smart object? Give an example? Why is Ethereum the appropriate platform for smart objects?
3. What is a smart contract? Come up with 3 smart contract use cases and discuss the merits of automating these transactions.
4. What is meant by blockchain 2.0? Is there a 3.0?
5. What is the difference between on-chain and off-chain governance? What are some of the pitfalls of each?
6. What are some of the current challenges for further developing Ethereum?
7. Go to https://ethgasstation.info/. What is the average wait time for running a transaction on Ethereum right now?
8. What is the process for making changes across the whole Ethereum network? What are some of the things that are currently changing?
9. Why did Ethereum go through a hard fork after The DAO hack? How is Dfinity seeking to avoid this?
10. What are the steps in developing and deploying a smart contract using the Solidity framework? Describe the tools used in the digital token example given in this chapter.

Tutorial: Developing a Dapp for Ethereum

Overview

There are many different kinds of computers in the world – from supercomputers to the smartphone in your pocket – each of which can do many different kinds of things through applications, or apps. Every day we use apps on our phones, laptops, and tablets. When we use a website, an app on our computer or phone (called a web browser) communicates with an app running on a powerful central computer (called a server). A typical shopping site, for example, runs on a server that has to keep track of shopping carts, billing information, all the items for sale, and much more – for everyone connected to this site, all at the same time! There is a lot being demanded of this app, and of the computer that it runs on. This is where the Ethereum Virtual Machine (EVM) comes in. Like every other computer, the EVM runs apps. These apps are decentralized software made up of smart contracts. The apps you use that run on Ethereum – called Dapps – are to the EVM what websites are to servers.

Ethereum's unique design makes the EVM an excellent server. Traditional servers can lose power, lose their Internet connection, become overloaded, be hacked, be stolen by pirates, and so on, rendering the apps that run on them useless. The EVM functions as a more resilient server, since smart contracts on the EVM will work as long as any of the nodes in the Ethereum network are working. The apps that run on traditional servers aren't downloaded by the people that use them. No one can see these apps or the code that they're made of; they can only see how the server acts. This is a problem: a hacker might break into the server of our shopping site and change the server app to send all of the credit card numbers people use to the hacker's computer and no one using the shopping site would know. There are two safeguards against this when using the public Ethereum network:

1. Immutability: Once someone sets up a smart contract, it can never be changed.

2. Transparency: A smart contract's code can be read by anybody. In fact, since smart contracts must be run by every node in the Ethereum network and anyone can join the network, it's not possible to hide a smart contract's code. (This doesn't mean that smart contracts can't deal with secrets; we'll talk about how this is done later.)

Running a Token Dapp

Better than thinking about Dapps is trying to actually deploy one yourself. This section highlights the usefulness of simulation for learning. Below is an exercise that will walk you through creating a "FUN" token.

Creation Process Steps of the Dapp

1. **Developing the smart contract source code**

Programmers materialize the logic and features of the Dapp idea by writing instructions for the EVM to execute. These instructions assembled together are essentially a formal human-readable specification that explains how the Dapp operates at the machine level. This formal specification is normally known as source code and the EVM uses it to execute transaction requests from network participants and update the state of the Dapp.

2. **Compiling the source code into its corresponding bytecode representation**

In order for the EVM to execute source code, the smart contract must first be converted into a format that can be understood at the machine level. This conversion process is called "compilation," and it utilizes a designated tool called a "compiler" that reads the source code and transforms it into bytecode. The compiler also acts as a code syntax checker and analyzer. If the code does not follow the rules of the Solidity programming language, then it cannot be converted into bytecode, and the compiler lists the "mistakes" that need to be corrected. With a sophisticated compiler, more useful information can be gained from the compilation process. For example, such a compiler could detect whether or not your code could be made shorter or more efficient, or possibly even warn you about potential sources of security vulnerabilities.

3. **Deploying the Dapp on the blockchain network**

After the Dapp source code has been compiled and verified, then it can run on the Ethereum blockchain network. The deployment process usually requires a client that communicates with the network on behalf of the user to carry out requests. The client can be a detached gateway or it can be a participating node in the network. The difference is usually in availability of network access and blockchain data. With a detached client, there is no waiting necessary to send requests to the network; whereas for a node client, it necessitates syncing with the network by downloading an entire copy of the blockchain, which, at the time of this writing, takes around 3-5 days.

Dapp Source Code

There are many token Dapps that have been deployed on the Ethereum network and have been used for various business use cases. Many of these Dapps have their tokens listed on the coinmarketcap.com website. A well-known location for token contracts is the Dapp source code repository provided by the open-source framework OpenZeppelin which was started and supported by the company Zeppelin which can be found at the following link:

https://github.com/OpenZeppelin/openzeppelin-solidity

For the sake of simplicity, we will take the token contract example from the official Ethereum website (https://www.ethereum.org/token) and run it in a simulated environment by using Remix, a simple and easy-to-use Ethereum network client and compiler. Because of its ease, this token contract has also been used by many ICOs, some of which have been fraudulent or made unachievable promises. Use solidity compiler version "0.4.21+commit.dfe3193c" and EVM version "compiler default." Here is the Ethereum basic token contract example source code:

```solidity
pragma solidity ^0.4.21;

interface tokenRecipient { function receiveApproval(address _from, uint256 _value, address _token, bytes _extraData) external; }

contract TokenERC20 {
    // Public variables of the token
    string public name;
    string public symbol;
    uint8 public decimals = 18;
    // 18 decimals is the strongly suggested default, avoid changing it
    uint256 public totalSupply;

    // This creates an array with all balances
    mapping (address => uint256) public balanceOf;
    mapping (address => mapping (address => uint256)) public allowance;

    // This generates a public event on the blockchain that will notify clients
    event Transfer(address indexed from, address indexed to, uint256 value);

    // This generates a public event on the blockchain that will notify clients
    event Approval(address indexed _owner, address indexed _spender, uint256 _value);

    // This notifies clients about the amount burnt
    event Burn(address indexed from, uint256 value);

    /**
```

```
/**
 * Constructor function
 *
 * Initializes contract with initial supply tokens to the creator of the contract
 */
function TokenERC20(
    uint256 initialSupply,
    string tokenName,
    string tokenSymbol
) public payable {
    totalSupply = initialSupply * 10 ** uint256(decimals);  // Update total supply with the decimal amount
    balanceOf[msg.sender] = totalSupply;           // Give the creator all initial tokens
    name = tokenName;                              // Set the name for display purposes
    symbol = tokenSymbol;                          // Set the symbol for display purposes
}

/**
 * Internal transfer, only can be called by this contract
 */
function _transfer(address _from, address _to, uint _value) internal {
    // Prevent transfer to 0x0 address. Use burn() instead
    require(_to != 0x0);
    // Check if the sender has enough
    require(balanceOf[_from] >= _value);
    // Check for overflows
    require(balanceOf[_to] + _value >= balanceOf[_to]);
    // Save this for an assertion in the future
    uint previousBalances = balanceOf[_from] + balanceOf[_to];
    // Subtract from the sender
    balanceOf[_from] -= _value;
    // Add the same to the recipient
    balanceOf[_to] += _value;
    emit Transfer(_from, _to, _value);
    // Asserts are used to use static analysis to find bugs in your code. They should never fail
    assert(balanceOf[_from] + balanceOf[_to] == previousBalances);
}
```

```
/**
 * Transfer tokens
 *
 * Send `_value` tokens to `_to` from your account
 *
 * @param _to The address of the recipient
 * @param _value the amount to send
 */
function transfer(address _to, uint256 _value) public payable returns (bool success) {
    _transfer(msg.sender, _to, _value);
    return true;
}

/**
 * Transfer tokens from other address
 *
 * Send `_value` tokens to `_to` on behalf of `_from`
 *
 * @param _from The address of the sender
 * @param _to The address of the recipient
 * @param _value the amount to send
 */
function transferFrom(address _from, address _to, uint256 _value) public payable returns (bool success) {
    require(_value <= allowance[_from][msg.sender]);     // Check allowance
    allowance[_from][msg.sender] -= _value;
    _transfer(_from, _to, _value);
    return true;
}

/**
 * Set allowance for other address
 *
 * Allows `_spender` to spend no more than `_value` tokens on your behalf
 *
 * @param _spender The address authorized to spend
```

* @param _value the max amount they can spend
 */
function approve(address _spender, uint256 _value) public
  returns (bool success) {
    allowance[msg.sender][_spender] = _value;
    emit Approval(msg.sender, _spender, _value);
    return true;
}

/**
 * Set allowance for other address and notify
 *
 * Allows `_spender` to spend no more than `_value` tokens on your behalf, and then ping the contract about it
 *
 * @param _spender The address authorized to spend
 * @param _value the max amount they can spend
 * @param _extraData some extra information to send to the approved contract
 */
function approveAndCall(address _spender, uint256 _value, bytes _extraData)
  public
  returns (bool success) {
    tokenRecipient spender = tokenRecipient(_spender);
    if (approve(_spender, _value)) {
      spender.receiveApproval(msg.sender, _value, this, _extraData);
      return true;
    }
}

/**
 * Destroy tokens
 *
 * Remove `_value` tokens from the system irreversibly
 *
 * @param _value the amount of money to burn
 */

```solidity
function burn(uint256 _value) public returns (bool success) {
    require(balanceOf[msg.sender] >= _value);   // Check if the sender has enough
    balanceOf[msg.sender] -= _value;            // Subtract from the sender
    totalSupply -= _value;                      // Updates totalSupply
    emit Burn(msg.sender, _value);
    return true;
}

/**
 * Destroy tokens from other account
 *
 * Remove `_value` tokens from the system irreversibly on behalf of `_from`.
 *
 * @param _from the address of the sender
 * @param _value the amount of money to burn
 */
function burnFrom(address _from, uint256 _value) public returns (bool success) {
    require(balanceOf[_from] >= _value);                // Check if the targeted balance is enough
    require(_value <= allowance[_from][msg.sender]);    // Check allowance
    balanceOf[_from] -= _value;                         // Subtract from the targeted balance
    allowance[_from][msg.sender] -= _value;             // Subtract from the sender's allowance
    totalSupply -= _value;                              // Update totalSupply
    emit Burn(_from, _value);
    return true;
}

}
```

The contract:

- Specifies the symbol, name, and total supply possible of the token in circulation. This total supply is initially assigned to the contract owner (the account that deployed the contract).

- Specifies the range of denominations that can be traded through the number of decimals.

- Stores the individual allowance of an account.

- Stores the balance of an account.

- Allows token owners to:
    - Make payments (in the form of token transfers)
    - Destroy their tokens (usually for deflationary purposes)
    - Authorize other users to spend their tokens

Compiling the Dapp

Open the Remix editor at the following address: https://remix.ethereum.org. You should be able to see the following:

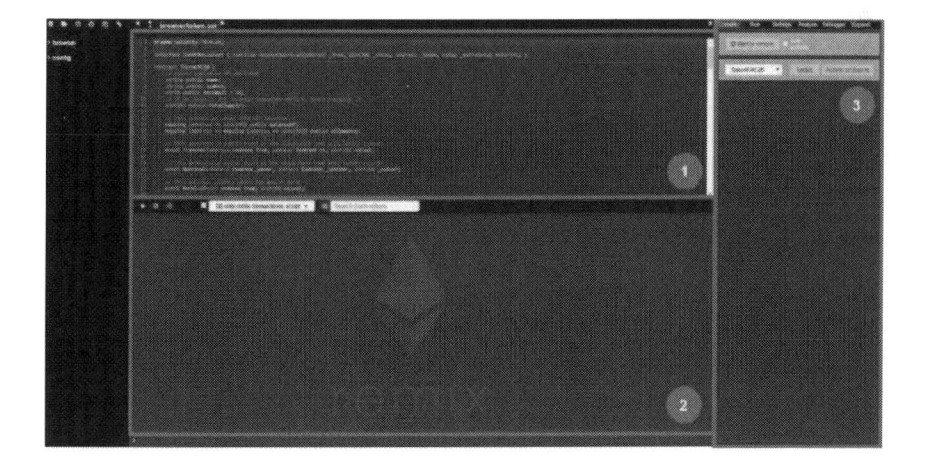

Figure 4-4: The Remix IDE is a relatively simple and convenient way to build and run

Solidity smart contracts

Remix UI Overview

1. **The Editor Panel** - used for writing and editing smart contract source code

2. **The Output Console** - displays transaction logs

3. **The Control Panel** - used for executing transactions and configuring the IDE

Let's get started by copying and pasting the token source code into the editor panel. If you are using a hard copy of this text, just go to https://www.ethereum.org/token and copy the code found there. Then, click on the "Compile" Tab in the Control Panel and press "Start to compile," as shown below. This will convert the source code into binary code which is stored locally.

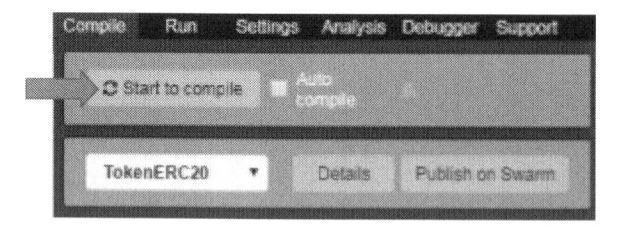

Figure 4-5: In the "Compile" tab you can compile your source code and look at compilation details

After compiling, you should get the following:

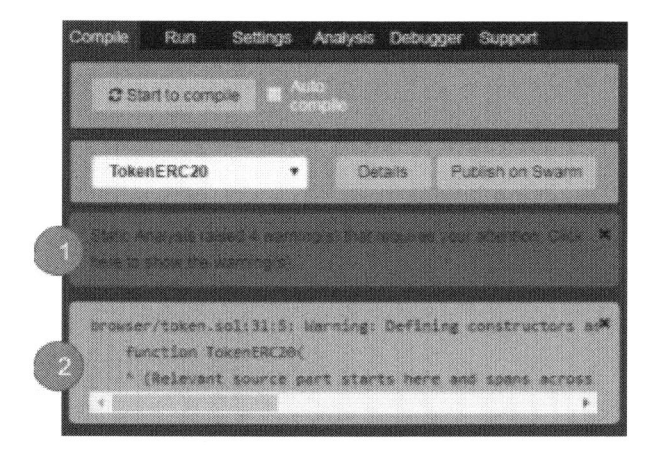

Figure 4-6: Response from Remix after a successful compilation (with no syntax errors)

Compilation Output

1. **Static Analysis** - gives you warnings regarding your code logic

2. **Warnings** - tell you how to better structure your code

You can view the compiled code and additional compilation information by clicking "Details".

If you did not copy the code correctly or made incorrect modifications, you would get the following screen, which lists compilation errors or "code mistakes" that you need to correct.

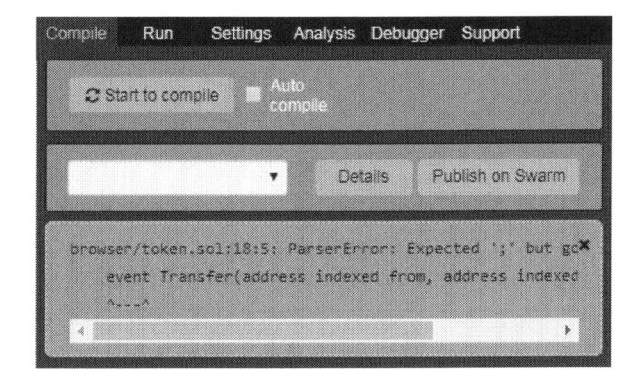

Figure 4-7: Response from Remix after an unsuccessful compilation

203

Deploying the Dapp

In the control panel, switch to the "Run" tab. As you can see in Figure 4-8, you are presented with options for deploying your smart contract.

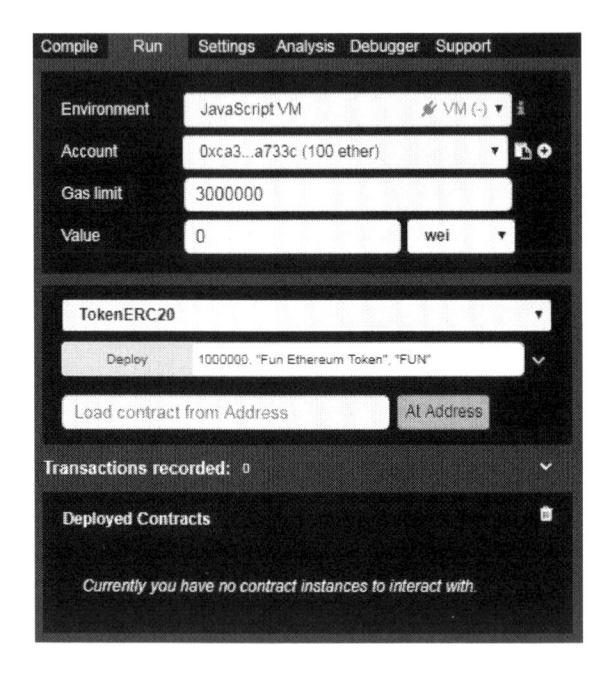

Figure 4-8: The Run Tab

The run tab allows you to not only deploy smart contracts but also interact with them. This is where you can send your transaction requests to the blockchain network.

Let's go over each individual option together and configure our deployment.

Environment. Specifies the network with which to communicate. At the time of this writing, there are three options listed:

1. JavaScript VM - This connects Remix to a simulated Ethereum blockchain network environment that runs on your computer. All blockchain activities are simulated and are instantaneous. This environment is completely isolated from the Internet, so any content you send over to this network cannot be accessed by anybody on the Internet. For our demo, we are going to pick this environment because it simplifies our process.

2. Injected Web3 - This connects Remix to the actual Ethereum mainnet. It is not recommended to send transaction requests using this method unless you know exactly what you are doing!

3. Web3 Provider - This connects Remix to an external client by specifying its url endpoint to communicate with via http. This is usually used when you want to connect to an unlisted Ethereum network. This can usually be Ropsten or Rinkeby, which are testnets maintained by the Ethereum Foundation, or it can be your own private Ethereum network that you deployed yourself.

Account. This lists the wallet accounts you own on the target Environment. This account is used for deploying the Dapp and executing transactions, which means, every time you execute a transaction, ether tokens will be withdrawn from the specified account. For the simulated environment, Remix creates several random accounts with 100 (simulated) ether on each. For other environments, the wallet accounts need to be connected individually. But again, it is not recommended unless you are certain of what you are doing! Pick a random account.

Gas Limit. Ethereum transactions have two types of gas limits: maximum gas limit and transaction gas limit. This option specifies transaction gas limit, which is the maximum amount of gas you are willing to spend to deploy your smart contract. If the gas cost exceeds the transaction gas limit, then the deployment process is halted and the gas used in deploying the contract is returned to the sender. Maximum gas limit is usually set by the miners through consensus. Leave this setting as is.

Value. This specifies which ether tokens are to be sent to the deployed contract in the given denomination. Useful if you want your contract to hold tokens to carry out various transactions. You can leave this at 0.

The next three fields specify:

1. Which subcontract to deploy (your smart contract source code can have multiple subcontracts). Leave the option at TokenERC20

2. The constructor arguments, or less formally, deployment parameters. For our contract, we are going to type in the following text:

1000000, "Fun Ethereum Token", "FUN"

You can also choose to expand the option and enter the values to each field individually.

3. The address of an already deployed smart contract. You can type here your contract address if you want to load a token you already deployed. We are not going to use this for our demo so leave it blank.

After you have finished setting these options, press the "Deploy" button and observe your contract getting deployed on the network!

What Happens During the Deployment Process?

Transaction Request Preparation. The Remix client assembles a transaction request that contains the compiled bytecode, constructor arguments, account address, gas parameters, and the tokens to be deposited that are specified in the "Value" field. It signs the transaction using the private key of the account, then sends the signed transaction to a node in the Ethereum network. The deployment will happen quickly because the simulated environment runs locally; thus, network processes such as consensus and confirmation (which usually take dozens of seconds) are therefore instant. However, if Remix was connected to an actual Ethereum network (the mainnet or a private network, rather than the testnet), then the deployment would take significantly longer, and you would have to wait for the deployment process to finish before you would see any visual updates.

Deploying the Contract. The node to which we sent the transaction request forwards the request to other nodes until it reaches the miners which look at the request and execute it. Miners execute additional transactions until the total cost of all transactions outnumbers the maximum gas limit. At this point, they mint a new block containing the smart contract we just sent as a Dapp and start working on a new block. The surrounding nodes forward the new block until the Dapp becomes generally available across the network to receive transaction requests. When the deployment process is finished you will see details about it as illustrated in Figures 4-9 and 4-10.

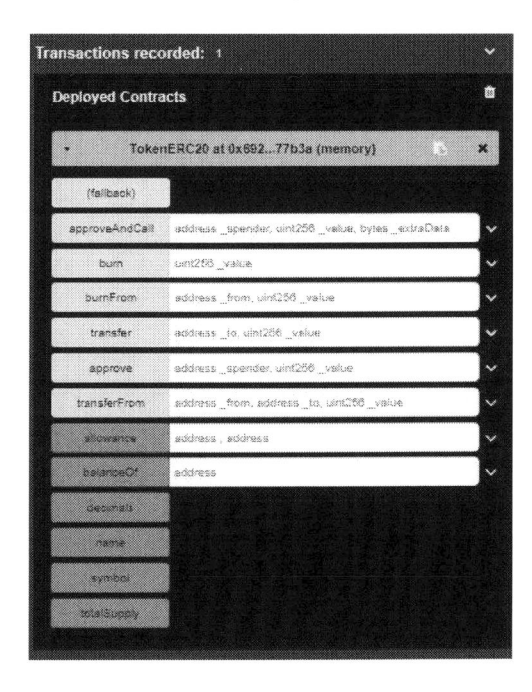

Figure 4-9: List of Deployed contracts

The token is added to the list of deployed contracts. You can click the listing to expand it. This will allow you to view intractable functions and properties.

Basics of Blockchain

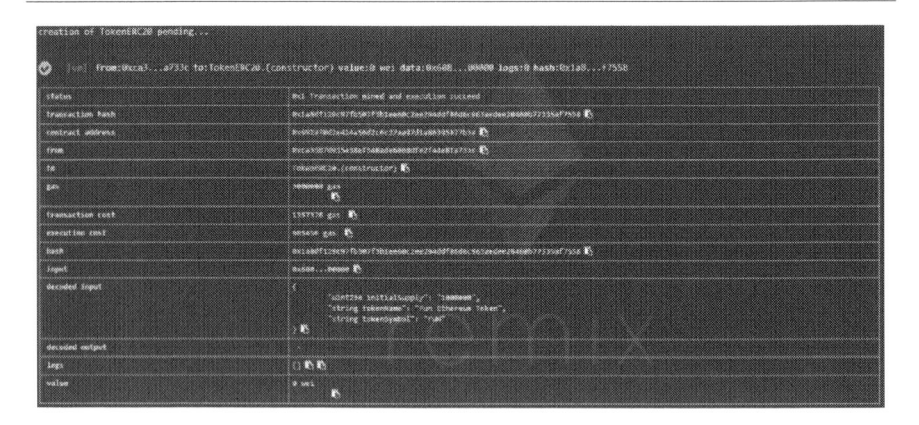

Figure 4-10: The console will output deployment transaction details. You can click the text output to view these details

Congratulations, you've deployed your first smart contract on Ethereum! It is a simulated Ethereum, but it is a great step nonetheless. Now it's time to interact with our Dapp.

Interacting with the Dapp

Viewing Dapp Properties

Before we run any transactions, let's first observe the state of our Dapp. In Figure 4-11, you can see the Dapp's properties in green. You can click on any property and see its value. If you click "totalSupply," you should see the number of tokens we specified during deployment (times 18 digits for decimal places, read below) as shown in Figure 4-11.

Note: Ethereum smart contracts do not support "decimal places" as we are normally familiar with them because it is costly for the EVM to support secure computation and storage of numbers with decimal places. Instead, Ethereum developers sided with converting the decimal places to digits and allowing Dapp developers to do the conversions necessary at the output level if they wanted to.

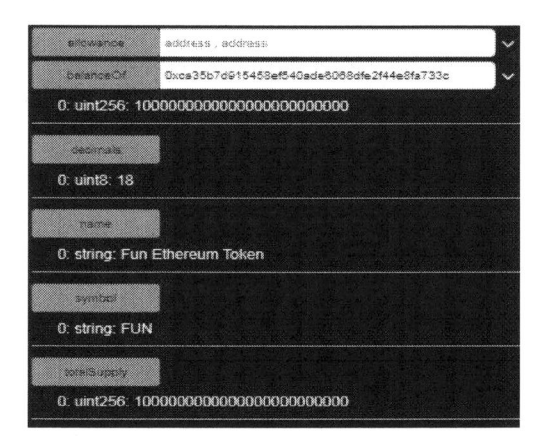

Figure 4-11: Viewing the values of the Dapp properties. If you view the balance of the account from which you deployed the contract, you can see it owns the entire supply of tokens

Executing Transactions

Now we can finally observe how our token acts like a currency. Let's make a token transfer between the main account and another account. In the control panel, expand the transfer function and add the address of the account you want to send FUN tokens to and enter the amount you would like to send as well. An example is provided below in Figure 4-12.

Figure 4-12: Input values for the transfer function

Basics of Blockchain

Click "transact". You should see output in the console similar to Figure 4-13.

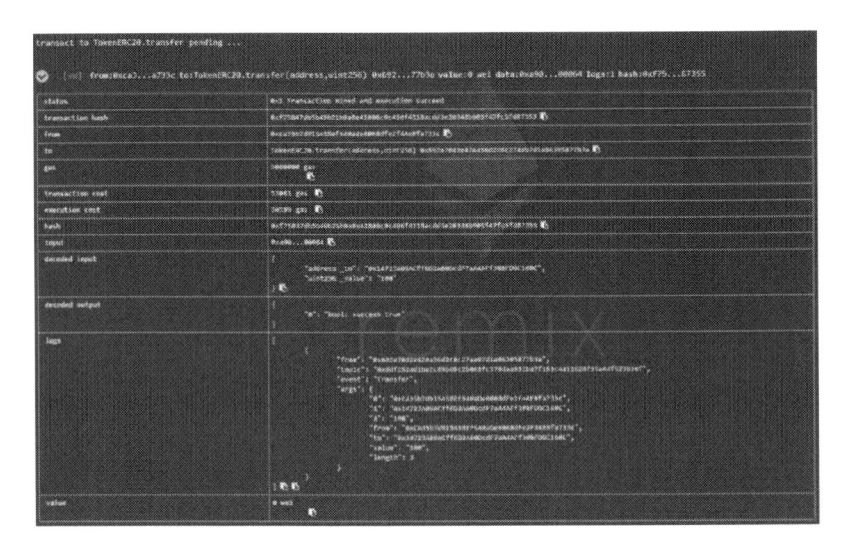

Figure 4-13: The output of the transfer transaction. Among other things, you can observe the address of the owner and the recipient, as well as the amount that was transferred

When you submit transaction requests to your token Dapp, a similar process happens when you deployed your Dapp. The Remix client takes the function parameters of your request, adds them to a transaction request that includes the "from" account address, the address of the deployed token smart contract, and gas cost configuration. It signs the request and then submits it to the Ethereum node it is connected to. The Ethereum node takes the request and forwards it until it reaches a miner, which executes the requests through the Dapp that it is running. This process takes time in a real Ethereum network, but in our virtual environment, it is instantaneous.

If you check the balance of the recipient, you should see a value of 100, as shown in the Figure 4-14 below.

Figure 4-14: Balance of the recipient should be 100

This wraps up our tutorial on running a token Dapp. In the next section you are going to learn how to interact with Dapps in the public Ethereum blockchain network (or mainnet), as well as how to develop your own smart contract from scratch. You might also want to take a look at the open source application called Orb Weaver. As discussed in the earlier chapters it will give a head start to build blockchain applications.[67]

Publishing and Using Your Token with MetaMask

The ERC-20 standard allows the ever-growing collection of Ethereum tools and Dapps to know that your contract is a token that can be sent from one person to another. Let's see one of those tools in action! There are several ways you can access the Ethereum blockchain from your web browser. The easiest and most popular is MetaMask: with MetaMask, you can create or import an Ethereum wallet and then send or receive ether right from your web browser. The websites you visit can also use MetaMask to call functions on smart contracts, bridging the gap between the traditional Internet and the blockchain. We're going to use MetaMask to:

• Make a new wallet for an account on the Ropsten test network. We'll get some (free!) test ether from MetaMask's faucet.

• Deploy our FUN contract to the test network.

• See our token balance right from the MetaMask main screen!

Note that MetaMask runs on Chrome and Firefox. Let's start by downloading MetaMask from the Chrome Web Store:

---

[67] Access Orb Weaver at https://animalventures.com/

Basics of Blockchain

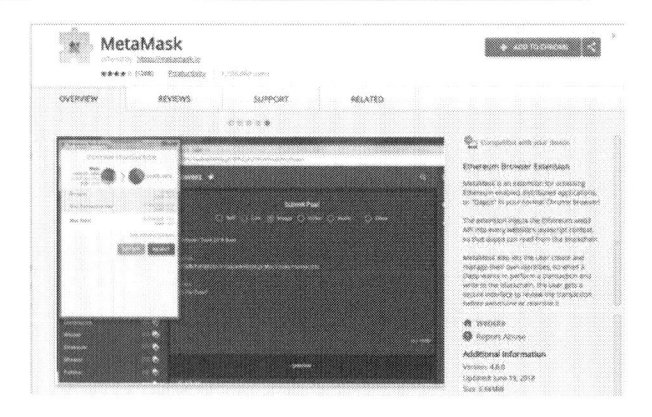

Figure 4-15: Downloading MetaMask from Chrome

After installing MetaMask, all of the websites you visit will have full and automatic access to smart contracts on Ethereum. But don't worry: sites won't be able to spend your tokens or ether without your permission.

Once you install the extension, click on the MetaMask icon at the top of your Chrome window. Before going any further, click on "Main Ethereum Network" at the top of this window and then switch to "Ropsten Test Network."

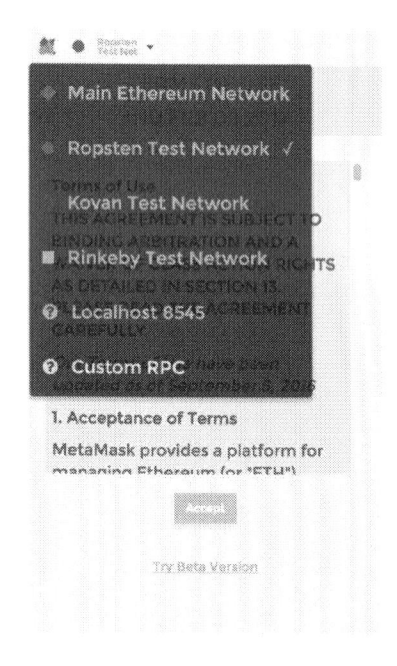

Figure 4-16: Ropsten Test Network View

After this, you'll be asked to accept MetaMask's terms and conditions, and to create a password. This password will be used to encrypt your private key for extra security, and you'll need to enter it before you submit a transaction to the Ethereum mainnet.

Figure 4-17: Ropsten Test Network Sign In

MetaMask then makes your private key for you and will show you a 12-word seed. To keep your account safe, it's best to write this seed down on paper; never upload this key to the Internet! Congratulations! You're the owner of a freshly minted Ethereum wallet. But we can't do much yet. We need ether to pay for uploading contracts and sending transactions, even on the Ropsten test network. Fortunately, test ether is given for free to anyone who asks for it. Using your MetaMask-powered web browser, navigate to https://faucet.metamask.io/ and request an ether from the faucet:

Basics of Blockchain

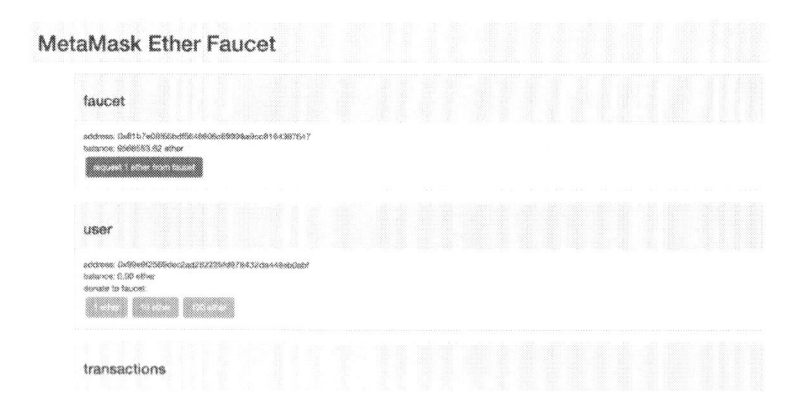

Figure 4-18: View of MetaMask Ether Faucet

A few seconds after you click on this button, a link will show up on the bottom of the page. Click on this link to see the transaction being mined:

Figure 4-19: View of transaction being mined

You're now 1 test ether ($0.00) richer! This is more than enough to deploy our FUN contract for the Ropsten-using world to see. Let's go back to Remix. Once you open Remix, you should see the token contract you entered in the last section. Like before, click on the Run tab. You'll see these options:

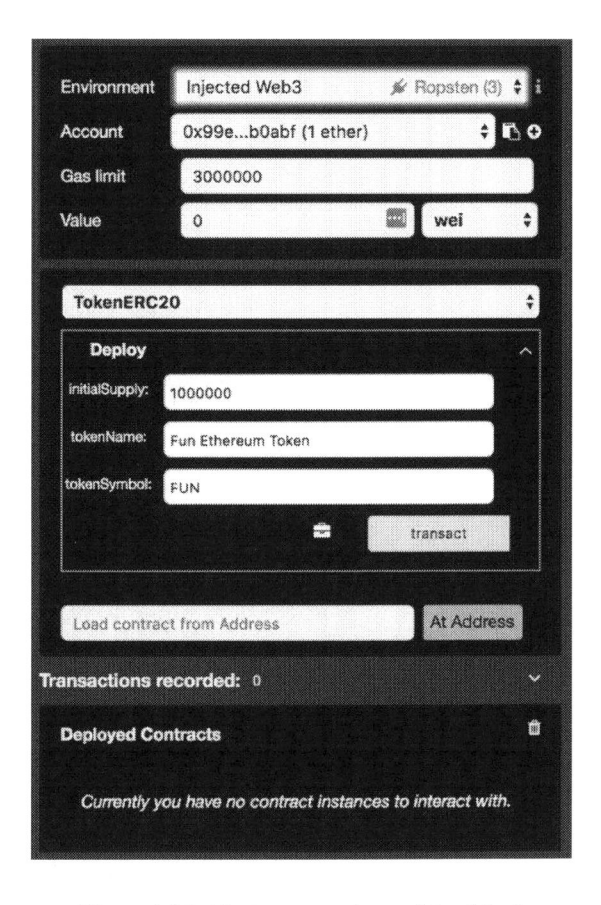

Figure 4-20: Environment view on MetaMask

Now that your browser has MetaMask, you'll have a new option in the "Environment" menu, "Injected Web3." This means that rather than using a simulated Ethereum network, Remix will use the connection to the real Ethereum network that MetaMask "injects" into your web pages. Make sure you choose this option. Next, fill out the information in "Deploy" just as you did before, and click on "transact". A window will pop up:

Basics of Blockchain

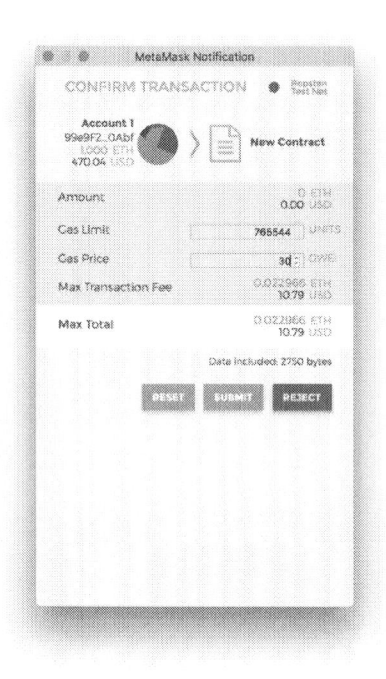

Figure 4-21: Transaction confirmation

MetaMask is telling us that something is trying to send a transaction that will cost us ether. Your smart contract will be created only after you click "Submit" on this page. Be careful, the "Gas Price" defaults to zero. If you click on Submit without adjusting it, you'll get an error in Remix that tells you your transaction was "underpriced." So, make sure you set a gas price. On both the test network and main network, a higher gas price results in a more expensive transaction, but miners will prioritize higher-priced transactions before lower-priced ones, and transactions that are too cheap will be ignored basically forever. When deploying contracts to the main network, developers use tools like https://ethgasstation.info/ to estimate the perfect gas price without wasting ether.

Since you're using the test network, feel free to set the gas price as high as you like – for instance, at the time of writing, 30 Gwei is enough to deploy a contract in about thirty seconds.

Once you click "Submit", you'll see a link to Etherscan in the Remix window, where you'll see your contract creation transaction being mined:

Figure 4-22: Etherscan transaction view

Now you really can send tokens to your friends – as long as there is just one Ropsten node connected to the Internet, anyone in the world will be able to send and receive your FUN token. We've deployed the token contract. Now let's use it the way anyone else would – with MetaMask, as you might have guessed. First, copy the contract address from Etherscan. Then, open MetaMask and click on Tokens. Click on "Add Token" and paste your contract's address:

Figure 4-23: Pasting token address

MetaMask will read the blockchain and automatically fill out the token's symbol and number of decimals for you – this is ERC-20 in action.

Basics of Blockchain

Once you click Add:

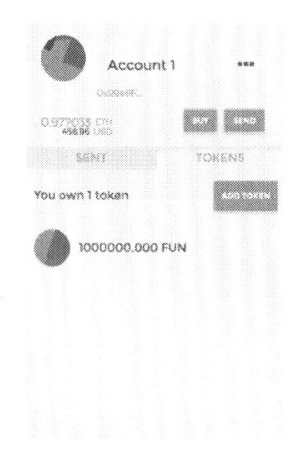

Figure 4-24: ERC-20 token in action

MetaMask will read your balance and show you just how much FUN you're having. You've now been through the complete, end-to-end process of going from a bit of Solidity code in a browser to a decentralized, censorship-resistant virtual currency accessible to anyone in the world, and one that can be integrated with other smart contracts and Dapps.

How to Write a Smart Contract

So far, you have seen what a Dapp looks like and how it runs on an Ethereum network. But how does one actually develop a Dapp? While this section will cover programming concepts, it will only do so for the purpose of explaining immediate functionalities and features of the code at hand. This section will not cover sophisticated subjects or advanced theory, which are normally the material of computer science or software development classes.

The current section will make references to the Solidity reference manual (http://solidity.readthedocs.io/en/v0.4.24/), which is the best place to check the rules and examples of the Solidity programming language.

Let's start with a very simple contract.

```
browser/token.sol
1  pragma solidity ^0.4.24;
2
3  contract SimpleContract {
4      uint value;
5      function setValue(uint _value) public{
6          value = _value;
7      }
8  }
```

Figure 4-25: View of simple contract

As you can observe, the contract only stores and updates the value number. Let's break the code line by line so we understand the purpose of each code statement.

1: This can be called a compiler and EVM directive. It specifies the EVM with which version of the Virtual Machine to execute the code. (Note: The Solidity Programming Language is spread out over multiple versions. This is done so that updates to the language and the EVM do not invalidate previous versions of smart contracts).

3: This line declares a subcontract of this Solidity file. All such declarations always start with the keyword *contract*.

4: This declares that the subcontract stores a variable called **value** of type uint. uint stands for *unsigned integer*, which in programmer lingo means that it is a positive number. **value** is called a variable because it is updatable, meaning its single value can be changed at any point in time.

5: This line declares a public function that takes as input an unsigned integer called **_value**. All function declarations start with *function* keyword. Functions enable users to execute transactions on the smart contract. All Dapp transactions happen through functions.

6: This updates the value of the contract with the value specified in the input parameter.

Finally, notice that each entity (contract, function) is surrounded by curly braces, and that each individual statement is ended with a semicolon. The curly braces and semicolons are entirely necessary as they tell the compiler how to differentiate between entities and statements. If you do not properly place the braces or semicolons, you will get compilation errors. You can take this contract and play with it in the Remix client. Now we have a contract, but how do we take this and turn it into the token Dapps we were playing with earlier, or even a DAO?

How to Write a Token Contract

Let's go over token contract essential characteristics:

1. Contract must specify the total supply of tokens and (optionally) number of decimals for denominations

2. Contract must store the balance of each account that has made a transfer using the token Dapp

3. Contract must allow accounts to make token transfers

Let's add each one of these characteristics at a time.

Contract must specify the total supply of tokens

If you recall from earlier in the chapter, we used the value variable to store a value for our SimpleContract. Whenever you code in Solidity, and you need to store any piece of information, you will need to use variables.

Let's modify our previous contract and add the totalSupply variable to it.

```
browser/token.sol
1   pragma solidity ^0.4.24;
2
3   contract SimpleContract {
4       uint totalSupply;
5       function setValue(uint _totalSupply) public{
6           totalSupply = _totalSupply;
7       }
8   }
```

Figure 4-26: Contract with TotalSupply variable

We replaced the value variable with totalSupply. If you compile and run the program, you can change the totalSupply. This isn't exactly what we want. We would like to specify the totalSupply only once. But how would we do that?

The answer: constructors.

```
browser/token.sol
1  pragma solidity ^0.4.24;
2
3  contract ERC20Token {
4      uint totalSupply;
5      constructor(uint _totalSupply) public {
6          totalSupply = _totalSupply;
7      }
8  }
```

Figure 4-27: Contract with constructor variable

We've changed the contract name and added the constructor. It's similar to a function, except it is executed only once when the contract is deployed. This is very barebones; let's now add some accounting.

Contract must store a list of balances

The variable type we've used so far is uint, but uint only stores one value at a time. For storing a list of values, we are going to use a special structure called mapping, which stores a list where each element of the list is mapped to an index of custom type.

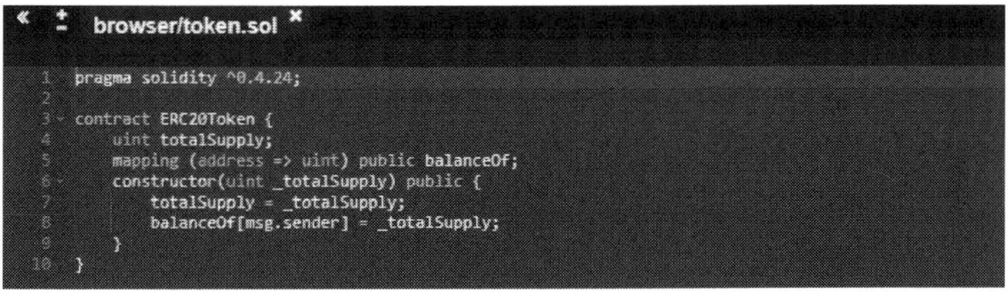

```
browser/token.sol
1  pragma solidity ^0.4.24;
2
3  contract ERC20Token {
4      uint totalSupply;
5      mapping (address => uint) public balanceOf;
6      constructor(uint _totalSupply) public {
7          totalSupply = _totalSupply;
8          balanceOf[msg.sender] = _totalSupply;
9      }
10 }
```

Figure 4-28: Contract with list of balances

We've added a mapping construct that maps a number (uint) to an address (usually account address). Even though the balances are not set, you can query them and they will show a value of 0 each time, except for the owner address, which shows the total supply.

Contract must allow accounts to make token transfers

For token transfers, we do not need to store anything but transfer numbers from one balance to another. A transfer is also a transaction, which means we will need to add another function.

```solidity
pragma solidity ^0.4.24;

contract ERC20Token {
    uint totalSupply;
    mapping (address => uint) public balanceOf;
    constructor(uint _totalSupply) public {
        totalSupply = _totalSupply;
        balanceOf[msg.sender] = _totalSupply;
    }
    function transfer(address _to, uint _value) public {
        require(_to != 0x0);
        require(balanceOf[msg.sender] >= _value);
        require(balanceOf[_to] + _value >= balanceOf[_to]);
        balanceOf[msg.sender] -= _value;
        balanceOf[_to] += _value;
    }
}
```

Figure 4-29: Contract allowing token transfers

Let's go over the transfer function together. It takes as input two parameters: _to, and _value. _to is the recipient of the token amount to be transferred; _value is the amount to be transferred.

Now notice the statement at line 10. **require** is an internal EVM function that acts as a failsafe validator. It takes as input a boolean expression and discontinues transaction execution if the expression is false. But what expression are we checking for at line 10? This is to make sure no transfer is made with address 0. Address 0 is reserved for deploying contracts. Nobody can gain access to that address.

Line 11 makes sure the sender has sufficient tokens to send over.

Line 12 checks for computational overflow. In most programming languages, Solidity included, number variables are bounded (they cannot be larger or smaller than a certain number). If you add a number to your variable, and the sum of both is higher than the bound of the variable, then the variable starts over from the lowest bound.

Line 13 subtracts the amount of tokens to be transferred from the sender.

Line 14 adds the subtracted amount from the sender to the receiver.

You can play with the contract and observe how the tokens are transferred from one account to another.

Going Forward and Best Practices

Having reached the end of our FUN token exercises, you may be wondering what else is possible with smart contracts such as these. Some additional activities include contract writing or editing and instantiating a contract. While our contract was only instantiated once, other contracts can be instantiated multiple times. In some cases, a smart contract can have its functionality defined by external contracts which are linked by their address, and this functionality can be updated. Contracts can even have a self-destruct mechanism built into them! Smart contract development is a very new field, but we are starting to see some best practices emerge. In particular, those related to the principles of defining access/authorization security. Additional best practices can be applied to drafting code as well, but these are generally supplemental (e.g. how to write clean functions, separation of concerns in contracts).

More advanced token features might include introducing fungibility. Our example card is currently fungible, and this is often desirable for tokens so that they can be exchanged easily. But a trading card game with one kind of card is boring. We want different kinds of cards, each of which has unique properties. To do this kind of advanced token development you can use standards like ERC-721 to give distinct tokens their own names. There are of course also advances in the features of the Solidity programming language itself, like strings, and these come up quite regularly.

If you develop an interest in building Dapps and smart contracts you can find communities and coding camps to help advance your abilities. As you learn more about Dapp development be sure to keep in mind that there are risks around security and bugs are common, just as in traditional software development.

Chapter 5 – Project Management, Use Cases, and Hyperledger

Learning Objectives
- Examine the overall process for leveraging a blockchain
- Learn about tools for deciding if a blockchain application would be appropriate
- Understand the different job skills needed for blockchain development
- Learn how to develop a blockchain use case
- Examine current use cases across industries and functional areas of business
- Develop a permissioned blockchain using Hyperledger Composer Playground

Blockchain in Action – Making Giving Better

Ever wonder if that $30 that you decided to give to help veterans get artificial limbs ever went to the right people? That money you gave may have helped to fund terrorists or buy yachts for corrupt administrators, how can you know? This is one of the biggest problems with giving money to any charity. Wouldn't it be nice if there were a way to make the whole process more transparent? Bitgive was one of the first philanthropic organizations to create a blockchain application for making donations. Since donations are visible on the transparent ledger donors can tell what happens with their money. Fees are low to non-existent and highly secure. On top of that, donors can see the impact of their giving in real-time. Right now, the organization only supports donations in bitcoin. Some more established philanthropic organizations such as Save the Children, United Way, and the Red Cross are also experimenting with accepting donations in bitcoin.[68] Alice.si has taken the concept of transparency to a new level too, by allowing donations to be made "conditional upon impact." Many donors prefer to see the results of their giving, and blockchain is making this possible in a new way. The technology can even help the organizations to document their work in order to apply to grant-giving institutions. The World Food Programme, part of the United Nations, has been using blockchain to ensure the correct individuals can take advantage of refugee aid programs. Even large corporations are looking to include blockchain in their charitable work. For instance, Alibaba connected their 445 million users to their own blockchain-based charity tool in 2016.

New "charity coins" are also starting to show up in the alt-coin space. These tokens are designed to give a portion of their proceeds to specific social causes. Clean Water Coin, for example, focuses on giving to clean water projects. Whereas Pinkcoin and ImpakCoin are more generally focused on social causes and are listed on some major exchanges. There is even a growing list of foundations being funded by the nouveau riche of the crypto world and talk of DAOs being formed to support nonprofits.

---

[68] Lamb, Paul. "Crypto-philanthropy: How Bitcoin and Blockchain Are Disrupting the World of Giving," Medium, February 12, 2018, https://medium.com/@pauljlamb/crypto-philanthropy-how-bitcoin-and-blockchain-are-disrupting-the-philanthropic-sector-80716dc7cb68

Project Management: Developing a Use Case

The following section is an adaptation of some of the processes used at the prototyping and advisory firm, Animal Ventures, to build blockchain-based products for Fortune 100 corporations and other clients. While not a perfect rubric for every project, it is a real-world method of approaching use case development and can help us explore a way to evaluate potential opportunities. You can do the following exercises with a team or on your own.

Identify a 10-Year, 5-Year, and 2-Year Vision

Roy Amara, a well-known Silicon Valley futurist coined the phrase, "We tend to overestimate technology's impact in the short-term and underestimate it in the long-term." Known as Amara's Law, the statement holds true for almost any new technology, and blockchain is no exception. In approaching a build, it is important to think far enough into the future to envision how your industry or company might be different a decade from now. While blockchain may be an exciting technology that deserves attention, it is not a panacea; it will evolve alongside changes in our businesses and industries. To make the most of the long-term impact of a new technology, as Amara suggests, we should do the work of imagining the future more broadly. Why just use a nascent technology to solve today's problems when you can use it to prepare to solve tomorrow's? You are probably already an expert in your own work or industry. So the best place to start is by envisioning your field and your business in the next 10 years. Where is your industry heading? How will technology be different then? Who will be the major stakeholders or players you need to contend with?

Vision Exercise

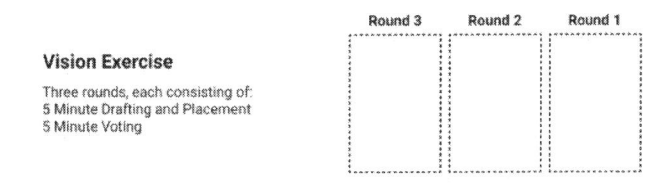

Three rounds, each consisting of:
5 Minute Drafting and Placement
5 Minute Voting

Figure 5-1: AV vision exercise

Vision Exercise: Headlines from the Future

Sit down with some sticky notes and a pen, and set a timer for 10 minutes. Write down as many headlines as you can about where you see your company or initiative in 10 years. These should be bold and yet also based on your strategic interests as an organization or project. Repeat for a 5-year vision, and then a 2-year vision, nesting one within the other.

Identify Beachhead(s)

You have listed out a 10-year, 5-year, and 2-year vision, but how should you narrow down toward the present day and actions you can take that align with that future? One of the best ways to do this is cribbed from military language, and is called targeting a "**beachhead**." A beachhead is a product entry point. For any given project, you can usually come up with many different beachheads that have different pros and cons associated with them. Maybe one entry point is with your customers, another is with your existing partners. Or perhaps you have plans to overhaul an existing product and can leverage that opportunity to build something new. You can usually identify many such beachheads for a given 2-year vision, because there are many possible paths that will help you to tackle your objective. Spend an hour drafting as many beachheads as you can think of – one idea per sticky note.

Once you have your beachheads identified, begin to rank them according to which one is most desirable and suits your 2-year vision best. You should keep track of the list of beachheads, since they can come in handy later on as a pipeline of ideas to pursue as additional experiments.

Identifying a set of Beachheads to support our 2-Year Vision

Figure 5-2: AV beachhead identification

Map the Technical Ecosystem

Now is your chance to get a bit more tactical. Once you have a top beachhead identified, you want to explore what is already going on that relates to your product entry point. What kind of technical infrastructure or systems are already in place that you would need to interface with? Who is involved and is there any strategic alignment? Mapping this ecosystem will help clarify some of the necessary real-world steps that would need to happen to use the beachhead as your starting place for a given project. Once you have created your technical ecosystem map, you can identify areas that might be ripest for intervention. If you are in a group, you can heatmap the best starting point. This is also a great exercise to perform if you have maybe three top beachheads and are trying to evaluate which one would be your best candidate for intervention.

Mapping the Technical Ecosystems for each Beachhead

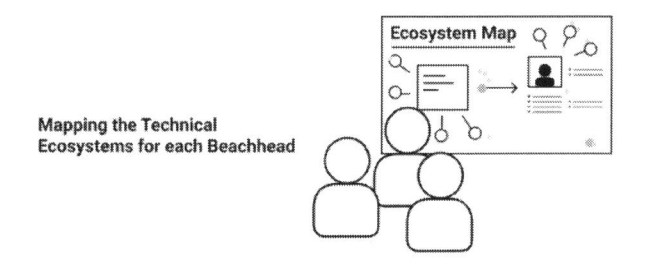

Figure 5-3: AV likes to map the technical ecosystem for any beachhead

Heatmapping the Ecosystems

Figure 5-4: AV uses heat mapping as a way to vet good starting points

Develop a Hypothesis and KPI

The best use cases start with a **hypothesis**. As the saying goes in Silicon

Valley, "a startup is an experiment to see if a company *should* exist." Whether using blockchain or any other tool, the experimental mindset is paramount. By now you should have a 2-year vision statement as well as a beachhead and its associated technical map in hand. Naturally, these are high-level brainstorming exercises and do not need to be perfect at this point; think of them as tools to help you define an experiment, which is your project.

We need to move from a 2-year vision down to something that can be built in 3 months. If you cannot build something in 3 months, you have not scoped your project to be narrow enough. 3 months represents a quarter of the calendar year, and it is also hard to predict variables (especially external ones) beyond the 3-month timeframe. The 3-month build cycle is your friend – it creates the necessary constraints to help you define a hypothesis statement that your project can test. Essentially, you want to know within 3 months if you are going down a path that is useful, or if you need to alter paths and perhaps choose a different beachhead to accomplish your vision.

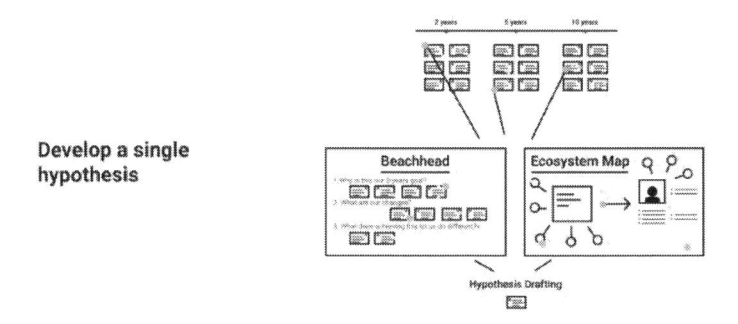

Figure 5-5: From vision to hypothesis

For our first domino, if we achieve (goal X), (Important metric Y) will improve.

Example - "If we can capture data at the raw source, we can increase speed to invoice setlement."

Figure 5-6: A hypothesis statement format

Your hypothesis statement and associated **Key Performance Indicator** (KPI) become your north star during a product build. This is the statement you will come back to again and again to reference and verify whether a decision you are making will help you answer the hypothesis. Often, during a product build phase, there are additional features that start to creep into a project, and these should always be weighed against the hypothesis – does it help test the hypothesis? If not, do not pursue these distractions at that time.

Sketch Out Prototype Ideas

Once you have done the work of a vision exercise, beachhead identification, and hypothesis drafting, you are ready to sketch out possible prototype solutions. This is really an opportunity to think creatively and draft solutions that could tackle your 2-year vision either holistically or in part. It is a great exercise to do with many people in order to bring diverse perspective on what kinds of tools, partners, and processes you could utilize to accomplish your goal. One way we like to frame this exercise is by using movie titles – see below.

Step 1: The Movie Titles

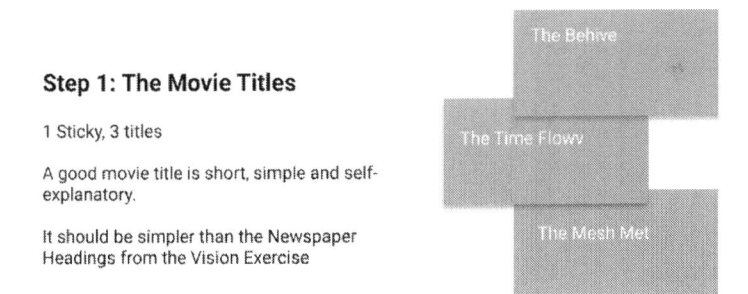

1 Sticky, 3 titles

A good movie title is short, simple and self-explanatory.

It should be simpler than the Newspaper Headings from the Vision Exercise

Figure 5-7: AV sketching exercise

Basics of Blockchain

Solution Sketch Recaps

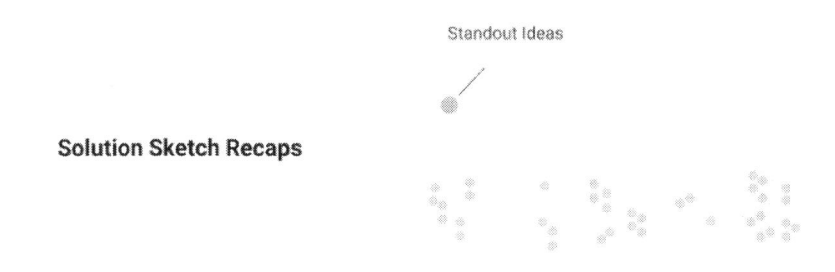

Figure 5-8: Sample gallery of sketches

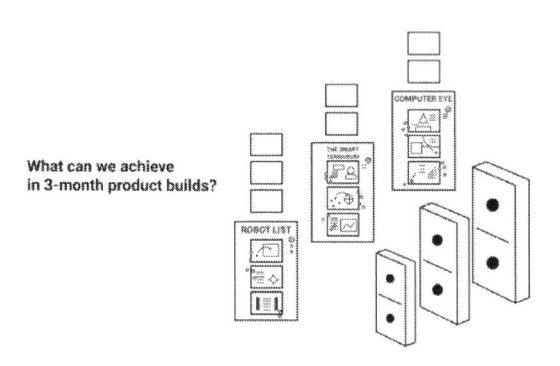

Figure 5-9: Dominos for product builds

Project Management: Lifecycle for Dapps

Because blockchain technology is industry agnostic, virtually every type of organization or area of business today is looking to benefit from implementing it. But the fact is that not all problems will require a decentralized application to solve them. Even a cursory review of some of the half-baked concepts for ICOs out there today bears this out. Before investing a lot of time and resources into a blockchain project, it is crucial to make sure that the problem justifies using or exploring blockchain at all.

Interest in developing **decentralized applications** (Dapps) is growing rapidly across industries. But because of the complexity and cross-functional nature of blockchain technology, the process for developing a blockchain application can be quite different from a normal IT application. Even the skills needed can be quite specialized and difficult for companies to find. With all of the options today regarding consensus protocols, security protocols, and development tools and platforms, it is more important than ever to have a project plan. The following section describes the phases in a blockchain project from a high-level perspective. Depending on the type of blockchain application being developed there may be dozens or hundreds of intermediate steps involved in each of the phases described. One way of viewing the development process is as a sequence of phases or steps like that shown in Figure 5-10 below.

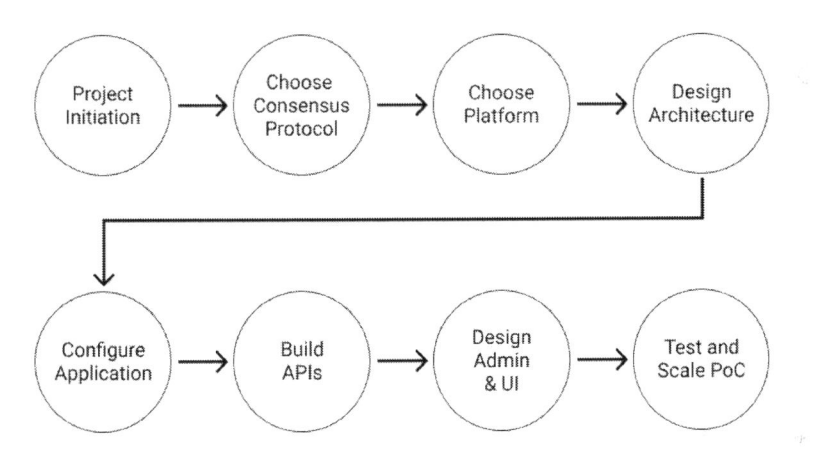

Figure 5-10: Phases in blockchain development

Do You Need a Blockchain?

You may have already decided that blockchain is an appropriate technology tool for your project. And while your vision, use case, and hypothesis should drive the direction of any product you plan to build, there is also value in gut-checking whether or not blockchain affords an advantage. There are a number of decision-making tools out there to help with this part of the process. The most popular blockchain decision models are the IBM model, the Lewis model, and the Suiches model.

By beginning with the question about whether a database is needed and what kind of write access is needed, the Suiches model is trying to focus on whether distributed ledger technology is needed here. If shared write access is not required for this problem, then we immediately know that it does not need a blockchain application. If the writers to the database are not known and unified, then this helps make the case for a blockchain solution. The other questions help to focus on third-party control and how consensus might be determined. What is also good about this model is that it gives the user some direction as to whether they should develop a public, hybrid, or private blockchain. If the answer is yes, then it might be worth trying to do some initial cost/benefit analysis to get a rough idea as to the economic feasibility of the project.

Evaluating Consensus Mechanisms

One of the areas in blockchain seeing significant innovation is in the design for achieving consensus. Choosing the correct design is very important because it will impact the overall features of the blockchain application, and carries certain dependencies. Most designs today implement a combination of protocols to achieve both **Sybil attack resistance** and **consensus** or decision-making for a coin or system. Many combinations are possible, though not all combinations make sense, and the design is dependent on your goals and security parameters. For instance, if **Proof of Work** is used as a Sybil-control mechanism (like in Bitcoin or Bitcoin Cash), you will need to attract a large number of computer users who will participate as full nodes in order to validate transactions and create new blocks. This means that appropriate rewards will have to be built into the design of the application in order to attract and motivate the miners. The same is basically true if you choose to use a **Proof of Stake** mechanism. For Ethereum, miners are rewarded for sharing their computer processing power rather than for solving a cryptographic puzzle. The idea is that this approach might be fairer and attract fewer mercenary computer users to join the network. Both of these protocols are popular for permissionless blockchain applications.

For hybrid and even private blockchain applications, there is less of a need for a huge network of validators to ensure the security of the blockchain. This is largely because private and/or permissioned chains delineate who is able to validate the chain. These systems often use protocols such as Practical Byzantine Fault Tolerance, Delegated Proof of Stake, Federated models, and Proof of Authority, which can be appropriate designs when validators are semi-trusted. Think of a consortium of banks or an industry such as trucking or pharmaceuticals using a blockchain-based system to create a shared reality. **Practical Byzantine Fault Tolerance** (PBFT) is currently used by the Hyperledger platform and is very efficient in terms of energy use and the speed of validating transactions. With PBFT, nodes have to be recognized before they can participate on the network. These recognized validators send messages to the other nodes about the validity of a particular transaction. If over 66% of the nodes agree that it is valid, the transaction is accepted, and the database can be updated.

The **Delegated Proof of Stake** (DPoS) protocol is an increasingly popular option that builds on the Proof of Stake mechanism. In the DPoS protocol, members vote for whom they want to serve as "Witnesses." These witnesses function as validators and block creators. A member's vote power is determined by the number of tokens they hold or their "stake." If a witness starts misbehaving or not doing their job, the members can vote them out. In the **Federated Byzantine Agreement** (FBA) protocol, each validator decides which other validators they trust. This creates a "quorum slice" which then overlaps with other slices on the network. A quorum of validators then comes to a consensus on the validity of a transaction for the network. Additionally, there is also **Proof of Authority (PoA)**, which is commonly used as a starting point in creating a permissioned network. It essentially allows a node to demonstrate that it has been granted participation authority in the network, which is awarded as a setup mechanism off-chain, through governance of the technology. There are many more variations on these protocols, and they are often paired with tools like Ben-Or, Tendermint/Cosmos, or Avalanche to make decisions. They represent an exciting area of protocol evolution in the blockchain space.

A very important note here is the golden rule in this space, and cryptography at large: "Don't roll your own crypto," which basically is sound advice. If you are a novice developer looking to build decentralized applications you should

Basics of Blockchain

leverage well-known and tested tools for cryptography, consensus mechanisms, and other core protocols. The space is growing rapidly, but there are also many ways to insert bugs or flaws into programs that have not been developed using industry standards.

Less Common Consensus Mechanisms

Proof of Activity (PoA)

Proof of Activity is a hybrid of Proof of Work (PoW) and Proof of Stake (PoS). Its mining process starts as a standard PoW process with various miners competing to write a new block. But after a new block is mined, a random group of validators is selected to validate or sign the new block. The likelihood of becoming a signer depends on the number of network tokens a validator owns, making it similar to PoS. Criticisms of Proof of Activity include that it still requires high computational power, meaning energy consumption, and also promotes token hoarding behavior by validators.[69]

Proof of Burn (PoB)

Proof of Burn is a consensus algorithm that allows miners to "burn" tokens in return for the right to write blocks in proportion to the tokens burnt. According to Iain Stewart, the inventor of the PoB algorithm, burnt tokens are "mining rigs" – by burning tokens, a miner is buying a virtual mining rig that allows him/her to mine blocks.[70] The "burning" actually involves sending tokens to a verifiably un-spendable address.

Proof of Capacity (PoC)

Proof of Capacity allows nodes on a blockchain network to utilize empty space on their hard drives for mining available tokens.[71] It works by storing a

---

[69] Frankenfield, Jake. "Proof of Activity (Cryptocurrency)," Investopedia, updated June 25, 2019, accessed June 25, 2019, https://www.investopedia.com/terms/p/proof-activity-cryptocurrency.asp

[70] Frankenfield, Jake. "Proof of Burn (Cryptocurrency)," Investopedia, updated April 4 2018, accessed June 25, 2019, https://www.investopedia.com/terms/p/proof-burn-cryptocurrency.asp

[71] Frankenfield, Jake. "Proof of Capacity (Cryptocurrency)," Investopedia, updated April 4 2018, accessed June 25, 2019,

list of possible solutions on a node's hard drive even before the mining activity commences. Having a larger hard drive gives a miner competitive advantage in winning the reward because it is possible to store more solution values that could match the required hash value.

Proof of Elapsed Time (PoET)

Proof of Elapsed Time is a consensus algorithm invented by Intel in 2016, and is used on some permissioned blockchain networks to determine mining rights or the block winners. PoET spreads the chances of winning mining rights across nodes similar to a lottery structure by using both "wait" and "sleep" times to randomly modulate which node mines. Simply put, the first node to complete a randomly chosen waiting time wins the reward and writes the new block. Nodes also go to sleep for randomly generated amounts of time, meaning the node assigned the shortest wait time will wake up first and win, committing a new block to the blockchain. The process repeats to discover each consecutive block. PoET offers a way to solve the computing problem of "random leader election."[72]

Proof of Importance (PoI)

Proof of Importance was put forward by the blockchain network NEM which launched in 2015, as a new consensus algorithm. Rather than the PoS system of staking, PoI rates a validator's importance in the network.[73] Importance is based on the number and quality of transactions a validator has previously performed. The importance score can be thought of as a kind of reputation score, where a higher score means the network trusts a validator more to verify transactions. It is calculated through a combination of variables: vested stake, transaction partners, and number and size of transactions over the past 30 days.

---

https://www.investopedia.com/terms/p/proof-capacity-cryptocurrency.asp

72 Frankenfield, Jake. "Proof of Elapsed Time (Cryptocurrency)," Investopedia, updated April 4, 2018, accessed June 25, 2019, https://www.investopedia.com/terms/p/proof-elapsed-time-cryptocurrency.asp

73 "NEM Technical Reference," Version 1.2.1, February 23, 2018, NEM Website, accessed June 25, 2019, https://nem.io/wp-content/themes/nem/files/NEM_techRef.pdf#section

Identifying a Suitable Blockchain Platform

The initial analysis of the problem being addressed will go a long way towards determining which blockchain platform to use. This, of course, assumes that you are not intending on programming a new blockchain network from scratch. Using an existing development platform will shortcut the development process and provide a host of tools for the project. After the initial analysis, you should have some idea about the type of blockchain application being developed. Will it involve smart contracts? Will it use digital tokens? What kind of consensus protocols will be used? Is processing speed crucial to the success and will it be scalable? These questions will dictate the platform and the overall architecture to be used for the application.

Bitcoin is an open-source blockchain application that was originally written in C++. It is good for financial transactions but is not really a good platform for developing new blockchain applications. Developers continue to fix program bugs and also create different kinds of bitcoin wallets. Bitcoin miners are continually working to gain advantages by programming better mining algorithms too. But if you need a smart contract as part of your Dapp, you need to look at a different platform.

There are a number of platforms that offer smart contract functionality. Some of the most popular of these include Ethereum, Hyperledger Fabric, and Openchain. Probably the fastest growing of all of these is the Ethereum platform (see Figure 5-12 below). Ethereum is popular because it offers the most flexible set of development tools and has one of the largest developer communities. It also has the widest variety of programming options for developers. They are always working to improve the platform and the Ethereum Foundation offers generous research funding for improvements to the technology. Having a built-in native digital token also makes it more flexible for handling transactions and smart contracts.

Aspect	Ethereum	Hyperledger Fabric	BigChainDB	Corda	Openchain
Open Source?	Yes	Yes	Yes	Yes	Yes
Main Purpose	Smart contracts; Dapp dev	Developing enterprise BC apps	Storing and processing data	Dev interoperable BC networks	Smart contracts; general asset mgmt
Permissibility	Both	Permissioned	Both	Permissioned	Both
Consensus	PoW / PoS	PBFT	Federation	Pluggable	Partitioned
Scripting Lang	Solidity; Go, Python, Java, Rust	Go, Java	Python	Java, Kotlin	Javascript
Data Focus	Smart contracts, etc.	Smart contracts, etc.	Transaction data	Transaction data	Smart contracts, etc.
Native Token	ether	N/A	N/A	N/A	N/A (free)

Figure 5-11: Characteristics of some popular blockchain development platforms

Some of these platforms are focused more on managing the data and processing database queries quickly (i.e. BigChainDB). While others are addressing the corporate market, which is more interested in private or hybrid blockchain applications involving a network of permissioned users. Hyperledger, while open-source and modular for enterprises, is seen as a bit of a kitchen-sink without some of the unique properties of other networks. Openchain tries to be more efficient and cheaper by getting rid of miners and having transactions validated by an "asset manager." It also uses a client server architecture as opposed to the peer-to-peer network proposed by Bitcoin and Ethereum. These efficiencies are intended to make it more appealing to enterprises who might want to develop a quick side chain application.

Design Architecture

The architecture of a blockchain network and/or application should consider both hardware and software characteristics. The options for the overall architecture ranges from running it in-house, having it completely hosted in the cloud, or some hybrid of the two. For larger companies with a complete IT department, developing and running it in-house might be a good option, depending on the level of expertise they may have. However, for most smaller companies, hosting blockchain applications in the cloud through platforms such as AWS or Azure will be the preferred option.

The decisions about the application architecture includes whether it makes sense to use a permissioned or permissionless blockchain, and who will be allowed to participate. Other general design considerations will involve how the transactions will be validated, whether a digital token will be involved, and how the application will be deployed. The pertinent APIs also must be identified since some will have to be custom programmed or existing ones modified. If a side-chain or off-chain data is involved, this should be part of the resulting design architecture. This phase will also present a general roadmap of the overall project and timeline for the release of the different versions (alpha, beta, production).[74]

Another important consideration for the architectural design is data management. What sources of data will be part of transactions and how will that data be accessed. The management of data is a separate consideration from the nodes running a permissioned blockchain – for instance, it will make sense for many enterprises to encrypt their data and use a blockchain as a control-access layer.

Configuring a Blockchain Application

Once the general design is in place, there are literally thousands of other parameters that need to be configured. At this point, we might be working on a Proof of Concept rather than a full-fledged application. Some of the parameters that need to be set include those around how consensus will work, how the various keys will be managed, how tokens are issued and possibly re-issued, and how nodes will function and communication on the network. Many of these tasks involve very technical knowledge that may not be readily available to your organization. This is often where expert consultants get involved.

Depending on what you are building, there are open-source libraries and suites available for building and testing your application. These include the

---

[74] Jain, Yogesh. "8 Steps to Start Blockchain Development and Get Your Dapp Ready," New Gen Apps, February 15, 2018, https://www.newgenapps.com/blog/8-steps-how-to-start-blockchain-development-DApp

Truffle Framework as well as OpenZeppelin.

Building APIs

Since blockchain is built on a peer-to-peer network running on the Internet, **APIs** or, Application Program Interfaces, are crucial to the smooth functioning of a blockchain application. And because blockchain technology is so new, many of these APIs have yet to be programmed. For example, if you want to accept bitcoin payments on your e-commerce site, there are many APIs already available for you to set this up. However, if you want to incorporate other tokens in your application, they may or may not have APIs set up already that would connect to the platform you are using. This is especially true for smart contracts. In order to execute a smart contract, the application may need to access data outside of the application that is stored on another system. For example, in the case of a betting smart contract for a football match/game, to retrieve data about football scores, the application may need to access these results from a trusted sporting website. This would require the use of some kind of API. If you want to connect your blockchain application to a specific wallet, you would need to use an API for this. Some common API use cases are:

- Generating key pairs and addresses

- Storing and retrieving data

- Enabling data authentication with signatures and hashes

- Managing the smart contract life-cycle

Some of the specific APIs that are especially popular with Web blockchain developers include the Coinbase API for adding bitcoin payment functionality to a website, Chain API for transferring digital assets in enterprise blockchain applications, and Bitcore API which is favored because it's especially fast and helps developers scale up their applications.[75]

Building Administrative and User Interfaces

Depending on the type of application being developed, there may be a variety of different users. These could include administrators, nodes, validators, and wallet accounts. All of these users will need different levels of access to the application, which means that multiple levels of security and data need to be built into the user interface. Often, developing these interfaces is about matching legacy architecture or governance frameworks to this new technology, and this step requires significant attention to details that may introduce new vulnerabilities.

Testing and Scaling

Because distributed applications can be very complex, they must go through a rigorous set of tests before they go into production. At the beginning of the project, the goal is to develop a **Proof of Concept** (PoC) version of the application. PoCs can vary in sophistication, but their goal is to test a hypothesis with some real data and, at some point, evolve to perform in a **staging environment**. Sometimes called the pre-alpha version, the idea is to develop a bare bones application without any of the side features or special UI enhancements. This is just to prove that the concept is feasible and works toward solving your initial hypothesis.

Assuming that the PoC is successful, after some more improvements, the application may go through an audit before proceeding to an alpha release. This is where formal testing of the internal software structures begins even though the application may not have all the bells and whistles yet. Specifically, they are looking for performances issues such as **latency,** storage or memory issues, and system crashes. After these issues are resolved, the application is

---

[75] "10 Best Blockchain API Providers for Developers," Applikey, January 11, 2018, https://applikeysolutions.com/blog/10-best-blockchain-api-providers-for-developers

completed and moves on to the beta release. In this phase, the application is released to a select group of outside users who do their best to expose any further problems, especially problems that may be associated with a high volume of processing requests. The resulting version is called a **release candidate**, since it may be one of several versions that are ready to go into production. When it finally does go into production, it must be deployed on the application servers. This can be further complicated by the fact that users functioning as nodes will have to install the core application and other users may have to set up accounts and install wallets, etc. After the initial deployment, there will be the inevitable series of upgrades to the software and even potentially enhancements such as AI, Analytics and IoT. The application should be designed to make it as easy as possible to make these future improvements.

Because this technology is so new, enterprises that seek to "productionize" a blockchain application may go through this life-cycle, but will most certainly continue to run their standard operations in parallel for some time. This is an important consideration in understanding costs and the true deployment staging involved in building new technology – it is not a simple flip of the switch to move over old infrastructure safely.

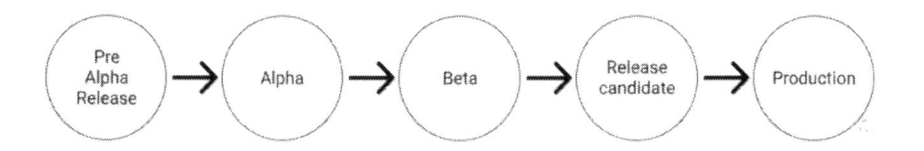

Figure 5-12: Blockchain release stages

Roles in a Blockchain Project

One of the most difficult aspects of a blockchain project is actually finding people with the correct skills to staff it. Surveys show that 23% of large corporations are now actively working on blockchain projects.[76] A typical

---

[76] Mearian, Lucas. "The top blockchain jobs you need to know about," ComputerWorld, June 5, 2018,

project might require hiring a manager, some designers, and developers. This is one reason that blockchain job listings grew over 6000% and were identified as the hottest IT job market out of a list of the twenty top IT jobs for freelancers.[77] And of course, blockchain jobs tend to average 20-30% more in terms of salaries being offered. The median rate for full-time blockchain developers was $140,000 as compared to $105,000 for general software developers. In Silicon Valley or New York City, the rate is closer to $165,000.[78]

Exactly what kinds of jobs would you encounter on a blockchain project? The technical skills that projects are most looking for include NodeJS, Go, APIs, Java, C++, Solidity, Truffle, CSS and HTML. This section describes some of the most common blockchain technology jobs currently being listed.

Blockchain Project Manager

The project manager is going to be the big picture person. They will be responsible for planning, supervising and delivering the blockchain project. As such, they will be interfacing with executives in the organization and will have to be able to translate their requirements into technical blockchain developer language and back again. They are often the first person brought on board for a new project.

Blockchain Developer

These workers are in the most demand for blockchain projects. They should have knowledge of database languages/tools including SQL Server and

---

https://www.computerworld.com/article/3277617/blockchain/the-top-blockchain-jobs-you-need-to-know-about.html

77 Mearian, Lucas. "The top blockchain jobs you need to know about," ComputerWorld, June 5, 2018,

https://www.computerworld.com/article/3277617/blockchain/the-top-blockchain-jobs-you-need-to-know-about.html

78 Mearian, Lucas. "Blockchain moves into top spot for hottest job skills," ComputerWorld, May 1, 2018,

https://www.computerworld.com/article/3235972/it-careers/blockchain-moves-into-top-spot-for-hottest-job-skills.html?nsdr=true programming languages such as Node.js, C++, and JavaScript.

Blockchain Quality Engineer

Quality engineers have a narrower focus for their work. They have the all-important task of planning, researching, and developing all of the testing standards and strategies. This is especially important since blockchain applications cover a lot of different technologies including networks, specific blockchain platforms, mobile and web-based technologies.

Blockchain Legal Consultant

Soon there will be a demand for people who have a combination of legal and technical skills. Currently, people with this kind of background are very rare commodities. A company might need to take counsel from a blockchain legal consultant about how to structure an ICO. Or whether sharing data across an industry interferes with anti-trust legislation, amongst any number of other legal concerns. With the rise in smart contracts there will be a need for legal advice on how to negotiate legal partnerships and write contracts for different jurisdictions.

Blockchain Web/UI Designer

Any company launching a new token will have to build a great website to help attract users and investors. If the project is an industry or enterprise-specific one, developing an intuitive user experience is important to ensure the integrity of the process and also help make sure that you are improving a previous experience by using blockchain.

Basics of Blockchain

Outsourcing Blockchain Development - Yea or Nay?

With the extreme shortage of experienced blockchain developers, many companies are turning to outsourcing their blockchain projects. Given that 57% of large corporations are now saying they are experimenting with or actively deploying blockchain projects, it comes as no surprise that blockchain talent is hard to find and retain.[79] Many companies are choosing to outsource some or all of their blockchain development. This is a good strategy to get up and running quickly. Not everyone has to be an expert in all of the minutiae of cryptographic protocols either. Though you may be surprised at how many of your IT people have been hacking away at blockchain in their free time! Consultants can also train the company's internal IT personnel as part of their contract. With a projected compound annual growth rate of 61.5% until 2021, the labor shortage for blockchain chain technology is only going to get worse.[80] And now that cloud platforms such as AWS and Azure can host your blockchain applications in the cloud, outsourcing the development just got even easier to do. Of course, if you decide to outsource to an offshore consulting firm, be prepared to deal with the potential language, cultural, and time-zone nuances.

Challenges of Blockchain Deployment

With all of the talk about the tremendous growth of blockchain applications, it is important to keep in mind that we are still in the very early stages of blockchain. Deloitte examined thousands of blockchain projects posted on GitHub and found that 92% of them had been abandoned and only the remaining 8% were being maintained at all.[81] Of course, GitHub projects may not be the best indicator of blockchain success but it is clear that organizations are still largely experimenting with blockchain technology. There are many barriers to adopting blockchain technology

---

[79] "5 Industries That Will Fuel The Blockchain Boom," Juniper Research, https://www.juniperresearch.com/document-library/white-papers/5-industries-that-will-fuel-the-blockchain-boom

[80] "Blockchain Market to Grow at CAGR of 61.5% by 2021–Analysis by Provider, Application, Organization Size, Vertical & Region – Research and Markets," BusinessWire, April 25, 2017, https://www.businesswire.com/news/home/20170425005753/en/Blockchain-Market-Grow-CAGR-61.5-2021--

[81] Harvey, Cynthia. "9 Challenges Slowing Blockchain Deployment," Information Week, March 1, 2018, https://www.informationweek.com/devops/project-management/9-challenges-slowing-blockchain-deployment/d/d-id/1331137?_mc=NL_IWK_EDT_IWK_daily_20180529&cid=NL_IWK_EDT_IWK_daily_20180529&elq_mid=84978&elq_cid=19995087

both organizational and technical. But the biggest obstacle is simply that there is still a lack of knowledge about blockchain and the use cases for it because of its recent development. Most of the popular press has surrounded the growth of cryptocurrencies and this has hindered the general adoption of blockchain for other uses.

Some blockchain applications may require that multiple organizations work together to create a network of users. While this may be the best scenario for using a blockchain (across non-trusting parties) the process of creating these industry consortia or partnerships may also take a lot of time and be an obstacle to the general adoption of blockchain. Implementing blockchain may also entail huge changes in the roles, processes, legal norms, and overall culture of the organizations involved. Many companies are struggling to come to grips with all of the potential changes in their firms and industries.

The uncertainties surrounding blockchain regulation have been stalling some blockchain projects, especially in the financial industry. Many companies are waiting for some definitive statements from governmental agencies about blockchain before moving forward with their projects. Similarly, the well-known issues around scaling blockchain transaction processing is causing some enterprises to hold back on deployment.

The lack of blockchain developers and developer tools is also holding back blockchain projects. This is a good indicator that we are still in the early stages of blockchain adoption. There is a general lack of documentation and tools for debugging, testing, IDEs, and security audit and deployment. There are some tools out there, but they are immature and need improvement. Being open-source means that the development of new tools is subject to time limitations of the core developers, who usually work on these projects on a volunteer basis unless they are awarded grants from the Ethereum Foundation or other groups. Look for lots of improvements in all these areas in the near future.

Use Cases

Everywhere you turn in the blockchain world, you hear people talking about **use cases**. The basic idea of the use case is to provide a high-level view of the overall objective of an application and how it will be used. It should include a clear statement of the problem being addressed by the application and may include a simple diagram of how the user will interact with the application. A good use case will give a quick overview of the application and make a case

Basics of Blockchain

for it by describing some of its potential benefits. The use case described in Figure 5-13 below depicts how a "health token" could be used to solve the problem of keeping patients on track with their doctor-prescribed treatment or fitness regimes. Interestingly, this is just one of many different use cases envisioned for the health-based smart contract applications.[82]

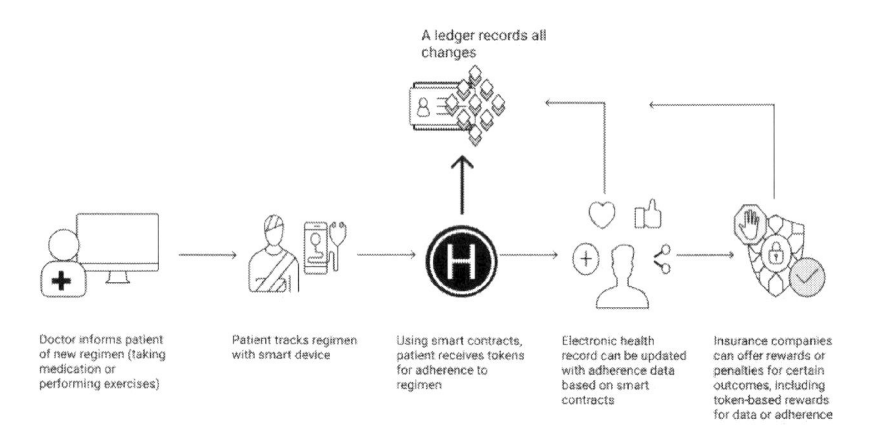

Figure 5-13: Health token use case

Blockchain use cases can vary widely in terms of the level of detail they provide. Of course, the more detail the better, though you don't want it to be so detailed or technical that it overwhelms the reader. When developing a blockchain use case, it is sometimes good to review the features of blockchain technology that make it unique. These include:

- Immutability – once a transaction is stored on blockchain it never changes

- Security – encrypted and very secure; identity is hidden

---

[82] Bennett, Brendan. "Healthcoin – blockchain-enabled platform for diabetes prevention," Blockchain Healthcare Review, April 3, 2017, https://blockchainhealthcarereview.com/healthcoin-blockchain-enabled-platform-for-diabetes-prevention/

- Verifiability – transactions are verified and provide a record

- Transparency – all transactions are shared among all the peer nodes

When coming up with a potential use case for blockchain one should look for areas where there may be potential "trust" issues, which in the past were resolved by the intervention of a third party. This is often the case when data is coming from external partners. The process of verifying the data can be very time-consuming and expensive and can be made more efficient with a blockchain application. Because of its immutability and verifiability, blockchain is also good when there is a need for auditing and compliance monitoring of transactions. Conceivably, auditors could do this in real-time by joining the network to get verification of the data. If the application involves a supply chain, all the participants can be linked via smart contracts which can be stored and verified from beginning to end.

Other considerations of what constitutes a "good" use case would include the barriers to entry, extensibility, feasibility, and potential benefits. If the use case requires a large network of users and verifiers, this could be considered a barrier to entry. A good use case should also have the possibility of being extended to create additional use cases. The health token use case above is an example of a blockchain use case that can be extended well beyond the one initially described. Good use cases should also have a high degree of technical and economic feasibility. If the use case requires the development of a whole new platform and supporting infrastructure, this adds considerably to the risks and becomes a barrier to entry. Of course, the use case should clearly show how users and stakeholders will benefit from the application. For many ICOs, this has been a major problem. Generally speaking, benefits will include reduction in costs for participants, streamlining of business processes, and providing security and real-time access to verifiable data. If the benefits to participants are clear, more users will join the network and increase the overall value of the blockchain application.

Cross-functional Blockchain Use Cases

One way to simplify our view of blockchain use cases is to categorize them.

Cross-functional blockchain use cases are ones that cut across virtually all areas of business and society. These general categories include **Identity Management**, **Asset Tracking** (**Provenance**), and **Internet of Things** integration or IoT.

Blockchain for Identity Management

Think of all the fraudulent activity that depends on someone spoofing or hacking another person's identity. Wouldn't it be nice to be confident that the company selling you designer sunglasses on eBay is legitimate and not some fake popup firm? As it turns out, the application of blockchain for identity is one of the biggest use cases being developed today and it cuts across many different industries (see Figure 5-14). While Bitcoin and other token networks are often built on pseudonymous transfers of value, where accounts are known but their owner identity is not, the ability to transact unique goods online through blockchains also opens up the ability to transact around the verifiability of a given identity as a piece of value itself. Identity and access management (IAM) attempts to validate an identity and allow it to be referenced and managed repeatedly without revealing all these details.

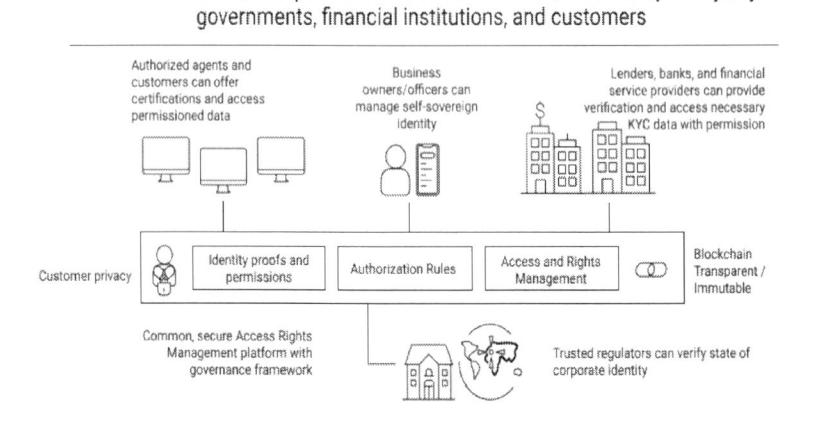

Figure 5-14: Identity use case for corporations

Figure 5-14 above shows an example of how an identity use case might work for a small business or corporation. The business would have its own verified smart contract stored on the blockchain which would possibly contain financial and sales data along with the rules governing access to this data by key partners, customers, government agencies, etc. Access to their data would be controlled by the small business owners themselves so that only the relevant data could be viewed by the right entity. This identity smart contract could be linked up to other smart contracts to create a more extensive application like in a supply chain.

Aspect	Home, Health, Family	Social & Leisure	Professional	Financial	Travel	Government & Legal
Daily / Weekly	Sign into accounts online	Online Shopping	Enter office buildings	Payments online with credit cards	Carry driver's license	Claim benefits
Monthly	Pay utility bills Collect Parcels from Post	Bar tab Club and memberships	Log-ins	Log into bank account	Rent a vehicle	
Yearly	Sign up for utilities or telco Collect prescription meds Receive Healthcare Book Doctor Appointments	Call centre support Download apps Pay utilities & telco products	Payroll Banking Hotel check-in	Apply for a banking or insurance product like credit card or insurance policy	Immigration Accomodation and hotel check-in Online Bookings	Pay taxes Apply for a license Voting
Infrequent	Online dating Name change Adoption / Guardian POA Purchase insurance Change address	Memberships Subscriptions Phone & Internet signup Sign up to online service	Pay tuition fees or loan Pay coaching Occupational license	Superannuation Apply for a loan Buy or claim insurance Credit scoring	Apply for a travel visa Sign up for loyalty program Travel cheques Register travel card	Birth certificate Death certificate Jury service Police check Pay fines

Figure 5-15: Industry-wide identity use cases

Figure 5-15 shows how widespread the application of identity use cases could be in the blockchain world. Anywhere where a proof of ID is needed, such as in healthcare, subscription services, or bookings, a blockchain application may improve the efficiency of the identity sharing and management process. In fact, identity applications in government for voting, benefit tracking, and paying taxes, may be areas where we see the most impact.

Blockchain applications for identity and access management are still in their early days of development. A large number of identity projects are currently underway. An example is the uPort identity framework meant to create a persistent identity for people, organizations, or objects (or bots) using the Ethereum network. Another example is the Civic Secure Identity Ecosystem, and a third is Sovrin. Newer proposals, such as the ERC-720 hope to create standards for identity management in the Ethereum network. Each of these is focused in a different way on a concept called **self-sovereign identity**. The idea here is that users have control over their personal information while potentially sharing parts of their information across a variety of industries. It's a way to have a portable identity online that represents different credentials that you can grant permission for others to view or reference. Credentials could be anything from a driver's license or diploma from a university, to an airline ticket. These types of applications are getting popular with a variety of governmental agencies around the world. Projects are being worked on in Spain, Switzerland, San Francisco, and Illinois. These applications should continue to expand.

Blockchain Use Cases for Asset Tracking

Another cross-functional type of blockchain use case is for tracking the history of any asset. This is called the **asset tracking** or provenance use case. Any time you have an asset worth tracking like artwork, real estate, conflict-free gemstones, degrees and certifications, or pharmaceuticals, you can make a case for using a blockchain application (see Figure 5-16).

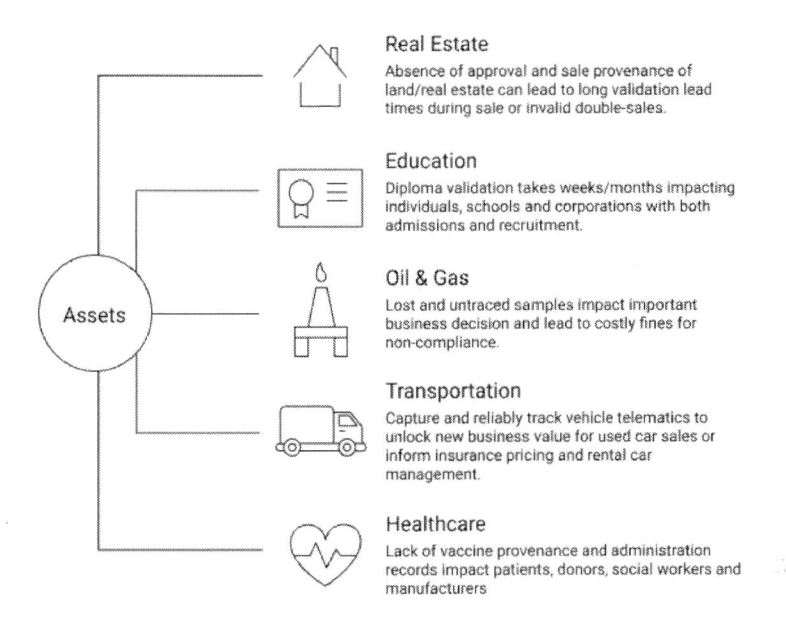

Real Estate
Absence of approval and sale provenance of land/real estate can lead to long validation lead times during sale or invalid double-sales.

Education
Diploma validation takes weeks/months impacting individuals, schools and corporations with both admissions and recruitment.

Oil & Gas
Lost and untraced samples impact important business decision and lead to costly fines for non-compliance.

Transportation
Capture and reliably track vehicle telematics to unlock new business value for used car sales or inform insurance pricing and rental car management.

Healthcare
Lack of vaccine provenance and administration records impact patients, donors, social workers and manufacturers

Figure 5-16: Cross-industry asset tracking use cases

The way a provenance blockchain use case would work is that the producer or original owner of the asset would register the asset on the blockchain. The asset has to be labeled with a unique code that can be verified by any of the other participants in the blockchain network. In the case of the blood diamond provenance application, over forty different measurements are taken of each diamond that will provide a fingerprint of the diamond for later verification.

Basics of Blockchain

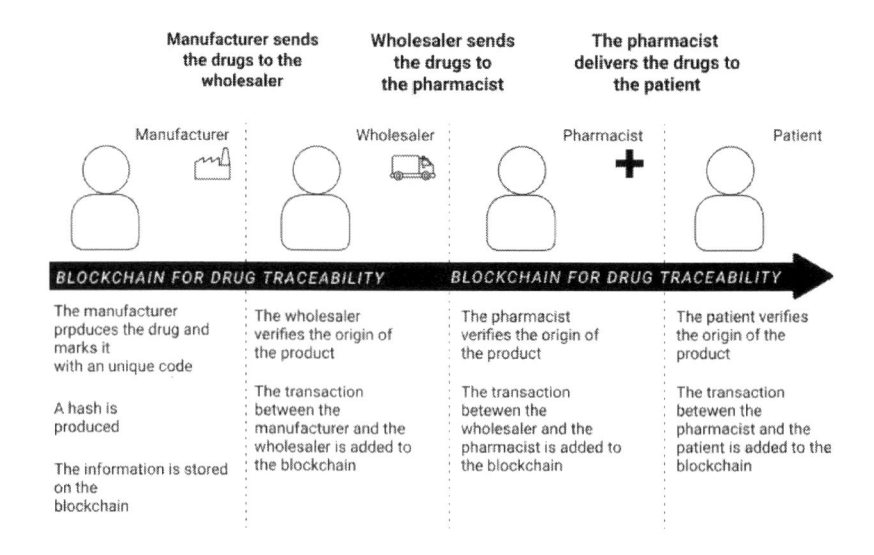

Figure 5-17: Provenance application for drug traceability

In the drug traceability blockchain shown in Figure 5-17, every time a stakeholder – such as a wholesaler, pharmacist, or patient – touches that particular drug, it can be verified and the new transaction data can be added to the blockchain. All kinds of information about the asset can potentially be shared with this type of blockchain. And the information would be transparent to the network participants. Given the huge amount of fraud and forgeries across all industries the cost savings could be immense. However, because it is a complex use case involving many participants, it may take more time for these types of applications to catch on.

Blockchain for Internet of Things (IoT) Integration

A little more futuristic, but potentially even more groundbreaking, is the idea that blockchain could be used to link up all the "smart" objects coming our way. Everyone has seen smart objects like their smartphones and smart thermostats and lights in their homes. However, intelligence is being added to cars, farm machinery, medical devices, guns, and even refrigerators! Making an object "smart" involves connecting it to the Internet and giving it some computer memory and processing power. In fact, by 2030, Gartner estimates that we may have over 500 billion connected smart devices.[83] The problem with this scenario is that these devices have security issues and are susceptible to being hacked. They also will overwhelm the current networks with the huge volume of data they could generate.

Enter blockchain. We already know that blockchain is growing in popularity because it is highly secure, verifiable, and decentralized. This makes it a good fit to solve some of the problems of the IoT. The encryption and verification features of blockchain makes it much more difficult to hack devices connected together on a blockchain. And since it is distributed, if one server on the network goes down, it won't cripple the entire network.

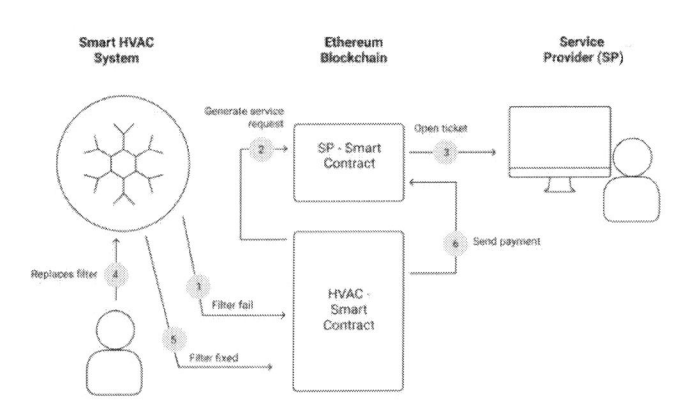

---

[83] Wood, Jon. "Blockchain of Things – cool things happen when IoT & Distributed Ledger Tech collide," Medium, April 20, 2018, https://medium.com/trivial-co/blockchain-of-things-cool-things-happen-when-iot-distributed-ledger-tech-collide-3784dc62cc7b

Figure 5-18: HVAC service IoT on blockchain use case

Another important advantage of running IoT projects on a blockchain network is the ability to process smart contracts. In the HVAC use case above, when the filter in the Smart HVAC System breaks, it can refer to its smart contract to contact the appropriate HVAC service provider in order to get service. After dispatching a technician who puts a new filter in, the smart system again refers to the contract for payment terms and a payment is transferred to the service provider. This is a relatively simple example, but it should become apparent that this same scenario could be replicated by thousands of different devices that might need servicing. And this is only a single use case. There are IoT use cases associated with Supply Chain Automation, automobiles, and many more scenarios.

Functional Area Blockchain Use Cases for Business

Another way to categorize blockchain use cases is to look at the various functional areas of a business. This includes Finance, Accounting, Marketing/Sales, Operations (SCM), and Human Resources (HR). Each of these areas is seeing tremendous interest in new blockchain applications. This further illustrates the wide impact that blockchain technology is having. It shows how these functional areas are being transformed and suggests new avenues for gaining competitive advantage.

Finance

The big elephant in the blockchain world is finance. Since its inception, Bitcoin was designed to disintermediate central banks and banking institutions. Bitcoin represented a new way of transacting value without the need for a third-party bank to function as a guarantor of the transaction. This was the first use case for blockchain. Since then, the financial applications have grown rapidly. Blockchain technology is being used in financial services for interbank transfers, cross-border payments, share trade processing and settlement, and trade finance. The qualities of blockchain can make all of these processes more efficient, secure, faster, and transparent. And doing all of these with significant cost savings. Some of these are more complex than others and involve linking together multiple smart contracts with possibly thousands of stakeholders. These, of course, will take longer time to come to fruition.

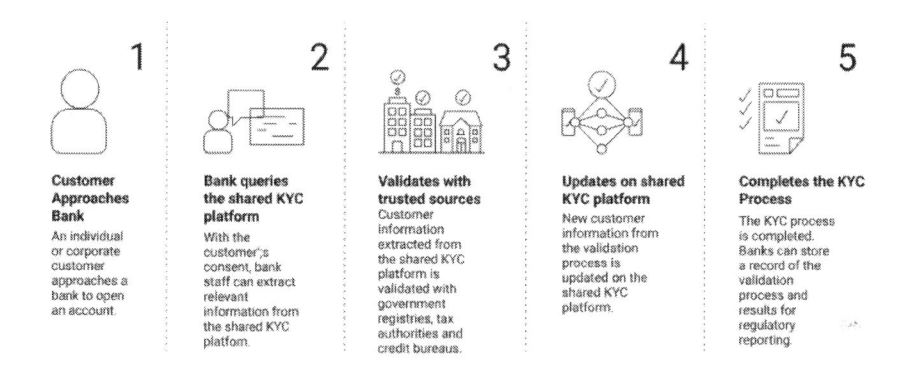

1	2	3	4	5
Customer Approaches Bank	**Bank queries the shared KYC platform**	**Validates with trusted sources**	**Updates on shared KYC platform**	**Completes the KYC Process**
An individual or corporate customer approaches a bank to open an account.	With the customer's consent, bank staff can extract relevant information from the shared KYC platform.	Customer information extracted from the shared KYC platform is validated with government registries, tax authorities and credit bureaus.	New customer information from the validation process is updated on the shared KYC platform.	The KYC process is completed. Banks can store a record of the validation process and results for regulatory reporting.

Figure 5-19: KYC use case for banking

One simple use case is found by applying the Identity Management concept to opening an account at a bank. If you have ever tried to open a new account at a bank, you know that it can take a lot of time and paperwork. And at the end of this, you will have to wait 3-5 business days to access any funds you deposit. Using a shared KYC (Know Your Customer) Platform, a person or even a corporate customer can consent to share with the bank all the relevant information needed to open a new account. Since the customer information has already been validated by credit bureaus, tax and government agencies, the bank can process their account quickly. The KYC records for the customer are then updated and stored again on the KYC platform. This way all parties can track their relevant information and get real-time updates and the customer knows that it was done in a highly secure manner.

Marketing/Sales

There are many fertile areas within marketing and sales for blockchain use cases. Some activity is already occurring around social marketing, content management, marketing management, e-commerce and marketing analytics. The most active area within the marketing function for blockchain is certainly in the advertising area. This is because of the relatively large number of middlemen in the digital media supply chain and its lack of transparency. The digital media supply chain involves a complex network of agencies, platforms, exchanges and publishers who provide very little value for every dollar spent by the brand being advertised. In fact, it is estimated that there is a 27% rate of fraud in the digital media supply chain.[84] The industry is full of undisclosed "fees" and techniques such as domain spoofing and bot traffic. Bots that generate fake clicks on digital ads are the source for an estimated $6.5 billion worth of fraud in 2017.[85] This makes the process of getting paid very long and drawn out since there is no transparency or one source of truth.

With the built-in transparency and verifiability of blockchain, some companies such as AminoPay are using it to try and clean up the fraud and waste built into the digital media supply chain. They have developed their own native token to help speed up the payment processing for the vendors on their supply chain. The transparency built into the network also helps to reduce discrepancies and also the number of disputes. They are now in the process of rolling this application out to the advertising world. Additional projects such as the Basic Attention Token project built on Ethereum and the separate Steemit network are working on restructuring the flow of content between creators and advertisers with blockchain-based incentive structures for certain actions on the network.

Supply Chain Management (SCM)

One of the most complex areas for blockchain applications is in Supply Chain

---

[84] Epstein, Jeremy. "Why 48 companies step up to Blockchain AdTech," Never Stop Marketing, August 1, 2018, accessed June 27, 2019, https://www.neverstopmarketing.com/why-48-companies-step-up-to-blockchain-adtech/

[85] "The Bot Baseline: Fraud in Digital Advertising 2017 Report," Association of National Advertisers and White Ops, May 2017, page 7, accessed June 27, 2019, https://www.ana.net/content/show/id/botfraud-2017

Management (SCM) and Logistics. With the increasing globalization of commerce, supply chains may involve dozens of transactions across multiple countries and currencies. There is a general lack of transparency and it can require many sets of complex documents and payments. When disputes arise over the terms of service and/or payments, it is very difficult and time-consuming to handle these since no one knows for sure what the other party did. Food supply chains are a particular example of this complexity. If Walmart wants to ship avocados from Guatemala to the U.S., it can take thirty days for the avocados to reach the markets. All the vendors downstream on the chain in turn have to wait for payment.

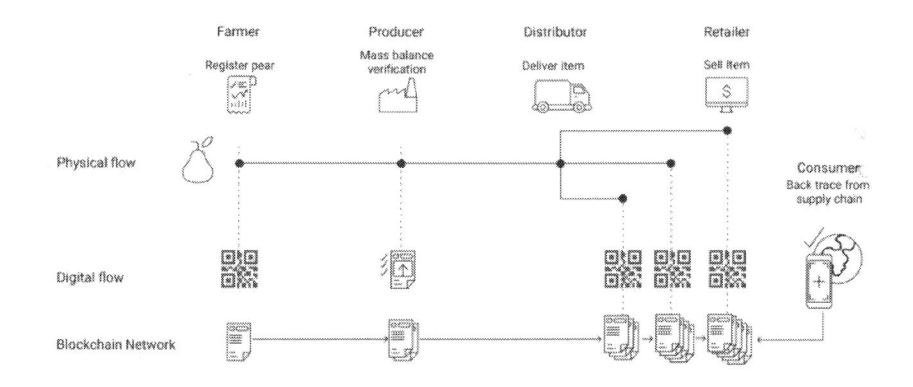

Figure 5-20: Blockchain for food supply chain

In fact, Walmart is already using blockchain for tracking pork shipments from China. This application records where every piece of pork came from, how it was processed and shipped. Given the transparency and verifiability built into blockchain, there are fewer disputes since all of the supply chain partners have access to the same copies of the blockchain records. The products are scanned and verified along each step of the chain. These records come in handy when there is a food recall and the retailers need to quickly ascertain the exact source of a specific item. The ability to quickly pay each supply chain partner using digital tokens on the chain also helps to reduce the costs and complexity of using bankers in multiple countries and currencies. Similar types of supply chain blockchain applications are spreading quickly throughout the food industry to companies such as Nestlé, Tyson, and

Dole.[86] In general, supply chains are ripe for blockchain use cases due to the need to connect the flow of product transactions across a number of partners and vendors that may or may not trust or know one another. Frequently there are dark holes in supply chain networks that cross many enterprises, since they do not share databases or relevant information that could make supply chains more responsive or efficient.

Accounting

Interestingly, since the core of blockchain revolves around a distributed ledger, blockchain technology aligns very well with accounting functions. All of the Big Four accounting firms are racing to figure out how it will impact them and their clients. The last revolution in accounting takes us back to the invention of double-entry bookkeeping in the Renaissance. This was a huge improvement in that it provided a way for managers within the organization to check the figures and make sure they were correct. However, the numbers could be manipulated and entered fraudulently, so external stakeholders required that the ledger be audited by independent agencies. This spawned a whole new industry of audit accounting which can be a very expensive, and time-consuming process.

Now imagine that your company has access to a new kind of ledger. One that cannot be altered or corrupted once the transactions are entered and that is continuously updated and verified in real-time. The distributed ledger behind blockchain may represent this next great leap in ledger technology. By entering each transaction between company A and Company B in a joint ledger running on blockchain, the process of verifying and encrypting this data performs a kind of **digital notarization** (Figure 5-21). This means that much of the auditing of standard transactions could be audited and the price of performing audits would decrease. Of course, the day of the fully automated audit may still be far away. There are other useful benefits of

---

86 Marr, Bernard. "How Blockchain Will Transform The Supply Chain And Logistics Industry," Forbes, March 23, 2018, https://www.forbes.com/sites/bernardmarr/2018/03/23/how-blockchain-will-transform-the-supply-chain-and-logistics-industry/#6bcd14005fec

blockchain for auditing. First, the immutability of the data on a blockchain makes it much easier to prove the integrity of the records. And the transparency of the blockchain makes it easier to trace the audit trails. This data can also be used by other external stakeholders for banking, tax and governmental actions. The fact that it is trusted and verified already will make these reporting processes much more efficient.

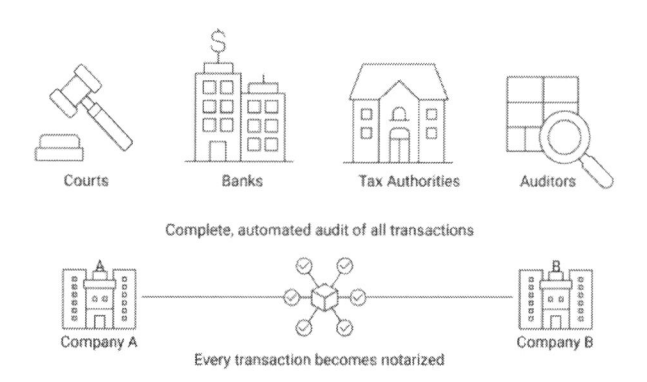

Figure 5-21: Basic audit use case

Does this mean that accountants will be going out of business soon? Probably not. They will evolve to provide valuable additional services. In fact, PricewaterhouseCoopers (PwC) is now offering a smart contract audit service for their clients that combines legal, accounting, and technology in its analysis.[87] However, it also means that accountants will have to evolve their skill sets or be left behind.

Use Cases for Human Resources

Not to be overlooked is the area of Human Resources management. Sadly,

---

[87] Vetter, Amy. "Blockchain is already changing accounting," Accounting Today, May 7, 2018, https://www.accountingtoday.com/opinion/blockchain-is-already-changing-accounting

Basics of Blockchain

this functional area often lags behind the other areas in terms of technical resources and applications. However, blockchain technology is still predicted by many to have a huge impact.[88] One major headache with the rise of the gig economy is tracking and managing part-time workers. Blockchain use cases have been proposed for this and also for paying taxes, tracking payroll, issuing paychecks, and managing employee contracts/benefits. Not only could it make paying taxes and employees more efficient and accurate, it can be more secure and transparent to all parties involved.

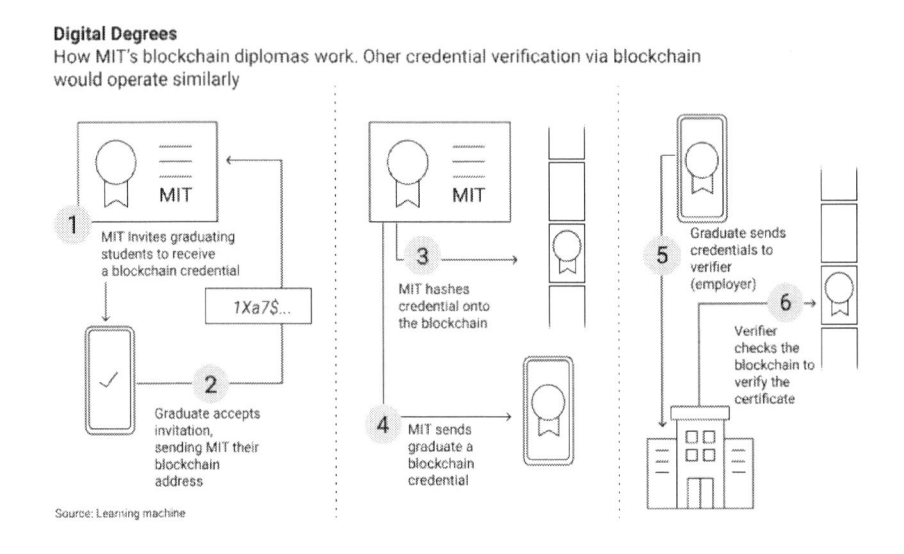

Digital Degrees
How MIT's blockchain diplomas work. Oher credential verification via blockchain would operate similarly

1. MIT Invites graduating students to receive a blockchain credential
2. Graduate accepts invitation, sending MIT their blockchain address
3. MIT hashes credential onto the blockchain
4. MIT sends graduate a blockchain credential
5. Graduate sends credentials to verifier (employer)
6. Verifier checks the blockchain to verify the certificate

Source: Learning machine

Figure 5-22: MIT's degree validation blockchain use case

It has been suggested that blockchain may help to make LinkedIn or other platforms obsolete by validating resumes, degrees and job skills.[89] MIT's degree validation use case (see Figure 5-22) was one of the first to propose blockchain for this purpose. They are now using this for their own graduates, and this model is expanding to other universities. Given the unknown number of fake degrees and certificates out there, this could be a game-

---

[88] Ahmed, Ashik. "How Blockchain Will Change HR Forever," Forbes, March 14, 2018, https://www.forbes.com/sites/ashikahmed/2018/03/14/how-blockchain-will-change-hr-forever/#1336d5e7727c

[89] Ahmed, Ashik. "How Blockchain Will Change HR Forever," Forbes, March 14, 2018, https://www.forbes.com/sites/ashikahmed/2018/03/14/how-blockchain-will-change-hr-forever/#1336d5e7727c

changer in the HR space.[90]

---

[90] Lova, Vicky. "Blockchain-based Project to Verify Education and Work Experience Information," Coin Telegraph, Feburary 1, 2018, https://cointelegraph.com/news/blockchain-based-project-to-verify-education-and-work-experience-information

> **Becoming Your Own Utility**
>
> Did you ever wish you could sell your extra power from your solar panels or your extra bandwidth? Probably not, which makes these use cases even more interesting. There are companies out there actually exploring the idea that you could sell your extra electrical capacity or bandwidth to other users on your network. Companies like Power Ledger and EnerChain are developing blockchain applications that allow for anyone with extra power to sell it others on in a peer-to-peer network.
>
> The same situation could generally apply to your bandwidth. Provided you are not on a pay-as-you go contract, your bandwidth may be another unused asset that is ready for a peer-to-peer blockchain app. According to Privatix, a blockchain startup for this, up to 90% of prepaid Internet bandwidth remains unused.[91] Using their blockchain app, you can rent this out to them and they will share it with other people via a VPN in order to help them avoid censorship. Similar blockchain apps are being created to resell unused computer power and storage capabilities.

Use Cases for Specific Industries

Beyond the traditional functional areas of a business, many specific industries are seeing a tremendous amount of interest in blockchain. Some of the most impacted ones include insurance, real estate, manufacturing and healthcare. Companies in these industries are developing use cases that may employ a combination of identity, asset tracking and IoT features. The following section gives an overview of some of these.

Insurance

McKinsey's 2018 report on blockchain highlighted the insurance business as one of the industries that will feel the greatest impact of blockchain

---

[91] Clancy, Tom. "This Blockchain Helps Users Sell Idle Bandwidth And Bypass Internet Censorship," CCN, October 18, 2017, https://www.ccn.com/blockchain-helps-users-sell-idle-bandwidth-bypass-Internet-censorship/

technology.[92] This makes sense because insurance companies function as a third-party guarantor of everything from people's lives to virtually any asset. But as anyone knows who has had an insurance claim, this can be a very complicated and expensive process. The verifiability, transparency and security of blockchain technology make it ideal for a variety of insurance functions. These use cases include:

- Health insurance

- Fraud detection

- Reinsurance

- Property and casualty insurance

Because of the many inefficiencies in the insurance process, it is ripe for fraud. You have probably heard stories of people who faked car accidents or made false property damage claims. In the U.S. alone the cost of insurance fraud (not including health insurance) is around $40 billion per year. One inherent roadblock to correcting this is the inability to share information across insurance companies themselves. Blockchain technology makes this possible in a secure manner. The leading industry consortium, has created an insurance group just for this purpose. The Institute's RiskBlock Alliance has signed up over 60% of American insurance firms to participate in developing blockchain applications for their industry. They are actively exploring applications for proof of insurance verification, first notice of loss, and claim settlement. The potential for disruption is huge and we are just in the early stages in this industry.

---

92 Carson, Brant and Giulio Romanelli, Patricia Walsh, and Askhat Zhumaev. "Blockchain beyond the hype: What is the strategic business value?" McKinsey & Company, June 2018, https://www.mckinsey.com/business-functions/digital-mckinsey/our-insights/blockchain-beyond-the-hype-what-is-the-strategic-business-value

Real Estate

Because blockchain is designed for transferring value, it is a surprisingly good fit for the real estate industry. If you have ever purchased a house you probably know how inefficient and expensive it is to go through with the transaction. From the endless inspections to the title transfer and insurance, there are quite a few middlemen involved and it adds significantly to the overall cost. In fact, the cost of purchasing real estate can be between 1.5-2.5% of the total value of the property.[93] This is enough to discourage many potential investors.

Even though there are significant obstacles, if there were a permanent record of real estate ownership using blockchain technology, there would be no need for title insurance and title searches. Transferring the title would be a simple matter as well, possibly involving smart contracts. This kind of universal property identifier is probably many years from being implemented. However, there are small scale experiments already going on with this in various parts of the world. This could also be a huge benefit in the developing world in particular, where property ownership and land title records may be difficult to ascertain or prove and may be holding back potential investors.

Besides paying your rent or mortgage with a cryptocurrency, real estate can also be tokenized. **Tokenization** of an asset such as real estate means that its value can be linked to a digital token. This makes for some interesting possibilities for investors. Smaller investors can micro-invest in real estate projects by buying the token linked to a project. Such a project was announced by Propellr and Fluidity, where a Manhattan condo development worth $30 million was tokenized.[94] In the future, real estate investments can be crowdsourced more easily and even bundled into various investment vehicles as with REITs today. Arguably, this could all be done securely and more efficiently on a blockchain.

---

[93] McDonald, Byron. "Use Cases for Blockchain in Real Estate," Medium, February 21, 2018, https://medium.com/@byron_17083/use-cases-for-blockchain-in-real-estate-f43daae745f9

[94] Wolfson, Rachel. "A First For Manhattan: $30M Real Estate Property Tokenized with Blockchain," Forbes, October 3, 2018, https://www.forbes.com/sites/rachelwolfson/2018/10/03/a-first-for-manhattan-30m-real-estate-property-tokenized-with-blockchain/#669860d84895

AirBnB and VRBO have revolutionized the property rental world by making it much easier for people with extra rooms to rent them out to travelers. These companies have opened up this industry by providing services for secure payments and search algorithms. However, just like Uber and Lyft, these companies can be further disintermediated by using smart contracts to allow owners to connect more directly with renters. The same holds true for the complex and expensive world of commercial leasing.

Healthcare

Healthcare today is characterized by a complex maze of independent and proprietary systems. From the pharmacist to the hospital to the physician and insurer, it is difficult to share important data among all these different systems. Boston alone has twenty-six different systems for tracking electronic medical records.[95] And, these systems have been notoriously insecure and susceptible to hacks. It is possible that blockchain technology could be the glue that holds all of these systems together.

At the center of any healthcare system is the patient record. In the past, patients did not have any control over their own data and it was bought and sold without much thought. With the introduction of blockchain, patients can control who has access to which pieces of their health records. Your acupuncturist doesn't necessarily need to know about your cholesterol levels. On the other hand, a patient could want the opportunity to sell their personal data to a pharmaceutical firm, participate in a study or trial using their data, or even offer access to genetic information for research.

A major proposal along these lines has been submitted by scientists from MIT. They are proposing a blockchain-based system for medical records that would be called MedRec that would help all of the disparate healthcare systems out there to exchange data.[96] It would be a private blockchain built

---

[95] Woolf, Nicky. "What Could Blockchain Do for Healthcare?" Medium, February 20, 2018, https://medium.com/s/welcome-to-blockchain/what-could-blockchain-do-for-healthcare-59c17245448e

[96] Woolf, Nicky. "What Could Blockchain Do for Healthcare?" Medium, February 20, 2018, https://medium.com/s/welcome-to-blockchain/what-could-blockchain-do-for-healthcare-59c17245448e

on the Ethereum platform, using smart contracts to set up protocols for sharing patient data. Patients give their consent by cryptographically signing their data. They can share data with specialists, insurers or any other healthcare providers. The system intends to be much more secure and flexible, and the data should be even more accurate and comprehensive since it will all be verified and stored in one place. Other proposed use cases for healthcare include tracking the complex trail of payments and services to help resolve disputes, and possibly cross-organization R&D collaboration.[97] This is certainly a fertile area for further development of use cases.

Energy

Several groups around the world are looking to innovate on the energy marketplace. LO3 in Brooklyn is leveraging the technology to store, buy, sell, or use energy at the local level using microgrids as well as legacy infrastructure hooked up to smart meters. In a different direction, the Australian blockchain startup Power Ledger (POWR) has a token, built on the Ethereum platform that allows individuals to buy and sell excess renewable electricity from other individuals and companies. Disintermediating local or national utility companies is quite a big deal, but part of the excitement is also about the secondary markets for green or solar energy.

---

[97] Bean, Randy and Grant Stephen. "How Blockchain Is Impacting Healthcare And Life Sciences Today," Forbes, April 2, 2018, https://www.forbes.com/sites/ciocentral/2018/04/02/how-blockchain-is-impacting-healthcare-and-life-sciences-today/#49c7b169738f

Ethical and Other Issues with Blockchain

By now, you probably have gotten tired of hearing how blockchain will have an impact on virtually every aspect of our lives and the economy in the future. Well, as with any technology, with the opportunities also come some drawbacks. One of the common criticisms to blockchain technology is that the technology is only good for funding terrorists, drug deals, and spreading child pornography.[98] In fact, some of these claims are true, including the final one. You can now pay for memberships in pornographic websites using various cryptocurrencies.[99] Sometimes the ethical considerations are not just about your direct action, but about what it means to be facilitating illegal activity simply by using a blockchain. For instance, if you are paying a miner a transaction fee and that miner is also funding terrorist activity in his or her personal life, are you abetting terrorism? Or, if you download and store the Bitcoin Core protocols, are you capable of storing illicit content such as child pornography on your computer even if you don't know it? The claim about child pornography received a boost from a study done in 2017 about how steganography could be used to embed secret data into the blockchain.

One example of this is the message that Satoshi Nakamoto embedded in the genesis block of Bitcoin. **Steganography** is the process of embedding secret messages into the digital code for public objects like photos, etc. With respect to blockchain this claim is a bit disingenuous since only text of 80 bytes or less can be sent from one node to another in the blocks. So it would be possible to embed a link to content but not the content itself. An analogous situation in the physical world might be if someone wrote an illicit website URL onto a piece of paper and dropped it on the floor of their local school or library. These are interesting questions that will need

---

[98] Bloomberg, Jason. "We Need To Shut Bitcoin And All Other Cryptocurrencies Down. Here's Why," Forbes, March 10, 2108, https://www.forbes.com/sites/jasonbloomberg/2018/03/10/we-need-to-shut-bitcoin-and-all-other-cryptocurrencies-down-heres-why/#6f6546191bca

[99] Buntinx, J.P. "Pornhub Looks Beyond Verge to Improve its Position Among Cryptocurrency Enthusiasts," CryptoMode, June 28, 2018, https://cryptomode.com/pornhub-looks-beyond-verge-to-improve-its-position-among-cryptocurrency-enthusiasts/

much greater exploration as we begin to understand the ethical ramifications and considerations in creating permanent distributed records.

Chapter Summary

This chapter was divided into three main topics; blockchain project management, blockchain use cases, and a Hyperledger tutorial. They are all important aspects of blockchain that will provide a solid basis for becoming blockchain literate. From a high level, the project management process – based on the Animal Ventures Build Cycle – described how to move from a bold vision down to a beachhead and hypothesis worth prototyping. We also described the life-cycle for deploying a proof of concept. Even before this, the Suiches decision model helps us to decide if we even need blockchain for a proposed application. Critical choices must be made about the architecture of the blockchain, the consensus protocols, and the development platform being used. These projects involve a wide variety of roles and skills that may be difficult to find.

Given that coming up with a viable use case is very important part of the development process, section two examined blockchain use cases in more detail. Use cases can be viewed as being cross-functional, functional, and by specific industries. The cross-functional use cases included Identity Management, Asset Tracking, and IoT Integration. Functional area use cases were examined for the business functional areas of Finance, Accounting, Supply Chain Management, Marketing/Sales and Human Resources. Some major industries that are seeing a big impact from blockchain include Healthcare, Real Estate, Insurance, and Energy.

The last section in this chapter introduced the Hyperledger developer framework and tools. Readers were guided through the concepts and process of creating the ChainCode for a permissioned blockchain application that would help to create a peer-to-peer college textbook marketplace.

Key Terms

Hypothesis
Key Performance Indicator (KPI)
Decentralized application (Dapp)
Suiches model
Sybil attack resistance
Consensus
Proof of Work
Proof of Stake
Practical Byzantine Fault Tolerance
Delegated Proof of Stake
Federated Byzantine Agreement
Proof of Authority
Proof of Activity
Proof of Burn

Proof of Elapsed Time
Proof of Importance
Application Program Interface (API)
Proof of Concept (PoC)
Staging environment
Latency
Release candidate
Identity Management
Asset tracking / Provenance
Internet of Things (IoT)
Self-sovereign identity
Digital notarization
Tokenization
Steganography

Questions for Further Discussion

1. What makes a good blockchain use case? What would be a possible barrier to entry?
2. What are some different consensus mechanisms and how do they differ?
3. When is it better to outsource the development of a blockchain application and when is it better to do it in-house?
4. What questions should you ask when deciding on a blockchain development platform?
5. Why are APIs important for blockchain developers?
6. Describe a use case for Identity Management, Asset Tracking, and IoT integration that was *not* described in the text.
7. What are the phases in a blockchain development project?
8. Describe a KYC use case for an industry other than banking.
9. How can blockchain be used to digitally notarize transactions?
10. What is tokenization? Describe another type of asset besides real estate that could be tokenized on a blockchain.

Tutorial: Introduction to Hyperledger and Interactive Example

Overview

Hyperledger is an umbrella project of permissioned blockchain technologies and related tools that was started in December 2015 by the Linux Foundation (an organization dedicated to promoting and maintaining open-source projects). One of the biggest contributors to Hyperledger today is IBM, and the systems integrator uses the technology across its blockchain projects. Hyperledger is popular with some traditional enterprises because it is seen as lower risk and more private than public blockchains (e.g. Ethereum and Bitcoin), and receives more attention and contributions than similar alternatives like R3's Corda and J. P. Morgan's Quorum.

Why Enterprise Blockchains?

While the Ethereum network can be accessed by anybody with a client, the Hyperledger blockchain network access requires authorization, which is one of the differentiating features that makes Hyperledger networks permissioned. The emergence of permissioned ledgers arose from a lack of certain characteristics inherent to public ledgers. Dominant platforms like Ethereum and Bitcoin are, in a practical sense, at the base protocol level, safe from hacking (but not from other types of attacks). Unfortunately, the same cannot be said about applications deployed on these networks, which are notoriously insecure. Attacks such as the DAO fiasco and the Parity Multisig Wallet hack caused immense anxiety among users and prompted U.S. government bodies like the SEC to intervene. These types of incidents can understandably make traditional enterprises feel reluctant about utilizing public blockchain networks. For traditional enterprises to utilize public blockchains, they would have to have significant control over the underlying protocol. Of course, this goes against the very essence of public decentralized blockchains, which by their definition, cannot be controlled by any entity. This market need gave rise to the less public and more permissioned distributed ledgers.

There are advantages and disadvantages to both public and private ledgers, and these can mirror early debates in the enterprise space about using the public Internet versus private intranets. Metaphorically speaking, intranets were corporate network ponds secluded from the large surrounding Internet ocean. Users of intranets, by being disconnected from the rest of the world, were unable to enjoy the full benefits of the public Internet. But they were also great tools for building communication infrastructure and digitizing workplaces before larger services made the Internet more useful for individuals (think search, cloud services, streaming, email, social networks, etc). Similarly, you can argue that permissioned blockchains have a purpose: to offer companies a sandbox environment to run experiments while protecting their core infrastructure and offering greater control than public blockchains. Another major advantage for using permissioned blockchains at the enterprise level is the ability to scale to greater numbers of transactions. Since these networks do not have to be fully decentralized, some network nodes can assume specialized roles, which can significantly increase the number of transactions that can be executed, unlike with current public networks.

Disadvantages exist as well, since permissioned ledgers are potentially more prone to being attacked and taken over at the protocol level, and more centralization of the network can give rise to more centralized points of failure. The large divide between public and private blockchains is a reflection of a mindset divide in the industry, and can even represent a much larger ideological dichotomy. For the time-being enterprises are geared toward more stable and experimentation-friendly platforms that offer a mode of privacy to learn and integrate blockchain into their work.

Technical Overview of Hyperledger Fabric

Hyperledger fabric is a permissioned blockchain distributed ledger with ChainCode (CC) capabilities (smart contracts), specialized node configurations, and a unique consensus mechanism. You can learn more about it at the following link: https://hyperledger-fabric.readthedocs.io/en/release-1.2/ Building and deploying a Hyperledger Fabric network with CC apps is a very involved process, and this chapter will only cover an online tool called Composer Playground to prototype and test Hyperledger Fabric applications. The online tool can be accessed at https://composer-playground.mybluemix.net, requires no account, and saves your progress.

Composer Playground

The chapter on Ethereum introduced an online tool called Remix to develop and interact with Ethereum Dapps. Composer Playground is the Remix for Hyperledger Fabric with the main differences being that no connection can be made to a live net, and that network configurations can also be defined. Composer will be used to both develop, deploy, and test what is called the business network, a collection of participants, assets, transactions, and access rules that will be embedded as part of a Hyperledger blockchain. The business network behaves similarly to a Dapp, with the difference that access is based on permissions that are embedded in the network.

A default business network is already provisioned when Hyperledger playground is first accessed. It is a very basic application, but we can use it to demonstrate how interactions would work on a hypothetical Hyperledger blockchain network. You can view the components of the application in the model file, as seen in Figure 5-23. It consists of a single asset called SampleAsset that has an owner and a value, a participant called SampleParticipant, which can own a SampleAsset, and a transaction SampleTransaction, which updates the value of the SampleAsset.

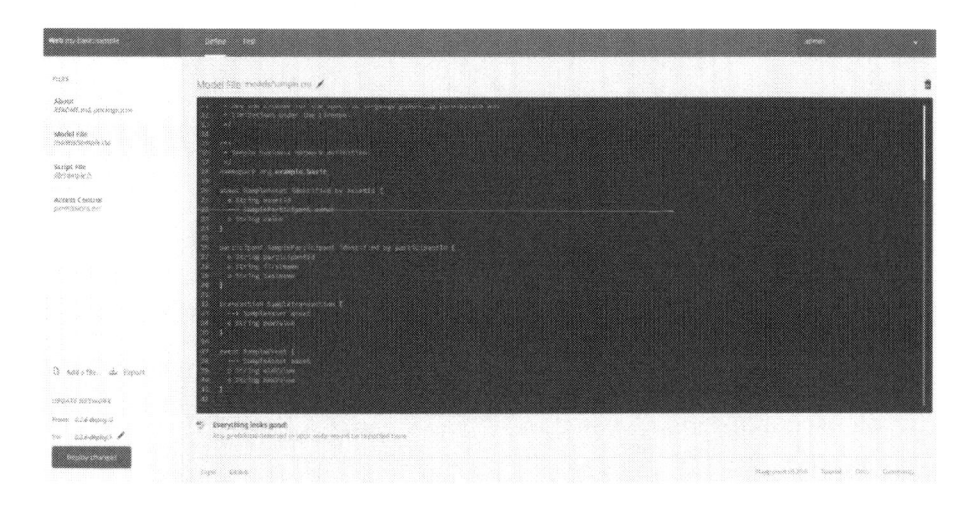

Figure 5-23: The model file contents of the sample application

The page where you manage assets, participants, and submit transactions is presented by clicking the *Test Tab* at the top of the screen. Click it so we can start interacting with our network.

Creating Participants

Creating a participant gives authorization to a user to access and interact with your application. Any number of participants can be defined with arbitrary permissions in the define section. Click on the Participants tab on the left if you have not already done so. Click the "Create New Participant" at the top right corner of the screen. This will open up a dialog. In the dialog, you will view the new participant's information in JSON format. Fill the fields for firstName and lastName, and then create your participant. The participant record will be listed after you are done.

Basics of Blockchain

Figure 5-24: Create a participant using JSON-formatted text

Creating Assets

Assets are created to represent and store information about physical or digital items that are important. Assets are owned and interacted with by participants. To create an asset, click on the assets tab, and then click the "Create New Asset" button. This will open a dialog to fill in information about the asset. Copy and paste the following text and create the asset:

{

"$class": "org.example.basic.SampleAsset",

"assetId": "2048",

"owner": "resource:org.example.basic.SampleParticipant#1694", "value": "1000"

}

Composer Playground assigns these assets by default to non-existing users. This would essentially mean assets are owned by the system and no actual participant. But, let's specify the actual owner of the asset by changing the number in the owner field to match the participantId field for our created participant.

Submitting Transactions

Hyperledger transactions are very similar to Ethereum transactions. They update the state of an entity. In this case, the entity is the asset. Click the submit transaction button on the left side of the screen, and fill the Text Box with the following information, then click submit.

{

"$class": "org.example.basic.SampleTransaction",

"asset": "resource:org.example.basic.SampleAsset#2048",

"newValue": "100"

}

Basics of Blockchain

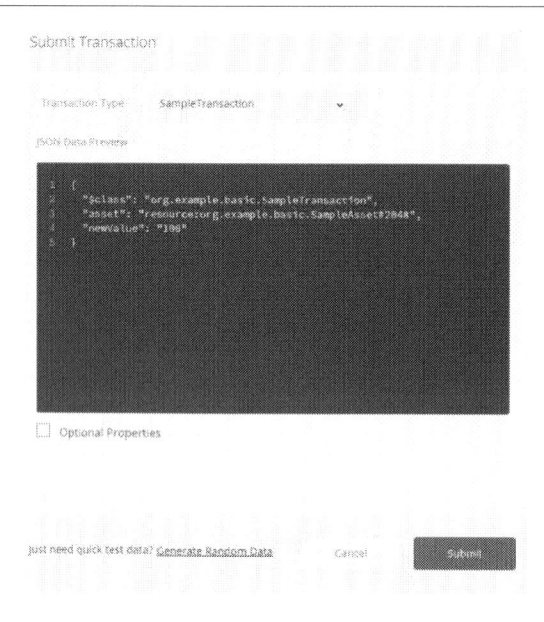

Figure 5-25: Submitting a transaction

Once you are done, you should see the asset's value updated. All the transactions that were executed can be viewed in the Transactions section. Composer Playground comes with predefined system transactions that are submitted under the hood whenever administrator-level changes are made (like adding participants or assets). Only application-defined transactions have to be executed explicitly.

Creating participants, assets, and submitting transactions will be the most commonly used activities in all your Hyperledger Fabric applications, even if you later decide to deploy a live net and hide the interactions under a pleasing user interface.

Implementing a Textbook Marketplace in Hyperledger

We've seen how we can use Composer Playground to interact with and test an application, but how can you actually go through the process of developing an application? First, we need to define a business use case to develop our application. Suppose you were one of the administrators of an exclusive textbook marketplace at a local college. The marketplace offers distinguished scholars and students the ability to trade textbooks as a secondary market. You would not want the textbooks to be accessed by people outside of the university setting, since access to this marketplace is one of the attractive features of attending the university. In order for such users to access your marketplace, you need to create accounts for them and list what books they own. The account is represented by a participant record, and the books they own are assets assigned to them.

A faculty member or student who wants to sell a book, requests one of the marketplace admins to create an asset for their physical book. After an asset is created, it can be removed again by the administrator. Administrators exclusively own this right in order to prevent people from fraudulently creating book assets.

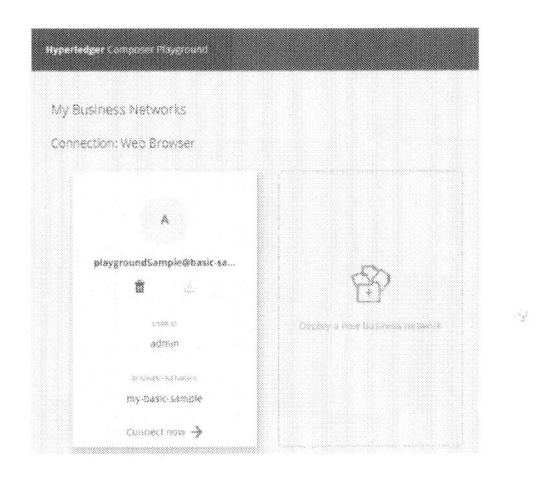

Figure 5-26: Hyperledger Composer Playground main dashboard

We will create a new project. Go to the main dashboard, as seen in Figure 5-27, and then click "Deploy a new business network". You will be directed to a page to set up your app. Here you can view a list of sample applications that you can deploy and play with, as seen in Figure 5-28. Under the "Choose a Business Network Definition to start with" section, pick "empty-business-network" and select "Deploy". You will have to also select "Connect now" to get to the developer screen. We will start from scratch.

Basics of Blockchain

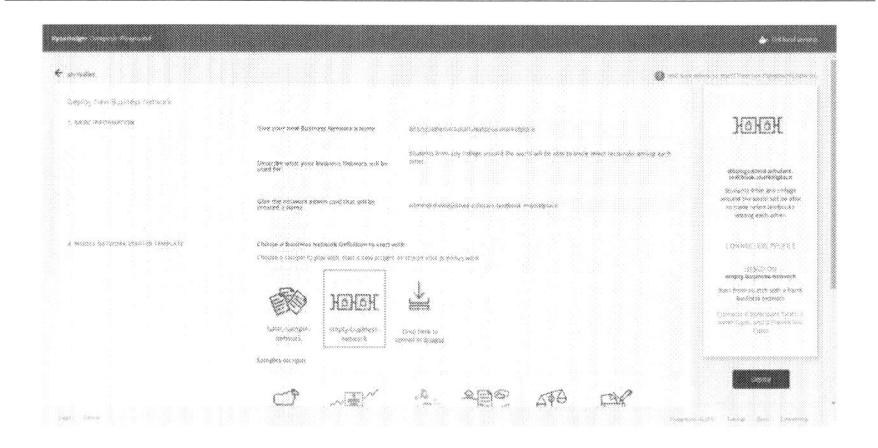

Figure 5-27: New business network page

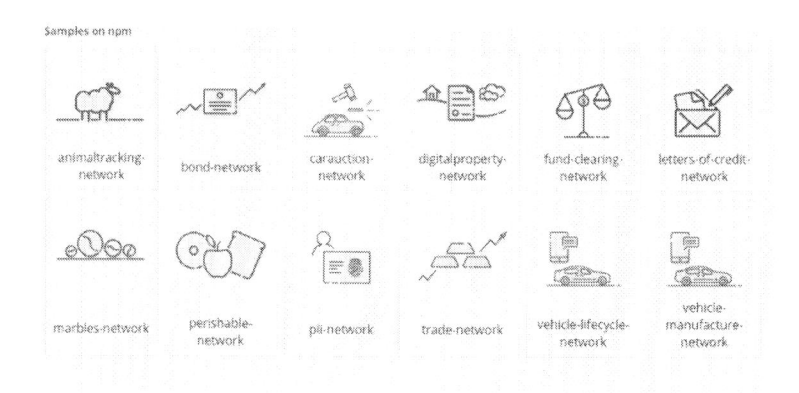

Figure 5-28: Sample applications

When you create an empty business network, you will be given an empty model file, no scripts file, and a small Access Control File. We will be developing our application by adding code to these files. The code structures that can be added can be discovered by following other examples or reading the official Composer Playground documentation at the following link: https://hyperledger.github.io/composer/latest/tutorials/playground-tutorial.html

Don't be too worried about the code and programming aspects of the exercise. They have been designed to be extremely simple to use for any type of user.

Model File

The model file is used to define the model of the business network. It consists of the following components: Assets, Participants, Transactions, Events, Enumerated Types, and Concepts. We will focus our attention on assets, participants, and transactions, and show how to define them for our application.

At the start of the file, replace the current namespace with the following line:

namespace edu.scholars.textbookmarketplace

We will use this namespace to reference our model components.

Assets

Textbook

The main asset of the application is the textbook since it is the trading commodity of the marketplace.

asset Textbook{

}

What information should this asset contain? Firstly, each textbook is unique, hence it needs to be identified by an ID. This can be an ISBN code or something custom.

asset Textbook identified by textbookId {

 o String textbookId

}

We also want to be able to store information about which participant owns the textbook and additional information about the physical textbook. This block of code should be copied and inserted in place of the default asset on your screen.

asset Textbook identified by textbookId {

  o String textbookId

  --> Scholar owner

  o String title

  o String author

  o String edition

  o String condition

}

We have defined a textbook asset with the minimum necessary information to be usable in the marketplace. Let's now define the participants.

Participants

Scholar

As mentioned previously, the main participant is a scholar; as such, we shall name it accordingly and give it an identifying property,

participant Scholar identified by studentId {

  o String studentId

}

We would like to store the name of the scholar. This is useful in special circumstances such as when a textbook is lost and needs to be returned. This block of code should be copied and pasted in place of the default participant in the example.

participant Scholar identified by studentId {

o String studentId

o String firstName

o String lastName

}

We now need to define what transactions participants can execute.

Transactions

Trade

Scholars can submit trade transactions to exchange textbooks.

transaction Trade {

--> Textbook textbook1

--> Textbook textbook2

}

ChangePricing

Sometimes scholars prize their textbook so much that they feel like the cost of exchange should be more expensive, or that contrary, their textbook is way too expensive and nobody is buying it.

The change pricing transaction allows the owners of the textbook to adjust the pricing of the textbook to their desire.

transaction ChangePricing {

--> Textbook textbook

o Integer newPrice

}

We have defined all the minimum necessary components to our model. Your model file should look something like this:

namespace edu.scholars.textbookmarketplace

asset Textbook identified by textbookId {

o String textbookId

--> Scholar owner

o String title

o String author

o String edition

o String condition

}

```
participant Scholar identified by studentId {

  o String studentId

  o String firstName

  o String lastName

}


transaction Trade {

  --> Textbook textbook1

  --> Textbook textbook2

}
```

Next, we need to define how our transactions get executed.

Scripts File

In the script file, we will create a script for each transaction.

Trade

```
/*

@param {edu.scholars.textbookmarketplace.Trade} tx

@transaction

*/

async function trade(tx) {

        // update owners
```

```
        const firstOwner = tx.textbook1.owner

        tx.textbook1.owner = tx.textbook2.owner;

  tx.textbook2.owner = firstOwner;



  // Get the asset registry for the asset.

  const assetRegistry = await
getAssetRegistry('edu.scholars.textbookmarketplace.Textbook');



  // update textbook and owner fields

  await assetRegistry.update(tx.textbook1);

  await assetRegistry.update(tx.textbook2);

}
```

Access Controls

The access control file you are given contains the following rules initially:

rule NetworkAdminUser {

  description: "Grant business network administrators full access to user resources"

  participant: "org.hyperledger.composer.system.NetworkAdmin"

  operation: ALL

  resource: "**"

  action: ALLOW

}

```
rule NetworkAdminSystem {
    description: "Grant business network administrators full access to system resources"
    participant: "org.hyperledger.composer.system.NetworkAdmin"
    operation: ALL
    resource: "org.hyperledger.composer.system.**"
    action: ALLOW
}
```

We only need to add one more rule, which stipulates that scholars own their textbooks:

```
rule OwnerHasFullAccessToTheirAssets {
    description: "Allow all scholars full access to their textbooks"
    participant(p): "edu.scholars.textbookmarketplace.Scholar"
    operation: ALL
    resource(r): "edu.scholars.textbookmarketplace.Textbook"
    condition: (r.owner.getIdentifier() === p.getIdentifier())
    action: ALLOW
}
```

We have finished defining our network. Go ahead and deploy the changes by clicking the "Deploy changes" button on the "Define" page and start interacting with your application.

Final Remarks

By this point you may be wondering how this application would differ from a traditional centralized web application. Firstly, you need to remember that the Composer Playground is meant as a test environment and does not fully resemble interactions with a production-level Hyperledger Fabric blockchain network. Additionally, if such an application was to be deployed on a production setting it would be far superior to a traditional application. Consider the case where there are multiple administrators controlling multiple nodes that store the ledger. What if some of the administrators cannot be trusted? The organization and structure of the network ensures corruption of the ledger is avoided, which means administrators can't freely manipulate the transactions. Such a feature does not exist in traditional applications.

Chapter 6 – The Future of Blockchain

Learning Objectives

- Gain a deeper understanding of how blockchain technology will evolve
- Examine predictions for blockchain adoption and impact
- Examine barriers to the adoption of blockchain technology
- Explain what artificial intelligence is and how it can be combined with blockchain
- Understand the impact of blockchain on legal and governmental services
- Discuss how blockchain is enabling globalization and its impact on the economy
- Understand the skills that will be needed to better manage blockchain in the future
- Integrate a predictive algorithm into an advanced smart contract in Ethereum

Blockchain in Action – Using Blockchain to Fight Fake News

The issue of "fake news" has been all over the media because of its impact on the 2016 American elections and also the United Kingdom's Brexit debates. One study from MIT found that Twitter users are 70% more likely to retweet false information than true information, and there is concern over the use of botnets and "click-farms" to propagate false stories.[100] It may not come as a surprise then, that many companies are talking about how to use blockchain technology to better detect fake news. The European Commission announced that blockchain was going to play a key role in their new Code of Practice on Disinformation, which is part of the EU's larger efforts at funding blockchain research.[101]

The idea is to take advantage of blockchain's transparency, security, and verifiability to track the sources of news stories. Blockchain technology would be combined with "the wisdom of crowds" to come up with a consensus about the source of news items. Users would be rewarded for identifying fake news when the crowd agrees and penalized when the crowd disagrees with their assessment. As a verifier in such a network you would have a reputation score that determines your level of influence and exposure. Articles would also be given scores to determine their exposure. All of this can be tracked on a blockchain to provide a permanent and transparent record. Those participants with high reputation scores may also receive other rewards depending on the platform being used. Additionally, other media outlets see blockchain as a possible solution component for logging news articles and journalism so that it cannot be tampered with by hackers trying to imitate or corrupt high-reputation media outlets. While concrete implementations have not emerged yet, this is an area where blockchain may prove valuable (or it may be just another news story!).

---

100 Bucho, Stephen. "Blockchain's Fight Against Fake News," Coin Central, March 26, 2018, https://coincentral.com/blockchains-fight-against-fake-news/

101 Partz, Helen. "European Commission to Fight Fake News With Power of Blockchain," Coin Telegraph, May 1, 2018, https://cointelegraph.com/news/european-commission-to-fight-fake-news-with-power-of-blockchain

Blockchain in the Future

With all of the talk about blockchain technology and its wide variety of use cases, it is worth taking the time to examine actual studies about its adoption, obstacles, and how it might impact society as a whole. This chapter will also review how the technology is evolving as it continues to move forward.

Blockchain may certainly be the most hyped technology since the dot-com bubble. It was one of the top priority topics at the Davos Economic Summit in 2017, where it was reported that 10% of the world's GDP would be stored on blockchains by the year 2027.[102] Governments around the world are announcing major blockchain initiatives and making blockchain a strategic necessity. Excluding the thousands of new ICOs being generated, venture capital continues to flow toward blockchain startups at an increasing rate. In 2017, investment approached $2.1 billion, with almost $1.5 billion invested in the first half of 2018 alone.[103]

Many people describe blockchain excitement as a bubble getting ready to burst and they argue that the reality can't possibly match the hype. Technologist and Apple co-founder, Steve Wozniak, is one such skeptic.[104] He compares the level of blockchain hype to the hype around e-commerce right before the dot-com bubble burst in the early 2000s. Wozniack went so far as to sell his bitcoin holdings in 2018, putting his "money" where his mouth is. However, the Internet came back even stronger after the bubble burst, and he agrees that the fundamental technology of blockchain will eventually be the "cornerstone for business in the future."[105] To many, including Wozniak, blockchain is immature and not quite ready for adoption,

---

[102] "Deep Shift: Technology Tipping Points and Societal Impact," World Economic Forum, September 2015, http://www3.weforum.org/docs/WEF_GAC15_Technological_Tipping_Points_report_2015.pdf

[103] Rowley, Jason. "With at least $1.3billion invested globally in 2018, VC funding for blockchain blows past 2017 totals," TechCrunch, 2018, https://techcrunch.com/2018/05/20/with-at-least-1-3-billion-invested-globally-in-2018-vc-funding-for-blockchain-blows-past-2017-totals/

[104] Paden, Romona. "Blockchain Hype Overstates Reality, Says Steve Wozniak," Bitcoin Magazine, June 29, 2018, https://bitcoinmagazine.com/articles/blockchain-hype-overstates-reality-says-steve-wozniak/

[105] Paden, Romona. "Blockchain Hype Overstates Reality, Says Steve Wozniak," Bitcoin Magazine, June 29, 2018, https://bitcoinmagazine.com/articles/blockchain-hype-overstates-reality-says-steve-wozniak/

leading to a sort of "blockchain fatigue." A recent Deloitte survey of over 1000 executives across the world found that 44% of Americans felt that blockchain was "overhyped"; up from 34% in a 2016 survey.[106] This may just be part of the after effect of the Bitcoin bubble bursting in 2018, since a majority still said they were exploring blockchain technology.

Despite this skepticism, blockchain technology continues to be adopted heavily by corporate actors. Walmart announced it will require its suppliers to upload data using IBM's Blockchain Platform (built on Hyperledger Fabric) by September 2019, to trace food quality issues. They claim this reduces food source queries from 7 days to 2.2 seconds.[107] This news is especially noteworthy since Walmart is a leader and technology innovator in the retail and supply chain spaces. Another indication that the blockchain tsunami is in fact continuing to bear down upon us comes from the pharmaceutical industry. A little-known 2013 law, called the Drug Supply Chain Security Act, is now forcing the industry's hand. The law requires pharmaceutical companies to be able to track drugs throughout the supply chain by 2020 in order to reduce counterfeiting and enable more efficient recalls.[108] Of course, the leading contender for this job is blockchain technology. The hype versus reality debate is not a new one for emergent technologies like blockchain (or Big Data, IoT, AI and others), and it should prompt consideration of futurist Roy Amara's law: "We tend to overestimate the effects of technology in the short run and underestimate the effect in the long run." To this end, blockchain as a science may be overly hyped in its infancy, but a game-changer in the advances that come for cryptography and decentralized computing as its swan song.

---

[106] "Breaking blockchain open, Deloitte's 2018 global blockchain survey," Deloitte, 2018, https://www2.deloitte.com/content/dam/Deloitte/us/Documents/financial-services/us-fsi-2018-global-blockchain-survey-report.pdf

[107] Miller, Ron. "Walmart is betting on the blockchain to improve food safety," TechCrunch, October, 2018, https://techcrunch.com/2018/09/24/walmart-is-betting-on-the-blockchain-to-improve-food-safety

[108] Leising, Matthew. "Blockchain hype may finally turn into reality in pharmaceuticals," The Inquirer, September 26, 2018, http://www2.philly.com/philly/business/pharma/blockchain-hype-may-finally-turn-into-reality-in-pharmaceuticals-20180926.html

> **Common Myths about Blockchain**
>
> A ground-breaking study by the McKinsey Group mentions five common myths about Blockchain.[109] These include:
>
> *Blockchain is Bitcoin*
>
> *Blockchain is tamper-proof*
>
> *Blockchain is 100% secure*
>
> *Blockchain is better than traditional databases*
>
> *Blockchain is a "truth machine"*

Of course, Bitcoin is just one of the most successful Dapps that make use of a blockchain architecture, as well as the first instantiation of a blockchain network. However, some of the negative press around bitcoin and other cryptocurrencies has spilled over into the reputation of the broader blockchain innovation space. The idea that blockchain is immutable and tamper-proof has been true up to this point, but disregards the idea that a 51% attack or other future manipulation could be used to rewrite some of the blocks. Blockchain itself is highly secure too, but the access points (such as crypto exchanges) and wallet technology seem to be sources of security issues. In terms of processing high volumes of transactions, blockchain is still not as good as a well-tuned, traditional database. And blockchain data is only as "truthful" as the off-chain data that applications supply to it or leverage. Blockchain is no panacea, but it offers a path to solve some of the pain points we face in our digital architecture status quo.

---

[109] Carson, Brant and Giulio Romanelli, Patricia Walsh, and Askhat Zhumaev, "Blockchain beyond the hype: What is the strategic business value?" McKinsey & Company, June 2018, https://www.mckinsey.com/business-functions/digital-mckinsey/our-insights/blockchain-beyond-the-hype-what-is-the-strategic-business-value

Adoption of Blockchain

One *Forbes* study found that all ten of the world's top public companies are already exploring blockchain technology.[110] They identified another 50 large firms that are investing billions of dollars into blockchain. These included companies such as IBM, which has already invested over $200 million and hired 1,000 new people specifically to work with blockchain. Another more recent study by Deloitte surveyed over 1,000 executives and found that 74% of them saw a "compelling business case" for the use of blockchain.[111] At the same time, only 34% of these same executives had initiated any kind of blockchain project. While 16% of the respondents said that the main benefit of blockchain was cost reduction, 28% said that a major advantage was the "new business models" that would result from it. Currently, most executives are not sure what to do with it, but 84% of respondents said that they were involved with blockchain in some manner. Another 29% have joined an industry consortium for blockchain. All of this indicates that we are still in the early stages of adoption, and that it is set for continued growth.

With many of the benefits of blockchain technology rooted in identity and security of transactions, it will help certain industries more than others. Some industries like insurance, for example, are inherently based on providing a centralized and secure foundation for all types of transactions. The McKinsey study identified the industries that will be most impacted by blockchain as: insurance, financial services, healthcare, property, public sector, agriculture, and utilities.[112]

At first, the most surprising of these leading industries for blockchain may be

---

110 del Castillo, Michael. "Big Blockchain: The 50 Largest Public Companies Exploring Blockchain," Forbes, July 3, 2018, https://www.forbes.com/sites/michaeldelcastillo/2018/07/03/big-blockchain-the-50-largest-public-companies-exploring-blockchain/#164621f92b5b

111 "Breaking blockchain open, Deloitte's 2018 global blockchain survey," Deloitte, 2018, https://www2.deloitte.com/content/dam/Deloitte/us/Documents/financial-services/us-fsi-2018-global-blockchain-survey-report.pdf

112 Carson, Brant and Giulio Romanelli, Patricia Walsh, and Askhat Zhumaev, "BLockchain beyond the hype: What is the strategic business value?" McKinsey & Company, June 2018, https://www.mckinsey.com/business-functions/digital-mckinsey/our-insights/blockchain-beyond-the-hype-what-is-the-strategic-business-value

the inclusion of agriculture. However, the potential impact on making our food supply chains safer and more efficient could benefit both farmers and consumers. According to the study, those industries that will feel the least impact from blockchain are predicted to be the arts and recreation, manufacturing, and mining. Even for the industries that are ripest for blockchain adoption, many estimate commercially viable blockchain solutions are three to five years away. Disruptor startups are emerging in each field, and many firms have recruited top industry talent to help them start fresh without being encumbered by the old models while maintaining industry know-how. One study by a Stanford researcher surveyed all of the current blockchain initiatives and found that those in the healthcare industry had the greatest potential for disruption, while governance initiatives were the farthest along.[113]

The (in)famous "hype cycle" chart for emerging technologies from the Gartner group identified blockchain in 2018 as having already passed the peak of "inflated expectations" as it makes its way towards the "trough of disillusionment."[114] Nevertheless, Gartner included blockchain as one of the key areas to watch as part of a trend toward "digitized ecosystems"; along with flying autonomous vehicles, 4D printing, and many other concepts. According to their research, general adoption of blockchain technology is still five to ten years away. The largest portion of companies are in the R&D phases of blockchain, while almost equal percentages are either doing nothing (14%) or have already gone live (15%) with their application.

---

[113] Edwards, John. "Calculating Blockchain's Impact," InformationWeek, May 15, 2018, https://www.informationweek.com/software/enterprise-applications/calculating-blockchains-impact/a/d-id/1331781?_mc=NL_IWK_EDT_IWK_review_20180518&cid=NL_IWK_EDT_IWK_review_20180518&elq_mid=84822&elq_cid=19995087

[114] Panetta, Kasey. "5 Trends Emerge in the Gartner Hype Cycle for Emerging Technologies, 2018," Gartner, August 16, 2018, https://www.gartner.com/smarterwithgartner/5-trends-emerge-in-gartner-hype-cycle-for-emerging-technologies-2018/

Blockchain Maturity Models

A **maturity model** is a tool for assessing how far an organization, industry, project, or specific technology has to go in order to be considered "mature." These have been applied to specific technologies such as smartphones, virtual reality, and artificial intelligence among others. For technology, it's a way of assessing how close it is to reaching general adoption. According to the blockchain maturity model presented by Accenture, blockchain has left the early adoption phase and moved into the phase of development.[115] A large percentage of projects are still in the Research phase (20%), and a smaller percentage are in the pilot stage (10%); about 15% have gone live with blockchain projects. This shows that there is still a lot of room for growth in blockchain applications.

A more macro view of blockchain maturity can be seen by analyzing its progression over a period of time. The Accenture report on blockchain shows a timeline of blockchain growth and adoption. In the *Exploration and Development* phase, organizations may do an initial assessment of the technology and relevant use cases. This provides the impetus for some firms to become early adopters, primarily for internal reconciliations. Once they see the value, this leads them to explore blockchain for external use along with more regulatory certainty. In the *Growth* phase, the deployment of blockchain for firms such as banks goes viral, as late adopters see the benefits that the early adopters obtained. Finally, in the *Maturity* phase, blockchain is considered to be a mainstream technology, used by the key stakeholders. At this point, blockchain may be so entrenched that it will be running behind the scenes, like the TCP/IP protocols of the Internet today. Interestingly, the consulting firm Accenture is predicting 2025 as the year when the technology reaches maturity. This is close to the amount of time it took for the general adoption of the Internet, which took about twenty years to reach maturity.

---

115 "Blockchain Technology: Preparing for Change," Accenture, 2015, https://www.accenture.com/t20160608T052656__w__/us-en/_acnmedia/PDF-5/Accenture-2016-Top-10-Challenges-04-Blockchain-Technology.pdf

Barriers to Adoption

Given that interest in using blockchain technology is very high, what factors are holding users back from adopting it today? One major study from PriceWaterhouseCoopers found that the top barriers to adoption centered around trust and regulations.[116] This is particularly ironic since blockchain is supposed to lower the need for trust in transactions. However, the association with mysterious figures such as the founder, Satoshi Nakamoto, the volatility of cryptocurrency prices, and hacks of exchanges like Mt. Gox – while often ancillary to the technology itself – can engender distrust. And depending on how government agencies around the world regulate crypto-assets, the market could change quickly. The biggest hurdle may be the disentanglement of blockchain as a form of nascent decentralized computing architecture from the cryptocurrency trading world (while relevant) that has grown around it. It is also so new that it requires a certain leap of faith to believe that a distributed ledger, running on a peer-to-peer network, could be more trustworthy than the many financial and third-party institutions that have established records of performance in society. Other major issues center around the scalability of blockchain and the problems associated with trying to get multiple blockchain networks working together.

The lack of regulation of crypto-assets and blockchain technology is seen as both a positive and negative indicator, depending on who you ask. Minimal regulations help to promote research and development, facilitate safe harbors for innovation, and lower the burden of hefty reporting structures or legal bills ahead of understanding best use cases for the technology. Inevitably, this also makes it a riskier trajectory for many people. Finding the right amount of regulation that would support blockchain best practices and not stifle its growth is still an open question. Both fear and hype around the thousands of ICOs and dark web use of cryptocurrencies keep many potential users away. Even though many of the security hacks have centered on how users access

---

[116] "Blockchain is here. What's your next move?" PwC Global Blockchain survey 2018, PwC, https://www.pwc.com/gx/en/issues/blockchain/blockchain-in-business.html

cryptocurrencies, this is a big concern as well.

For the enterprise adoption of blockchain, most of these same barriers apply. However, companies have additional concerns beyond the consumer-level issues. To experiment with blockchain, companies often choose to build custom blockchain applications and even networks from scratch. This can get very expensive since there is a general scarcity of blockchain developer talent. And those that are top notch are usually working on broader ecosystem initiatives or their own startups. Costs can range from $10,000 for building a very basic application, to $800,000 for more complex blockchain apps.[117] This is one reason that some software vendors are racing to develop more options such as Blockchain-as-a Service (BaaS); betting that many enterprises would rather use IBM, Microsoft or other providers of this service than spin up their own nodes. Adoption is also slowed because of a general aversion to change. Many people are afraid that jobs will be lost amid all the industry disruption. This may be a short-term consequence, but some new jobs will be gained too as the applications evolve. This is already happening in different parts of the world such as Switzerland and China, where blockchain booms have been underway.

The Continuing Evolution of Blockchain

One of the mistakes that some experts make when criticizing blockchain is neglecting to take into consideration how the technology is evolving. The previous section discussed many of the current barriers to adoption, but many, very smart people are working diligently at solving these issues. Since blockchain grew out of a combination of many disciplines – computer science, distributed system architecture, game theory, cryptography – its evolution will also have to factor in the rapid changes of the various blockchain components from these fields, as well as more general advances. We can see that blockchain technology has already evolved substantially from its bitcoin roots with the introduction of Ethereum and smart contracts.

---

117 Hjønnevåg, Joakim. "The 3 Biggest Obstacles to Business Adopting Blockchain Technology," Hackernoon, August 7, 2018, https://hackernoon.com/the-3-biggest-obstacles-to-businesses-adopting-blockchain-technology-d0e3dc52842d

Now, the platforms needed for constructing more advanced smart contracts and linking them are being put into place. This in turn will encourage more industries to adopt and develop further forms of the technology.

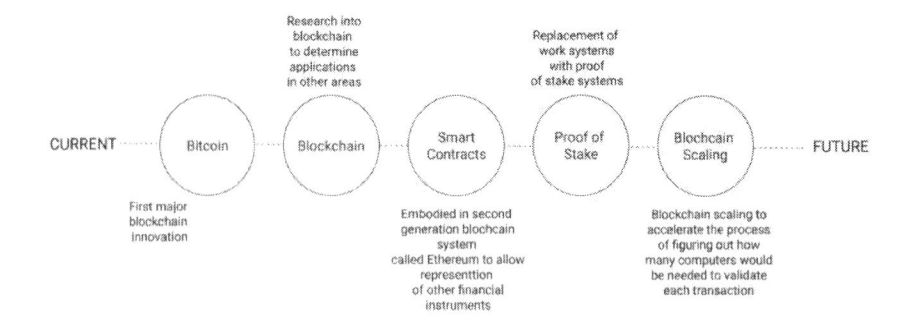

Figure 6-1: Evolution of blockchain innovation

Scalability

Whenever you talk to a knowledgeable person about blockchain, the issue of **scalability** comes up. The problem is that for blockchain applications to continue growing in usage, they must be able to handle more transactions. With the recent success of Bitcoin and Ethereum, their networks have been struggling to process the surge in applications. Since Bitcoin miners can verify and create blocks of about 2000 transactions every ten minutes, this come out to processing about 60 transactions a second. This is far short of the standard set by Visa which handles over 47,000 transactions per second using finely-tuned traditional database technology. Bitcoin Cash was the result of a hard fork in Bitcoin that was motivated by trying to improve the transaction processing problem. By quadrupling the size of the blocks being created to 4 MB, the idea was that this would speed up the transaction verification process. But this has been a short-term solution to the problem and didn't effectively change the issue for Bitcoin.[118]

---

[118] "Blockchain Scalability: The Issues and Proposed Solutions," BitRewards, Medium, April 25, 2018,

Proposed solutions to the scalability problem generally seem to involve reducing the number of trusted nodes used for verifying transactions by using the SegWit protocol, Plasma, and other sub-chain or off-chain architectures to speed up the processing. You could think of the problem as analogous to if your homework had to be graded by all the professors in a university rather than one or a few. This would ensure that it was graded properly but it might take a long time to know your grade and get it back. However, if only a few, trusted professors grade your paper, it might be easier to corrupt their grading process. This creates a potential tradeoff between the security and the scalability of the process. If each node is required to process the transactions of a blockchain, it becomes challenging to increase their throughput.

Another possible solution for the scalability problem is the **Lightning Network**. This is a payment protocol that primarily works on top of Bitcoin to verify transactions using the Segwit protocol. It avoids having a majority of Bitcoin miners verify transactions by having a few trusted miners perform this task instead. This happens in a separate channel and the main channel blocks are updated at a later time. Transactions are supposed to be instantaneous. It has been tested and is currently growing at a rate of about 15% per month.[119]

The Ethereum network has experienced some of the same scalability issues as Bitcoin. The global craze for the CryptoKitties Dapp created a crisis on the Ethereum network when it slowed the whole network down. When the game went viral late in 2017, the network saw a six-fold increase in pending transactions. This caused a controversy because of the concern that serious transactions were being delayed due to a game.[120] One of the solutions proposed for Ethereum is based on the concept of **sharding**. The basic idea of sharding is that the main chain is broken into shards or subsets, that are maintained by fewer miners. This would hopefully speed up the validation process since it would not require that thousands of miners verify each transaction. Again, this would involve a trade-off between the security of having many nodes verifying all the transactions and trusting that a smaller

---

https://medium.com/@bitrewards/blockchain-scalability-the-issues-and-proposed-solutions-2ec2c7ac98f0
119 "Lighting Network," Wikipedia, https://en.wikipedia.org/wiki/Lightning_Network
120 "CryptoKitties craze slows down transactions on Ethereum," BBC News, December 5, 2017, https://www.bbc.com/news/technology-42237162

group of them will suffice. This is also part of the reason that Ethereum is moving towards a Proof of Stake protocol, in order to mitigate these concerns about corruptibility. Ziliqua is a very promising new platform being developed in Singapore that is designed around this concept of sharding. They have shown a peak ability to process 2,488 transactions per second on Ethereum.[121]

Regulatory Issues

Another factor that is impeding the adoption of blockchain is the overall perception of the technology. Consumers perceive it to be the domain of anarchists and drug lords with hackers just waiting to prey on unsophisticated newbies. This perception is bolstered by the understandable bugs found in the early stages of technology development. One MIT study of almost 1 million smart contracts found that about 34,000 of them had significant security vulnerabilities.[122] Unfortunately, it seems that the only likely improvement to the reputation of blockchain will be through some form of regulation. Regulating a technology that has decentralization at its core is challenging from a technical standpoint (part of its purpose it to function without the need for intermediaries or censorship) and also from a governance standpoint (how best to manage risk without creating new externalities due to regulatory burdens or interference).

A patchwork of regulations across the globe has begun to form, mainly relating to tokens or cryptocurrencies. These range from outright banning digital currency transactions (e.g. Indonesia, India, and Brazil) to actively supporting them (e.g. Switzerland). Some countries, such as China and Korea have banned using tokens for crowdsales and fundraising via ICOs altogether, but are very supportive of the blockchain industry. Japan, Russia, and Saudi Arabia are working towards requiring new tokens to register with the

---

[121] "Zilliqua And Global Brain Blockchain Announces Intelligent Partnership," BlockchainExchangeGuide, https://bitcoinexchangeguide.com/zilliqua-and-global-brain-blockchain-announces-intelligent-partnership/

[122] Orcutt, Mike. "Ethereum's smart contracts are full of holes," MIT Technology Review, March 1, 2018, https://www.technologyreview.com/s/610392/ethereums-smart-contracts-are-full-of-holes/

government.[123] Alternatively, Canada is actively recruiting blockchain-related firms with their hands-off approach. In fact, a new blockchain ETF was recently launched there. Some very small countries such as Lichtenstein, Gibraltar, and Bermuda are working hard to brand themselves as crypto-friendly jurisdictions. In their efforts to disengage from global capitalism, and amidst a failing economy, Venezuela has gone even further and issued its own cryptocurrency, the Petro or Petromoneda, in 2018. The United States, United Kingdom, Japan, and Singapore are trying hard to keep a hands-off attitude towards blockchain. However, the SEC in the U.S. did rule that cryptocurrencies should be considered "assets" and should be regulated like assets. These regulations change almost daily and it is almost impossible to keep up with new regulatory developments. At the website http://map.bitlegal.io , all of cryptocurrency regulations are kept up-to-date and linked to a clickable map of the world. The countries in green are friendly to cryptocurrencies, while those in red are more hostile. Those colored in black are unknown.

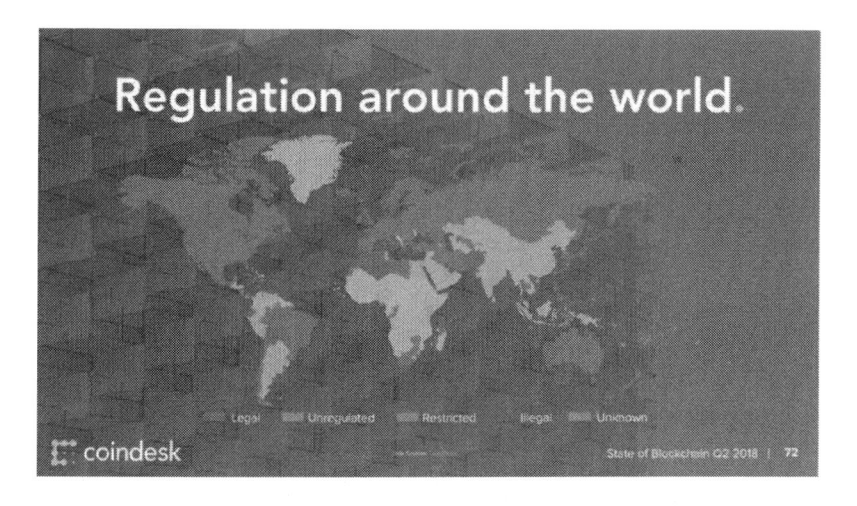

Figure 6-2: Blockchain regulation around the world

---

[123] "Blockchain Regulation: Technology Is Welcomed, Cryptocurrency Regulated," Intellectsoft, April 23, 2018, https://www.intellectsoft.net/blog/blockchain-government-regulation

Twenty-two countries within the European Union recently agreed to establish a European Blockchain Partnership in order to become a global leader in blockchain-related technologies. They have already allocated over $400 million toward blockchain projects and research in both public and private sector applications.[124]

The new **General Data Privacy Regulations (GDPR)** issued by the European Union were designed to allow consumers to have greater control over what personal data they wanted to share, and recourse in dealing with digital data held by companies. This caused widespread disruption to the global software community. At first glance, it seemed these regulations could be in direct opposition to the structural implementation of blockchain technology. This is because the new rules mandated that people essentially had "the right to be forgotten," or request data be removed from digital media and the Internet. Blockchains were designed to be immutable, and so a requirement for removing data from a blockchain was perceived to be a problem. In the past, this issue was resolved by doing a hard fork and starting a new main chain. However, this would be problematic for all the potential people who might want to delete their personal data. But new alternative blockchain applications are being rapidly developed that improve how firms adhere to these data regulations.[125] One approach is to create a private blockchain that is editable by a few trusted intermediaries. However, this may defeat the original intent of a decentralized blockchain network. Another would be to do all of these edits off-chain, which is the approach of a project called "Teechain" which is trying to solve the GDPR problem with the addition of trusted hardware for securing off-chain transactions with personal data.

---

[124] "Blockchain Regulation: Technology Is Welcomed, Cryptocurrency Regulated," Intellectsoft, April 23, 2018, https://www.intellectsoft.net/blog/blockchain-government-regulation

[125] Lima, Claudio. "Adapting Blockchain for GDPR Compliance," InformationWeek, August 7, 2018, https://www.informationweek.com/strategic-cio/security-and-risk-strategy/adapting-blockchain-for-gdpr-compliance-/a/d-id/1332499?_mc=NL_IWK_EDT_IWK_daily_20180809&cid=NL_IWK_EDT_IWK_daily_20180809&elq_mid=86185&elq_cid=19995087

Interoperability Issues

With the massive growth in blockchain platforms and applications, one could rightly worry that the field might fall victim to a "balkanization" effect in which data on one chain would be inaccessible to another chain that needs to use it. For example, a smart contract on one chain may require information from another chain in order for it to be executed. This is the root of what is called the "interoperability issue" of blockchain. **Interoperability** refers to the ability of different systems to be able to exchange information. It could be devices from different manufacturers, or even different software packages like Mac and Windows programs. In the world of blockchains, it is cumbersome to move an asset from one network to another. This is the reason that some of the crypto exchanges have been created.

Arguably, the lack of interoperability is slowing down the adoption of blockchain at this point. Some firms such as Parity Technologies are working on Polkadot framework to create master relay chains that connect blockchains of different governance architecture. Plasma is a similar effort in Ethereum to tackle child and parent chains that interoperate. Others like the Cosmos blockchain are developing a hub for a new "Internet of Blockchains." Yet others, such as Ark and Interledger, are working on less ambitious solutions to allowing payments across cryptocurrencies. Some of the potential use cases for interoperable blockchains, or chains of chains, include making assets more portable, allowing cross-chain contracts, and leasing assets for specific periods of time.

The Next Wave of Decentralized Computing

While we may be starting to get used to the concepts that come together to enable blockchains like Bitcoin and Ethereum to work and execute transactions without third parties, these methods and ideas will not stay static. **Third-generation blockchains** and computing technologies are emerging that push some of the components of this innovation further in new directions. Beyond evolving the existing platforms to handle greater transaction volume or interoperability, we are starting to see attempts at decentralized computing fabrics that do not fully resemble the early blockchains. For example, Dfinity has been working on a framework that removes much of the crypto-economic game theory of blockchains like Bitcoin, by using an alternative structure for creating randomness in how blocks are validated. Also, World Wide Web founder Tim Berners-Lee is working on a project called Solid, with the hopes of reshaping the Web to separate user data from applications, and turn the Web into a read-write tool. Others are working on **fog computing** as the evolution of cloud technology, and incorporating blockchain to decentralize these tools.[126] New technologies grow and iterate in a variety of ways, often meaning they end up requiring new categorization over time, such as the emergence of deep learning and machine learning for Artificial Intelligence. The technology nomenclature and taxonomy will change as its capabilities extend and shift over time. We may soon be talking less about blockchain, and more about decentralized computing fabrics or frameworks.

Blockchain Hardware

One way that blockchain might evolve is through the development of specialized **blockchain hardware**. One company, Gradient, is already working on embedding the ability to generate a private key into the very chips at the heart of every device.[127] Their goal is to solve the trust problem by embedding blockchain cryptography and identity into silicon chips. The private key generator is secure and hidden even from the original manufacturer to avoid fraud. This would mitigate the need for a network of verifying nodes and speed up the processing of transactions. This new type of network, based on the "remote attestation" built into the hardware, does not rely on any consensus mechanisms involving Proof of Work. Cryptographically secure identity is built into the chip and can provide a digital fingerprint for any assets or supply chains. More of these hardware-

---

[126] Sharma, Pradip Kumar and Muyen Chen and Jong Hyuk Park. "A Software Defined Fog Node Based Distributed Blockchain Cloud Architecture for IoT," IEEE Access Volume 6, September 29, 2017, https://ieeexplore.ieee.org/document/8053750

[127] Wentz, Christian. "Introducing Gradient," Medium, August 23, 2018, https://medium.com/gradient-tech/introducing-gradient-715e11be685b

specific projects are underway as the bridge between the real world and the digital world becomes increasingly important for verification and transactions.

Quantum-Resistant Blockchains

Imagine that no passwords currently in existence were safe. And no encryption schemes were unhackable. This could be a fatal blow to the evolution of blockchain which relies heavily on public/private key encryption to ensure its security and anonymity. **Quantum computing** is the threat that looms over not just blockchain security, but the entire architecture of our encrypted world. In a nutshell, quantum computing does not rely on silicon-based technology that we use today. Qubit chips are being developed that manipulate the energy level of atoms to create a vast increase in computing power. Companies such as IBM, Microsoft, Google, and even Alibaba are working on variations of this technology, as are certain governments. Estimates vary between three to ten years as to when this technology will become commercially viable.[128]

Efforts are already underway to make blockchains quantum-resistant. For new and existing blockchain applications such as Bitcoin, new digital signature schemes are being developed to replace the old public key cryptography. These post-quantum signature schemes are based on solving even more complex mathematical problems. Of course, by making the digital signatures larger and more complex, new problems arise around the performance and scalability of blockchains. Scientists at evolutionQ are taking a unique approach to this challenge. They are using the power of quantum computers to create new cryptographic schemes that even quantum computers can't break. This new breed of "quantum cryptography" makes use of new quantum keys that can detect any attempts at eavesdropping and will automatically generate a new quantum key as a deterrent. And so the cryptography race goes on, and the future of blockchains will be tied to these

---

[128] Gheorghiu, Vlad and Sergey Gorbunov, Michele Mosca, and Bill Munson. "Quantum-Proofing The Blockchain," Blockchain Research Institute, November 2017, https://www.evolutionq.com/assets/mosca_quantum-proofing-the-blockchain_blockchain-research-institute.pdf

advances.

Blockchain and AI

One of the other major movements in the world of technology today surrounds the use of **artificial intelligence** (AI). There are major implications for combining blockchain and AI to create a whole new type of application. Wouldn't it be wild if smart contracts could become cognitive? Currently, smart contracts require the use of an **oracle** to determine when the contract terms have been met. This is a feed from the real world into the digital world of external data necessary for triggering events in a smart contract. For example, if a contract stipulated that a travel insurance policy pays out based on a flight delay, an oracle could be the application FlightAware which updates flight status and details. In the future, oracles might not be feeds but rather intelligent agents that could take over this duty.

What Is AI?

The basic concept of AI is that we use computer technology to mimic various intelligent behaviors. This includes learning, reasoning, vision, movement, hearing, speech, and smell. If you have asked a question from Siri via your iPhone or Amazon's Echo in your home, then you are already experiencing one type of AI application, based on voice recognition and natural language processing. Other successful applications of AI have been used to detect credit card fraud and eliminate spam emails. Though these technologies have been around for a number of years, only recently has the quality and volume of data available for AI applications grown enough to start becoming more robust. Machine Learning is a subset of AI, and usually requires large data sets which are used to train learning algorithms. Today, especially in the corporate world, interest in all kinds of new AI applications is very high, and new applications are being developed across all functional areas of business.

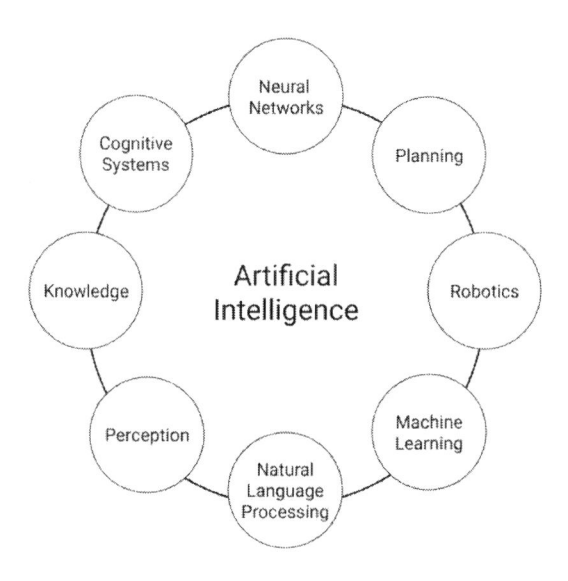

Figure 6-3: Domains within artificial intelligence

One of the things that blockchains do well is to verify and secure data. This quality creates a natural link between the two technologies: infrastructure and auditing can meet intelligence. On the one hand, AI techniques could also be used to make blockchain applications "smart," as in the smart oracle example mentioned above. Additionally, because blockchain mining takes so much energy, AI could be used to optimize the energy consumption of the mining process. It also could be used to learn techniques to make the data sharding process more efficient across nodes in a blockchain. On the other hand, AI can benefit from blockchain architecture as well. The trust-minimization of a blockchain architecture creates the rules and context in which smart machines, robots, and algorithms can perform transactions more autonomously. Especially as large data set computing is increasingly performed in the cloud on platforms like Azure or AWS, some researchers believe blockchain can act as a computational log of all the steps being performed so that checking the work of these outsourced machine learning structures is possible. That's the concept behind BlockSci, an open-source project by Princeton's Center for Information Technology Policy, which allows you to analyze blockchains more easily.[129] In the future, AI learning tools could also be combined with the decentralization of blockchain to create **federated learning systems** from the machine learning field.[130] This posits a future of virtual agents that can create, operate, and maintain new ledgers!

A particular use case we are fond of is for AI to be embedded in smart contracts to help manage IoT connections. The tutorial section offered at the end of this chapter shows how you can embed a basic regression algorithm along with data in a smart contract. Going forward, the ability to use blockchain to offer a portable identity management framework may help open up data sets for more machine learning applications. This is something of high importance, especially in the healthcare industry. By using verified data from a blockchain which can be audited, this could improve the reputation of AI overall, and remove fears around the traceability of computations or data sources.

Ultimately, the biggest impact that blockchain can have on AI is to enable it to function in a decentralized manner. For the most part, AI technologies in the past have been created to run on a centralized device or server. Data scientist, Francesco Corea, has categorized these various AI and blockchain initiatives into the following areas:[131]

- **Decentralized intelligence** – where AI tools and techniques actually run on the blockchain are used to gather data and enable interconnected devices. They could be given a variety of intelligent skills such as voice recognition, vision, and the ability to reason and even negotiate. They could become "smart objects." One of the leading startups in this area is SingularityNet. They are also the creators of the famous Sophia robot, whose social skills continue to

---

[129] Kalodner, Harry. "BlockSci: a platform for blockchain science and exploration," Freedom to Tinker, September 11, 2017, https://freedom-to-tinker.com/2017/09/11/blocksci-a-platform-for-blockchain-science-and-exploration/

[130] Corea, Francesco. "The convergence of AI and Blockchain: what's the deal?" Medium, December 1, 2017, https://medium.com/@Francesco_AI/the-convergence-of-ai-and-blockchain-whats-the-deal-60c618e3accc

[131] Corea, Francesco. "The convergence of AI and Blockchain: what's the deal?" Medium, December 1, 2017, https://medium.com/@Francesco_AI/the-convergence-of-ai-and-blockchain-whats-the-deal-60c618e3accc

grow.

- **Prediction Platform** – Augur uses blockchain and AI to make predictions about everything from elections to stock prices. Users can propose a topic for prediction and access the collective knowledge of the blockchain participants.

- **Conversational Platform** – This is where sophisticated chatbots are created for various industries such as healthcare and home energy advising. This is of special interest for financial services too. SingularityNet and Talla are two of the leading firms in developing these types of applications.

- **Provenance** – These intelligent agents actually search blockchain data for potential fraud related to fake goods and information. Two startups working on this problem are KapeIQ and Priops. You could also imagine intelligent supply chains running in conjunction with blockchain technology. They will use machine-learning to collect data, analyze it, and make decisions to make supply and demand more equal through autonomous transactions.

Recently, it was reported that traders had created bots targeting the crypto markets.[132] Since there is little oversight in these markets, they are ripe for manipulation. Some traders have developed AI bot programs that look for arbitrage opportunities between different cryptocurrencies. These bots will place large buy or sell orders above or below the current price. This placing of fake orders is called "**spoofing**" and is just one way that traders are using AI tools such as bots to manipulate prices in crypto markets.

Blockchain and Society

Given the breadth and scope of the potential impact of blockchain, it is

---

[132] Vigna, Paul and Alexander Osipovich, "Bots Are Manipulating Price of Bitcoin in 'Wild West of Crypto,'" The Wall Street Journal, October 2, 2018, https://www.wsj.com/articles/the-bots-manipulating-bitcoins-price-1538481600

worthwhile to take the time to consider some of the broader implications of blockchain and our society today. This includes how it is impacting the legal profession, governments, the global economy, and the future of work itself.

Blockchain Revolution and Legal Services

With all of the talk around smart contracts, the legal services industry may be seeing a substantial impact from blockchain integration. Though the impact is still far from clear, the larger, global firms are gearing up now in anticipation of this. The leading area of interest in blockchain for law firms is in "transactional" legal services.[133] These services are focused on blockchain startups and intellectual property, and reflect a recent uptick in blockchain patent applications.

High-value legal services category represent 31% of the interest from law firms, which includes functioning as in-house counsel for larger corporations. And general business support services, representing 21% of firm's plans to use blockchain, relates to tasks such as drafting legal documents and offering legal opinions to businesses.

At this nascent point in the adoption of blockchain by law firms, it is still unclear how it will disrupt the industry. Much of the legal work on blockchain today is with R&D organizations which are often operating on new blockchain applications in stealth mode. One of the use cases of most interest to law firms is how blockchain can be used to track intellectual property rights. This is especially difficult when calculating royalty payments for streaming media. Blockchain's ability to track ownership is also important for disentangling other property ownership legal issues.

Once smart contracts take hold in the industry, the need for commercial and dispute resolution services will gradually disappear or significantly change in

---

[133] "Time for Change, PwC Law Firms' Survey 2017," PriceWaterhouseCoopers, 2017, https://www.pwc.fr/fr/assets/files/pdf/2017/12/law-firms-survey-report-2017.pdf

scope. The need for lawyers to perform due diligence in reviewing contracts may also be greatly decreased as templates become more standardized. This is partly the goal of LegalZoom's project in collaboration with Clause, Inc to provide tools that extend computable contracting technologies (both blockchain-based and not) to consumers.[134]

Add better AI tools to the mix and this could make paralegals, banking lawyers, and litigation support roles obsolete.[135] But alongside the adoption of blockchain we will see an increased need for lawyers with a technical background – future "lawyer-coders" – to review and structure the best smart contracts. As smart contracts are increasingly linked together to create DAOs and DACs, questions of liability and regulation will have to be tested, including in the court systems. Also, with the rise in asset-based cryptocurrencies, there is a need for lawyers who understand the ins and outs of these growing global markets.

Blockchain and Government

With its emphasis on trust-minimization and security, blockchain would appear to be a perfect fit for government; allowing auditability and accountability to citizens and potentially decreasing corruption. Many countries are already experimenting with it for a variety of governmental services. The U.S., UK, Estonia, Switzerland, and Gibraltar all have blockchain initiatives underway. Dubai has already mandated that every possible government service that could work on a blockchain should be running on blockchain by 2020. Some countries such as China and Russia are viewing blockchain as a national security issue and are investing heavily in it, potentially to have greater understanding and control. Some of the public services being put on blockchain include voting, healthcare records, taxes, and land registries. The UK is using blockchain to track beef in slaughterhouses

---

134 "LegalZoom to Offer Smart Legal Contracts With Clause," PRNewsWire, September 17, 2018, https://www.prnewswire.com/news-releases/legalzoom-to-offer-smart-legal-contracts-with-clause-300713717.html

135. Shah, Sooraj. "How blockchain is revolutionising the legal sector," Raconteur, February 7, 2018, https://www.raconteur.net/risk-management/blockchain-revolutionising-legal-sector

for quality assurance. The EU also has a big initiative to use blockchain to reduce the number of counterfeit products on the market.[136] These are early and small initiatives – mostly in pilot phase – but they are picking up momentum.

Across the U.S. various cities, states, and agencies are working on blockchain as well. The city of Atlanta has announced its intention of becoming a hub for blockchain research and development. At the state level, Illinois also shared its plans for becoming the first blockchain-enabled state government. Delaware, known as a corporate law haven, is pushing to clarify legal frameworks to allow incorporation of blockchain companies in Delaware more easily. Government agencies at all levels purchase many goods, and are working to operate their supply chains on transparent blockchain networks to prevent corruption and help repair the reputations. These goods range from vehicles for the military to furniture and information technology. With confidence in governmental institutions at an all-time low, blockchain-based processes may help restore transparency and accountability.

The e-Stonia Example

Estonia is a small Baltic country of about 1.3 million people. When the Soviet Union collapsed in 1991 and the nation won its independence, fewer than half of Estonians had a basic telephone. But now, by investing in education and technology, the small nation has leapfrogged many developed countries and is providing an example to the world of how new technologies, including blockchain, can improve the way government functions.

Ditching the legacy Soviet systems and the "legacy thinking" it fostered, Estonia took the opportunity of independence to begin with a clean slate. To date, Estonia has the fastest broadband infrastructure and more startups per capita than any country in the world.[137] Most of its citizens pay taxes online,

---

[136] Macaulay, Tom. "How governments around the world are using blockchain," ComputerWorldUK, October 2, 2018, https://www.computerworlduk.com/galleries/applications/how-governments-are-using-blockchain-3680393/

[137] Adams, Colin. "Estonia, A Blockchain Model For Other Countries?," InvestInBlockchain, January 4, 2018, https://www.investinblockchain.com/estonia-blockchain-model/

store health records in the cloud, vote online and store land records on blockchain infrastructure. All schools are fully computerized and children as young as five are taught how to program. This amazing transformation is continuing with new blockchain applications and is providing a potential roadmap for the rest of the world.

> **Blockchain for Voting?**
>
> Public angst over election fraud and accountability is on the rise across the world. And it was probably inevitable that a tool that offered a high level of security and transparency like blockchain would be proposed as a component to a voting solution. While the topic of online voting for elections has been discussed for many years, it has gained new traction with the rise of blockchain. Several blockchain startups such as Democracy Earth Foundation, Milvum, and Follow My Vote have recently proposed a blockchain-based voting scheme. The hope is that blockchain can perform the holy grail of individual privacy protection while creating auditability that helps eliminate fraud or tampering. Some believe it can even increase voter turnout and convenience (say for absentee voting), while also reducing the cost of elections.
>
> West Virginia became the first state in the U.S. to experiment with using blockchain for voting. A small test was run in a primary election where voters were allowed to vote using mobile devices after they used biometric scans of their thumbprints. The votes were validated by a third party and then added to a publicly verifiable blockchain record of all votes.[138] This blockchain use case is certainly not without controversy. For one, third-party involvement is part of what blockchains aim to replace. Additionally, as with any electronic voting system, there is the inherent security concern that since it is electronic, it carries much greater vulnerability for hacking than say, paper ballots, which are relatively secure and auditable. An article in Scientific American pointed out some of the flaws in the argument for using blockchain for voting in elections.[139] This included concerns about the security of the user and device used, as well as the open question of private key management to ensure key loss wouldn't lead to disenfranchisement. Also, since such a voting scheme would likely be built on a hybrid consortium model that didn't rely on a large community of verifiers, there would be the possibility that a few of the validating nodes could corrupt the process. There are many other e-voting solutions that do not make use of blockchain that may be more suitable for managing the whole "end-to-

---

[138] Desouza, Kevin C. and Kiran Kabtta Somvanshi. "How blockchain could improve election transparency," Brookings Institute, May 30, 2108, https://www.brookings.edu/blog/techtank/2018/05/30/how-blockchain-could-improve-election-transparency/

[139] Dunietz, Jesse. "Are Blockchains the Answer for Secure Elections? Probably Not," Scientific American, August 16, 2018, https://www.scientificamerican.com/article/are-blockchains-the-answer-for-secure-elections-probably-not/

end voting" process. For all intents and purposes, a solution to this complex problem is still several years off.

Blockchain and Globalization

In a time of rising nationalism, it may seem odd to contemplate how blockchain is enabling further globalization. Of course, the initial impetus for Bitcoin was to support the sharing of value across the globe without any bank or governmental intervention, connecting global producers and consumers in a new way. The overall architecture of a Dapp, with its backend global network of computers, is also designed to share data by creating a single truth across borders. Even though it represents only a tiny fraction of overall transnational payments, according to people at Davos 2017, it is estimated that by 2027, 10% of the world's GDP will be stored on a blockchain.[140] This rise of cryptocurrencies means that central banks are having a harder time controlling the money supply and fewer tools for actively managing the economy. The biggest difficulties in using blockchain for cross-border transactions stem from possible compliance issues with the various taxing and regulatory agencies involved, as well as limitations of the technology scaling fast enough.

One hope is that blockchain adoption will lead to a true **sharing economy**; especially in lesser-developed countries that could leapfrog the instantiation of large institutional bodies that act as economic middlemen. For example, with a transparent supply chain, it will be easier for creators of value such as growers, to receive appropriate compensation in a timely manner, potentially connecting their wares to a decentralized global marketplace. Another example is the ability to allow the large population of unbanked individuals to participate in the economy both locally and across borders, no matter the quantity of assets under their control. Some economists have floated the idea of a pre-distribution of economic goods via the blockchain as opposed to the redistribution of economic resources. This is often discussed as part of a

---

[140] "Realizing the Potential of Blockchain," World Economic Forum, June 2017, page 30, http://www3.weforum.org/docs/WEF_Realizing_Potential_Blockchain.pdf

broader Universal Basic Income scheme, that poses a potential solution to the changing nature of work due to automation of low-skill jobs.[141]

Blockchain: Job Killer or Opportunity Generator?

Every new technology brings along the inevitable question of whether it will eliminate available jobs or create new ones. There are many examples of jobs that have disappeared because of improvements in technology that led to fundamental shifts in the economy. Economists call this **structural unemployment** as opposed to **frictional unemployment,** which occurs as people move between temporary jobs. Factory workers are being rapidly replaced by robots. Toll booth collectors and switchboard operators are also on the way out. A new generation of autonomous cars and trucks is now threatening to make drivers obsolete. Grocery cashiers may not be far behind. Given the extent of potential disruption stemming from the adoption of blockchain, people are curious about its economic impact on jobs. Can we identify jobs that will become endangered by the general adoption of blockchain?

We already know that blockchain is a way to automate some manual processes that require a third party to validate and manage transactions. But this is all somewhat abstract. Earlier in this chapter, a McKinsey study was cited stating that the industries most impacted by blockchain included insurance, financial services, healthcare and property. Specific jobs that might be impacted in the area of property/real estate might include real estate brokers, mortgage brokers, and title agents. In financial services, any jobs involving payments, banking, and security (as well as back-office work) may be affected.[142] With reduced fraud comes the lessened need for insurance in various industries. Smart contracts may also require less manual oversight and

---

141 Berggruen, Nicolas. "Here's how blockchain can reduce inequality," The Washington Post, January 29, 2018, https://www.washingtonpost.com/news/theworldpost/wp/2018/01/29/blockchain/?noredirect=on&utm_term=.790d53baf381

142 Temple Schrant, Kimberly. "Will Blockchain Impact Jobs? Three Things You Need To Know," Inquisitr, January 6, 2018, https://www.inquisitr.com/4721900/will-blockchain-impact-jobs-three-things-you-need-to-know/

time spent writing contracts and negotiating deals.

Yet, as always, for every taxi driver that has been displaced, there are ten new Uber drivers working in the gig economy. For every movie projectionist job lost, there were thousands more people earning money from posting their own videos on YouTube. Improving the efficiency of financial transactions may lead to an explosion of new financial services focused on fractionalized assets. There are approximately two billion "**unbanked**" people in the world, without any access to banks or financial institutions.[143] In a blockchain-enabled world, micro-investing will make it feasible for people to open accounts and invest with as little as $1.00.[144]

And what happens when Blockchain and AI are combined? Will this impact our current generation of knowledge workers? Blockchain combined with AI has the potential to disrupt legal services and the audit function. But even there, we will likely still have a need for auditors or lawyers to certify smart contracts and to certify that the validators in a permissioned corporate blockchain consortium are doing their jobs. This may even spawn a whole new specialized field. But contrary to other technology disruptions, the combination of AI and blockchain could hit knowledge workers such as accountants, lawyers, insurers, and financial managers harder than it hits manufacturing labor.

While it is still very early in the blockchain lifecycle, whole new industries and business models are already emerging. Greater efficiencies and disintermediation may lead to ride- and home-sharing services to decentralize even further on a blockchain. Amazon, Facebook, and Google are also all looking at how their business models may be undercut or altered by blockchain technologies. Utilities may be bought and sold on a peer-to-peer blockchain network. Who knows what new industries will be enabled by running IoT devices on a blockchain with AI capabilities? Blockchain startups

---

[143] Hodgson, Camilla. "The world's 2 billion unbanked, in 6 charts," Business Insider, August 30, 2017, https://www.businessinsider.com/the-worlds-unbanked-population-in-6-charts-2017-8

[144] Shin, Laura. "Transform Everything From Banking To Government To Our Identities," Forbes, May 26, 2016, https://www.forbes.com/sites/laurashin/2016/05/26/how-the-blockchain-will-transform-everything-from-banking-to-government-to-our-identities/#6fc1f653558e

are being announced almost every day across all industries and VC dollars are flowing into them to bolster their success.

Leadership in a Blockchain World

Whether you are a CFO, entrepreneur, or a state legislator, to be a leader in these times of accelerating technological disruption will require a deeper understanding of where we might be heading. Leaders from all industries need to understand this transition to a more decentralized economy, the key technologies underpinning this shift, and what the impacts might be to their organizations. They need to be thinking about potential gains and losses, potential workforce implications, long-term investment decisions and overall strategy in the context of a decentralized economy.

The disruption from blockchain technology means that leaders will have to abandon "legacy thinking" and adjust the way they currently do business. Since almost every product (whether physical or digital) has a supply chain and is part of a global trade infrastructure, it can be helpful to look at how blockchain might affect supply chains in particular. Leaders in the area of supply chain management will need to manage the flow of actual objects and assets alongside their digital twins within a supply chain. This will likely require collaboration with software engineers more than usual, implementation of smart contracting, and architecting new governance that allows for vendor permissioning and transparency. If a **self-policing asset** governs itself via a smart contract, the business leaders will need to inform the smart contract programmer of the conditions and parameters the asset will use to make decisions. For example, how will an autonomous vehicle interact with a blockchain-based "bill of lading" to perform last-mile delivery for products?

To prepare for supply chain disruption, leaders also need to invest in people who can program decision-making logic and optimize this logic with AI. For example, they might formalize decision-making logic for purchasing and partnering decisions. They can map out industry and provider partnerships for marketplace creation so that there is a workable framework for some of this logic to be built into machines and operations themselves. This may require taking inventory of existing physical capital and to evaluate which portions make sense to repurpose, re-invent, or eliminate.

We also know that the decentralized economy will see a talent shortage of lawyer-coders (smart-contract developers). With the emerging IoT, every smart IoT device will have to be programmed and there will be many companies with armies of smart contract developers programming these devices. There will be a high demand for people with this skill set, and the advent of smart devices will only increase this demand, as well as the demand for necessary secure hardware components. Leaders must also have the skills to consider the legal ramifications and liabilities of smart devices.

Artisans who specialize in some form of design will be the most sought out free agents in the decentralized economy. The decreased need for human intermediaries across the different functions of a supply chain means that the importance of the design function (intellectual property generation) for value creation will increase. Leaders will need to be extremely good at training, sourcing, and managing potential design talent.

The ability to learn and unlearn quickly will be the most coveted skill for people, objects, and entities looking to thrive. Vitalik Buterin, one of the founders of Ethereum, is a well-known polymath. In addition to understanding mathematics, economics, and computing languages, he also speaks several languages and reads ancient Greek and Latin. What attracted him to the study of blockchain initially was the fact that you had to master a wide variety of fields in order to understand it.[145] This begs the question as to how we can develop these skills or hire and train people to have these abilities.

The ability to build coalitions will also become a highly prized leadership quality. This will be especially important in supply chain applications where a dynamic and diverse group of partners must collaborate. Additionally, managing our reputations in the decentralized economy will be imperative: bad actors in supply chains will be represented by unalterable unique digital

---

[145] Tapscott, Don and Alex Tapscott. Blockchain Revolution: How the Technology Behind Bitcoin and other Cryptocurrencies is Changing the World (2nd ed), Penguin Publishing Group, 2018.

tokens in perpetuity.

Naturally, supply chains are not the only realm where we will see change based on technology implementation such as blockchain, AI, and IoT. But it should help us begin to understand where and how roles and responsibilities might shift as future transaction capabilities are further built out into our businesses.

Ethical and Other Issues with Blockchain

Just when you thought there couldn't possibly be any more use cases for blockchain, here comes the field of human genomics. Documenting the genetic sequence of individuals could take "Know Your Customer" applications to a whole new level. And the commercial applications of genetically-personalized products in medicine, but also retail, is likely to grow significantly. If Facebook has figured out how to make money off of the personal data of a profile, just imagine what could be done with the information available from DNA. A new area called blockchain genomics is looking at how blockchain can interface with human genetic information in various ways.

One ambition is to use blockchain technology as a means for securing personal DNA sequences and protecting them from being exploited.[146] While 99.9% of all human DNA is identical across our species, the information in the 0.1% variation can tell geneticists how susceptible we are to diseases or other features that make us unique. Today, many patients willingly sign over access to their DNA to researchers in hopes of finding treatments or cures for rare diseases that do not receive funding for significant research. However, drug companies use that human genomic data to design completely new drug therapies, making a handsome profit that is not shared with research subjects: by 2025 this is expected to generate $27.6 billion. Currently genomic data is stored on proprietary systems, which are not always secure and are also not very portable for research on projects beyond the original scope of a pharmaceutical company or trial.

The hope is that blockchain can tackle some of the challenges in genomic data collection by securing the privacy of the individuals and simultaneously allowing for researchers to have access and monetize that access. Safeguarding personal DNA information is important to patients in part because insurance groups are increasingly paying attention to this data to

---

[146] Huillet, Marie. "Life's Code: Blockchain and the Future of Genomics," Coin Telegraph, September 3, 2018, https://cointelegraph.com/news/lifes-code-blockchain-and-the-future-of-genomics

potentially deny insurance coverage based on pre-existing traits.[147] Additionally, patients may want to control their DNA data themselves, in order to provide access to it more portably and selectively. Therefore, similar to the identity management use case for blockchain, the technology is being viewed as a possible solution to securing and validating genomic data. It even provides a way of monetizing DNA data by issuing digital payments from researchers who make use of your personal DNA code. Several startups in the field of blockchain genomics are already working on applications in this area, such as Nebula Genomics.

One of the obstacles they must overcome is the sheer size of DNA databases, which can contain several petabytes of data. Additionally, many security researchers are concerned about the linkage between biometrics of any kind and blockchain applications, because the sensitivity of this information puts its treatment at a very high standard and key management for individuals and companies is still difficult.

---

[147] Huillet, Marie. "Life's Code: Blockchain and the Future of Genomics," Coin Telegraph, September 3, 2018, https://cointelegraph.com/news/lifes-code-blockchain-and-the-future-of-genomics

Chapter Summary

It is easy to get caught up in the excitement of blockchain as an emerging technology. In this chapter, several studies and blockchain maturity models were presented which show that blockchain is still in the early stages of adoption. Many firms are just beginning to develop use cases and explore different applications. However, the general adoption of blockchain technology is being held back by uncertainty over regulations and perceptions that it is the domain of illicit activity. Other barriers to adoption include issues of scalability and the cost of mining and developing newer validation and governance protocols. The thing that many critics seem to overlook, is that these issues are being actively researched and worked on by many different researchers and startups. The fact that blockchain is evolving so rapidly even makes writing a textbook on it somewhat challenging!

Some industries such as finance, insurance, banking, and healthcare are going to be impacted more than others early on. One particularly dynamic new area of research involves the combination of blockchain and artificial intelligence (AI). AI attempts to replicate intelligent behaviors such as speech, movement, vision, and reasoning and these features can enable a whole new breed of blockchain applications. Another promising, while maybe surprising, areas for blockchain adoption is in government services. Estonia is leading this initiative by showing how medical records, land records, social services, taxes, and voting can all be run by implementing blockchain applications. These approaches could have the potential to reduce government corruption and restore confidence in these institutions.

While healthy skepticism is important in analyzing a new technology, if current predictions hold true, blockchain will have a major impact on the global economy, the nature of our work, and society in general. A new generation of blockchain leaders and managers with a special set of skills will be needed to bring these applications and many more unknown ones to reality.

Key Terms

Scalability
SegWit
Lightning Network
Sharding
General Data Privacy Regulations (GDPR)
Interoperability
Third-generation blockchain
Fog computing
Blockchain hardware
Quantum computing
Artificial intelligence

Federated learning system
Decentralized intelligence
Prediction platform
Conversational platform
Provenance
Spoofing
Sharing economy
Structural unemployment
Frictional unemployment
Unbanked
Self-policing asset
EVM

Questions for Further Discussion

1. What is a maturity model for blockchain? In which phase of the maturity spectrum would you place blockchain technology today?
2. Describe two major barriers to blockchain adoption. How are these being addressed?
3. How is blockchain evolving?
4. Some governments are claiming that being at the forefront of blockchain research is a national security issue. Would you agree or disagree and why?
5. Go to http://map.bitlegal.io. Which countries are listed as hostile to cryptocurrencies? Some are listed as being "contentious" towards cryptocurrencies. How might this change?
6. What is artificial intelligence? How is it being combined with blockchain technology?
7. Go to http://singularitynet.io. Describe two use cases they are working on that combine AI and blockchain.
8. What is the difference between frictional and structural unemployment? Will blockchain be a job killer or a job creator? Explain.
9. How will blockchain impact the legal services industry? Describe a new job in legal services that will be created by blockchain.
10. What are the potential global impacts of blockchain? Will blockchain increase or decrease economic inequality? Why?

Tutorial: AI and Blockchain

Overview

The following tutorial is designed to illustrate how blockchain and AI might be combined for more advanced applications. This tutorial shows you how to create an advanced smart contract application on the Ethereum platform. It is designed so that anyone, even new users, can work through the steps to get a better feeling of how such an application can work. Having completed it, think about other types of AI applications that could be developed to take advantage of blockchain technologies going forward.

Interactive Example: Using AI to predict coffee sales

As we've mentioned, it's difficult to run the most sophisticated machine learning algorithms directly in the blockchain: the **EVM** won't be learning from cat pictures on the Internet in the near future! However, it's still possible for us to write smart contracts that can learn from data and present what they've learned in a useful way.

Dave, who runs a coffee shop downtown, has recently started accepting ether (ETH) for payments. Customers send ETH to his smart contract and, when the transaction is mined and confirmed, receive piping hot espresso in return. To demonstrate how the contract works, we will be using Remix (https://remix.ethereum.org/), which is an online solidity compiler and Ethereum client for deploying and executing smart contracts. We will run Dave's smart contract code and simulate some transactions. Compiler version used is 0.4.24+commit.e67f0147 and solidity version used is ^0.4.7. Right now, his smart contract looks like this:

Basics of Blockchain

```
contract CoffeeShop {

  address public owner;

  modifier onlyOwner() {
    require (msg.sender == owner);
    _;
  }

  constructor() public {
        _owner = msg.sender;
        }

  function () public payable {
  }

  function withdraw(uint amount) onlyOwner returns(bool) {
    require(amount <= this.balance);
    owner.transfer(amount);
    return true;
  }

  function getBalance() constant returns(uint) {
    return this.balance;
    }
}
```

Figure 6-4: Base Smart Contract for Dave's Coffee Shop

Learning about smart contracts and becoming involved in the Ethereum community has piqued Dave's interest in openness and decentralization. An important part of his business is forecasting sales: since if his sales are growing or shrinking, he will need to respond accordingly. But, even though the Ethereum blockchain provides a tamper-proof record of his sales, investors and suppliers must still trust Dave to produce forecasts.

Let's produce an intelligent smart contract that keeps track of Dave's sales in ETH on a day-by-day basis and predicts his sales for the days to come. First, we'll need to keep track of how much ETH he makes per day:

```
contract CoffeeShop {
###
  address public owner;

  uint dayEarnings;
###
  modifier onlyOwner() {
    require (msg.sender == owner);
    _;
  }
###
  constructor() public {
      owner = msg.sender;
  }
###
  function () public payable {
      dayEarnings += msg.value;
  }
###
  function withdraw(uint amount) onlyOwner returns(bool) {
    require(amount <= this.balance);
    owner.transfer(amount);
    return true;
  }
###
  function getBalance() constant returns(uint) {
    return this.balance;
  }
}
```

Figure 6-5: Dave's Coffee Shop Smart Contract with daily earnings tracking

Let's start learning! Here's the contract we'll use to do our predictions:

```solidity
pragma solidity ^0.4.7;
# # #
contract LinearRegression {

  int256 constant internal ONE = 1000000000000000000;
# # #
  int256 public covariance;
  int256 public variance;
  int256 public numDataPoints;
  int256 public meanX;
  int256 public meanY;
# # #
  function _updateCovariance(
    int256 oldCovariance,
    int256 oldMeanX,
    int256 oldMeanY,
    int256 x,
    int256 y,
    int256 newNumDataPoints
  ) internal pure returns (int256 newCovariance) {
    require(newNumDataPoints > 1);
    int256 scaledUpdateFactor =

      ((x - oldMeanX) * (y - oldMeanY) / ONE);
    return oldCovariance +

      ((newNumDataPoints - 1) * scaledUpdateFactor / newNumDataPoints);
  }

  function _updateVariance(
    int256 oldVariance,
    int256 oldMean,
    int256 newMean,
    int256 x
  ) internal pure returns (int256 newVariance) {
    return oldVariance + (((x - oldMean) * (x - newMean)) / ONE);
  }

  function _updateMean(int256 oldMean, int256 x, int256 newNumDataPoints)
```

```
  internal pure returns (int256 newMean) {
    require(newNumDataPoints > 1);
    return oldMean + ((x - oldMean) / newNumDataPoints);
  }

  function predict(int256 x) external view returns (int256 predictedY) {
    require(numDataPoints > 1);
    return ((covariance * (x - meanX)) / variance) + meanY;
  }

  function addTrainingPoint(int256 x, int256 y) external {
    numDataPoints = numDataPoints + 1;
    if (numDataPoints > 1) {
      covariance = _updateCovariance(

        covariance, meanX, meanY, x, y, numDataPoints);
      int256 newMeanX = _updateMean(meanX, x, numDataPoints);
      variance = _updateVariance(variance, meanX, newMeanX, x);
      require(variance != 0);
      meanX = newMeanX;
      meanY = _updateMean(meanY, y, numDataPoints);
    } else {
      meanX = x;
      meanY = y;
      covariance = 0;
      variance = 0;
    }
  }
}
```

Figure 6-6: "AI" Smart Contract uses an algorithm called "linear regression" to learn from data and make predictions

This contract finds the straight line that gives the "best" fit to a collection of points (x, y). Here x will represent the number of the day Dave received ether on, and y will represent the amount of ether.

There is a tricky caveat with this contract: the mathematics of linear regression require that numbers can be divided into fractional parts. Solidity as a programming language doesn't support this yet. Therefore, in order to make this contract work we have to fake decimals the way token contracts and ether itself does: by representing 1 as 1e18 (1 with 18 zeros).

```solidity
pragma solidity ^0.4.7;
###
import "./LinearRegression.sol";
###
contract CoffeeShop {
###
  address public owner;
###
  uint dayEarnings;
###
  // We'll use this to keep track of whether a given day has been sent to addTrainingPoint
  // in linearRegression.
  mapping(uint256 => bool) public dayRecordedInLinearRegression;
###
  LinearRegression public linearRegression;
###
  modifier onlyOwner() {
    require (msg.sender == owner);
    _;
  }
###
  constructor() public {
        owner = msg.sender;
        linearRegression = new LinearRegression();
        }
###
  function () public payable {
        dayEarnings += msg.value;
  }
###
  function withdraw(uint256 amount) public onlyOwner returns(bool) {
    require(amount <= address(this).balance);
    owner.transfer(amount);
    return true;
```

```
}
###
  function getBalance() public view returns(uint) {
    return address(this).balance;
  }
###
  // Send the total amount for a given day to the linear regression contract.
  function submitTotalForDay(uint256 dayNumber) public {
        require(dayRecordedInLinearRegression[dayNumber] == false);
  // The total should not have been submitted already.
        // Remember that the numbers going in to linearRegression get
  divided by 1000000000000000000.
        // We don't need to do anything to dayEarnings--the division
  converts the amount to eth.
        linearRegression.addTrainingPoint(

    int256(dayNumber * 1000000000000000000),

    int256(dayEarnings)

  );
        dayRecordedInLinearRegression[dayNumber] = true;
        dayEarnings = 0;
  }

  function predict(int256 day)

  public view returns (int256 totalPredictedSales) {
    return linearRegression.predict(day * 1000000000000000000);
  }
}
```

Figure 6-7: The final Dave's Coffee Shop Smart Contract utilizing the functions from the "AI" Contract

Using the Contract

Customers will be paying for coffee by sending wei to the fallback function of the contract. The contract will store the payments until Dave executes the submitTotalForDay transaction whenever his working day ends. That will trigger the AI to process the earnings for the day and update its internal model.

We will be sending multiple payments to Dave over three days to see how the AI will predict prices on subsequent days. First, deploy the CoffeeShop contract. All our interactions will happen through this contract. To send wei currency to the contract, you have to fill the Value field at the top right-hand side and click the "fallback function." See Figure 6-8.

Let's keep things simple and assume each coffee costs 100 wei. Submit 2 payments for the first day, and then execute submitForTheDay function with value "1". For day 2 submit 3 transactions.

Two days of transactions should be sufficient to start having predictions. You can now click "predict" and observe what the AI will think the cost will be for the following days. The result should be the same as in Figure 6-9.

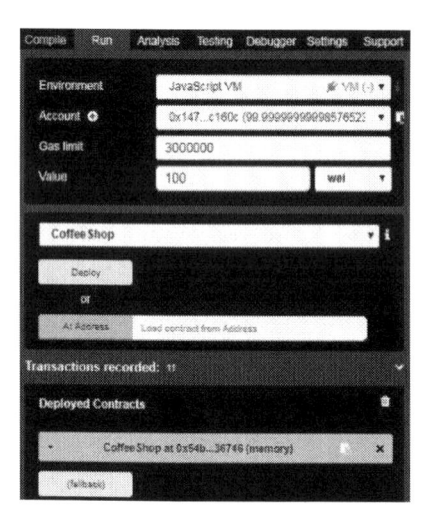

Figure 6-8: You need to set the Value field whenever you want to send wei to a contract

Let's observe how the predictions change if sales drop over the coming day.

For day 3, submit only 1 sale transaction. The predicted value should decrease to 100 for day 4, and 50 for day 5, and become negative for later days, which might seem a little strange. There are two reasons for this. First, the predictions seem a little small considering that for the first 2 days sales have been 2 to 3 times bigger. Second, how is it possible that the prediction consists of sales made from half a coffee? Most AI algorithms used in the industry require vast amounts of data to be able to make consistent and valuable predictions. The model that we used is no different. For Dave to get better predictions over time, he has to keep submitting sales made during each day to the contract. Additionally, our AI looks solely at sales and does not take into consideration the fact that sales are a factor of number of coffees sold. Perhaps, you could help Dave by either updating the AI Contract, or even changing the data learned from sales during a day to be the total number of coffees sold during a day. You should probably try either option and see what happens.

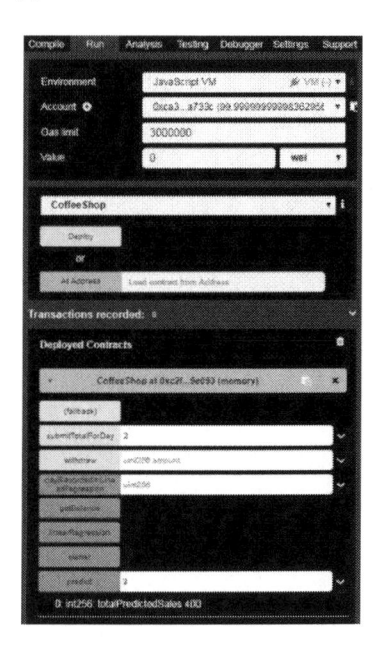

Figure 6-9: Sales predictions for day 3

Final Remarks

We have seen how a contract with AI embedded in it would work in a familiar setting. Some readers may be wondering how this would differ from just simply passing the data to an off-chain AI to perform the calculations. The answer is that an on-chain AI is more trustworthy because it provides complete internal visibility, access controls, and a secure execution model. Off-chain AI would not sufficiently meet such guarantees. This may not be completely obvious (or necessary) for a coffee shop example, but it becomes relevant in more complex settings, where the success of a business hinges on a third-party AI's ability to perform objectively.

One such example includes having a decentralized online service analyze your personal health information and be able to provide helpful advice for treatment and/or diagnostics; without the security and transparency guarantees, such a service could either produce wrong information over time if not properly maintained, or even worse, it could be manipulated by a malicious entity to produce skewed (and potentially harmful) results, such as marketing a cheaper but contraindicated medicine based on your health profile in order to achieve monetary gain.

Another good example is having a similar service that loans you currency based on a very sophisticated personal credit score. If the reasoning engine of the service became compromised, it could serve people unfairly by either denying credit to people who deserve it, or giving more credit to people who wouldn't otherwise be eligible to receive any credit at all!

Basics of Blockchain

Table of Figures

Chapter 1

Figure 1-1: Animal Ventures diagram of Agrarian to digital-era trade. "Agrarian to Digital-Era Trade." Reprinted courtesy of copyright holder. Copyright 2019 by Animal Ventures LLC.
Figure 1-2: *Example of double-entry ledger from J. and H. Hadden and Company Limited*. Reprinted courtesy of copyright holder. "Double-entry ledger from J. and H. Hadden and Company Limited, Hosiers, Nottingham (Ha A 7/2)." *The University of Nottingham*.
Figure 1-3: Visualizing the checkbook analogy of blockchain transactions. "Checkbook Analogy of Blockchain Transactions." Reprinted courtesy of copyright holder. Copyright 2019 by Animal Ventures LLC.
Figure 1-4: Progression to one-to-one trade at scale using blockchain technology. "One-to-one Trade at Scale." Reprinted courtesy of copyright holder. Copyright 2019 by Animal Ventures LLC.
Figure 1-5: Example of a massive organizational chart; army service forces supply. Adapted courtesy of copyright holder. Millet, John D. "The Organization and Role of the Army Service Forces," Center of Military History United States Army, Washington, D.C., 1998. June 13, 2001. Accessed June 12, 2019. https://history.army.mil/books/wwii/ASF/chapter22.htm
Figure 1-6: The rise of the Internet versus company intranets. "The Intranet vs. The Internet." Reprinted courtesy of copyright holder. Copyright 2019 by Animal Ventures LLC.
Figure 1-7: Simplified tech stack of the Internet. "Simplified Tech Stack of the Internet." Reprinted courtesy of copyright holder. Copyright 2019 by Animal Ventures LLC.
Figure 1-8: Features of top blockchain platforms for enterprise. "Enterprise Blockchain Features." Reprinted courtesy of copyright holder. Copyright 2019 by Animal Ventures LLC.

Chapter 2

Figure 2-1: Comparing the Internet and blockchain technology stacks. "Comparing the Internet and Blockchain Technology Stacks." Reprinted courtesy of copyright holder. Copyright 2019 by Animal Ventures LLC.
Figure 2-2: Table of blockchain terminology. "Table of Blockchain Terminology." Reprinted courtesy of copyright holder. Copyright 2019 by Animal Ventures LLC.
Figure 2-3: The many layers of blockchain. Adapted from "On Silos," by Vitalik Buterin, Ethereum Blog, December 30, 2014, https://blog.ethereum.org/2014/12/31/silos/
Figure 2-4: Value creation across the blockchain technology stack. "Value Creation Across the Technology Stack." Adapted courtesy of copyright holder. Copyright 2016 by Animal Ventures LLC.
Figure 2-5: Diagram of transactions on a blockchain. "A Transaction on a Blockchain." Reprinted courtesy of copyright holder. Copyright 2019 by Animal Ventures LLC.
Figure 2-6: Ava's participation options in KoffeeKoin. "Ava's Participation Options in KoffeeKoin." Reprinted courtesy of copyright holder. Copyright 2019 by Animal Ventures LLC.

Figure 2-7: Trezor hardware wallet. "Trezor One by SatoshiLabs." Reprinted courtesy of copyright holder. Copyright 2012-2019 by SatoshiLabs s.r.o., https://trezor.io.

Figure 2-8: First bitcoin transaction with Satoshi Nakamoto's Note. Retrieved August 14, 2019, from https://www.reddit.com/r/Bitcoin/comments/6wru6l/satoshis_vision/. Screenshot by Authors.

Figure 2-9: How text compression works. "Decoding Exercise." Reprinted courtesy of copyright holder. Copyright by Code.org, https://curriculum.code.org/csp-18/unit2/2/

Figure 2-10: SHA-256 demo. Retrieved August 14, 2019 from https://blockchain.adesso.ch/#/sha256. Screenshot by Authors.

Figure 2-11: SHA-256 demo with change to the data input. Retrieved August 14, 2019 from https://blockchain.adesso.ch/#/sha256. Screenshot by Authors.

Figure 2-12: SHA-256 demo with changed nonce value. Retrieved August 14, 2019 from https://blockchain.adesso.ch/#/sha256. Screenshot by Authors.

Figure 2-13: Simplified blockchain. "Simple Blockchain Sequence." Reprinted courtesy of copyright holder. Copyright 2019 by Animal Ventures LLC.

Figure 2-14: Block creation data. Retrieved May 25, 2018 from https://blockchain.info. Screenshot by Authors.

Figure 2-15: Block details. Retrieved May 25, 2018 from https://www.blockchain.com/btc/block-height/524360. Screenshot by Authors.

Figure 2-16: Bitcoin genesis block. Retrieved May 25, 2018 from https://blockchain.info. Screenshot by Authors.

Figure 2-17: Bitcoin mining calculator. Retrieved August 15th, 2019, from https://99bitcoins.com/bitcoin-mining/bitcoin-mining-calculator/. Screenshot by Authors.

Figure 2-18: How IPFS works. Reprinted courtesy of copyright holder. Copyright by Protocol Labs, https://ipfs.io/#how

Chapter 3

Figure 3-1: Simple taxonomy of token classification and usage. "Taxonomy of Tokens." Reprinted courtesy of copyright holder. Copyright 2019 by Animal Ventures LLC.

Figure 3-2: Top ten tokens by market capitalization Summer 2018. Retrieved June 3, 2018 from http://coinmarketcap.com. Screenshot by Authors.

Figure 3-3: Hard and Soft Fork diagram. "Hard and Soft Fork Diagram." Reprinted courtesy of copyright holder. Copyright 2019 by Animal Ventures LLC.

Figure 3-4: "Doge" meme that influenced dogecoin. Reprinted courtesy of Wikimedia Commons. "File: Doge homemade meme.jpg," Wikimedia Commons, CC0 1.0, accessed June 15, 2019 from https://commons.wikimedia.org/wiki/File:Doge_homemade_meme.jpg

Figure 3-5: Analysis of decentralization of top tokens. Retrieved June 15, 2018, from https://AreWeDecentralizedYet.com. Screenshot by Authors.

Figure 3-6: Coinbase exchange. Retrieved August 15th, 2019, from http://www.coinbase.com. Screenshot by Authors.

Figure 3-7: Bitcoin price history. Retrieved June 16, 2018 from https://www.buybitcoinworldwide.com/price/. Screenshot by Authors.

Figure 3-8: Volatility of bitcoin over time. Retrieved June 16, 2018 from https://www.buybitcoinworldwide.com/volatility-index/. Screenshot by Authors.

Figure 3-9: Amberdata analytics. Retrieved August 15th, 2019 from https://amberdata.io. Screenshot by Authors.

Chapter 4

Figure 4-1: Ethereum Foundation logo. Reprinted under Creative Commons Attribution 3.0 Unported license. Retrieved June 18, 2018, from https://www.ethereum.org/assets.

Figure 4-2: Meme on smart contracts. "Smart Contractify All The Things." Reprinted courtesy of copyright holder. Retrieved August 10, 2019 from https://monax.io/blog/2015/04/28/smart-securitisation/

Figure 4-3: Comparing Bitcoin and Ethereum (June 2019). "Comparing Bitcoin and Ethereum (June 2019)." Reprinted courtesy of copyright holder. Copyright 2019 by Animal Ventures LLC.

Figure 4-4: The Remix IDE is a relatively simple and convenient way to build and run Solidity smart contracts. Screenshot by Authors.

Figure 4-5: In the "Compile" tab you can compile your source code and look at compilation details. Screenshot by Authors.

Figure 4-6: Response from Remix after a successful compilation (with no syntax errors). Screenshot by Authors.

Figure 4-7: Response from Remix after an unsuccessful compilation. Screenshot by Authors.

Figure 4-8: The Run Tab. Screenshot by Authors.

Figure 4-9: List of Deployed contracts. Screenshot by Authors.

Figure 4-10: The console will output deployment transaction details. You can click the text output to view these details. Screenshot by Authors.

Figure 4-11: Viewing the values of the Dapp properties. If you view the balance of the account from which you deployed the contract, you can see it owns the entire supply of tokens. Screenshot by Authors.

Figure 4-12: Input values for the transfer function. Screenshot by Authors.

Figure 4-13: The output of the transfer transaction. Among other things, you can observe the address of the owner and the recipient, as well as the amount that was transferred. Screenshot by Authors.

Figure 4-14: Balance of the recipient should be 100. Screenshot by Authors.

Figure 4-15: Downloading MetaMask from Chrome. Screenshot by Authors.

Figure 4-16: Ropsten Test Network View. Screenshot by Authors.

Figure 4-17: Ropsten Test Network Sign In. Screenshot by Authors.

Figure 4-18: View of MetaMask Ether Faucet. Screenshot by Authors.

Figure 4-19: View of transaction being mined. Screenshot by Authors.

Figure 4-20: Environment view on MetaMask. Screenshot by Authors.

Figure 4-21: Transaction confirmation. Screenshot by Authors.

Figure 4-22: Etherscan transaction view. Screenshot by Authors.

Figure 4-23: Pasting token address. Screenshot by Authors.

Figure 4-24: ERC-20 token in action. Screenshot by Authors.

Figure 4-25: View of simple contract. Screenshot by Authors.

Figure 4-26: Contract with TotalSupply variable. Screenshot by Authors.

Figure 4-27: Contract with constructor variable. Screenshot by Authors.

Figure 4-28: Contract with list of balances. Screenshot by Authors.

Figure 4-29: Contract allowing token transfers. Screenshot by Authors.

Chapter 5

Figure 5-1: AV vision exercise. "Animal Ventures Vision Exercise." Reprinted courtesy of copyright holder. Copyright 2019 by Animal Ventures LLC.

Figure 5-2: AV beachhead identification. "Animal Ventures Beachhead Identification Exercise." Reprinted courtesy of copyright holder. Copyright 2019 by Animal Ventures LLC.

Figure 5-3: AV likes to map the technical ecosystem for any beachhead. "Animal Ventures Technical Mapping Exercise." Reprinted courtesy of copyright holder. Copyright 2019 by Animal Ventures LLC.

Figure 5-4: AV uses heat mapping as a way to vet good starting points. "Animal Ventures Heatmapping Exercise." Reprinted courtesy of copyright holder. Copyright 2019 by Animal Ventures LLC.

Figure 5-5: From vision to hypothesis. "Animal Ventures Vision to Hypothesis Exercise." Reprinted courtesy of copyright holder. Copyright 2019 by Animal Ventures LLC.

Figure 5-6: A hypothesis statement format. "Animal Ventures Hypothesis Exercise." Reprinted courtesy of copyright holder. Copyright 2019 by Animal Ventures LLC.

Figure 5-7: AV sketching exercise. "Animal Ventures Movie Headline Exercise." Reprinted courtesy of copyright holder. Copyright 2019 by Animal Ventures LLC.

Figure 5-8: Sample gallery of sketches. "Animal Ventures Sample Sketch Gallery." Reprinted courtesy of copyright holder. Copyright 2019 by Animal Ventures LLC.

Figure 5-9: Dominos for product builds. "Animal Ventures Dominos Diagram." Reprinted courtesy of copyright holder. Copyright 2019 by Animal Ventures LLC.

Figure 5-10: Phases in blockchain development. "Potential Phases in Blockchain Project Development." Reprinted courtesy of copyright holder. Copyright 2019 by Animal Ventures LLC.

Figure 5-11: Characteristics of some popular blockchain development platforms. "Characteristics of Some Popular Blockchain Platforms." Reprinted courtesy of copyright holder. Copyright 2019 by Animal Ventures LLC.

Figure 5-12: Blockchain release stages. "Blockchain Release Stages." Reprinted courtesy of copyright holder. Copyright 2019 by Animal Ventures LLC.

Figure 5-13: Health token use case. "Health Token Use Case." Reprinted courtesy of copyright holder. Copyright 2019 by Animal Ventures LLC.

Figure 5-14: Identity use case for corporations. "Corporate Identity Use Case." Reprinted courtesy of copyright holder. Copyright 2019 by Animal Ventures LLC

Figure 5-15: Industry-wide identity use cases. Adapted courtesy of copyright holder from "White Paper: A Frictionless Future for Identity Management," The Australia Post, December 2016, page 9, https://auspostenterprise.com.au/content/dam/corp/ent-gov/documents/digital-identity-white-paper.pdf

Figure 5-16: Cross-industry asset tracking use cases. "Cross-industry asset tracking use cases." Reprinted courtesy of copyright holder. Copyright 2019 by Animal Ventures LLC.

Figure 5-17: Provenance application for drug traceability. "Drug Traceability Using Blockchain." Reprinted courtesy of copyright holder. Copyright 2019 by Animal Ventures LLC.

Figure 5-18: HVAC service IoT on blockchain use case. "HVAC Blockchain." Reprinted courtesy of copyright holder. Copyright 2019 by Animal Ventures LLC.

Figure 5-19: KYC use case for banking. Adapted courtesy of copyright holder from https://asianbankingandfinance.net/banking-technology/in-focus/how-blockchain-unchained-in-singapore

Basics of Blockchain

Figure 5-20: Blockchain for food supply chain. "Food Supply Chain on a Blockchain." Reprinted courtesy of copyright holder. Copyright 2019 by Animal Ventures LLC.
Figure 5-21: Basic audit use case. "Basic Audit Use Case on a Blockchain." Reprinted courtesy of copyright holder. Copyright 2019 by Animal Ventures LLC.
Figure 5-22: MIT's degree validation blockchain use case. "Sample of MIT Credential." Reprinted courtesy of copyright holder. Copyright 2019 by Animal Ventures LLC.
Figure 5-23: The model file contents of the sample application. Screenshot by Authors.
Figure 5-24: Create a participant using JSON-formatted text. Screenshot by Authors.
Figure 5-25: Submitting a transaction. Screenshot by Authors.
Figure 5-26: Hyperledger Composer Playground main dashboard. Screenshot by Authors.
Figure 5-27: New business network page. Screenshot by Authors.
Figure 5-28: Sample applications. Screenshot by Authors.

Chapter 6

Figure 6-1: Evolution of blockchain innovation. "Evolution of Blockchain Innovation." Reprinted courtesy of copyright holder. Copyright 2019 by Animal Ventures LLC.
Figure 6-2: Blockchain regulation around the world. "Regulation Around the World." CoinDesk's State of Blockchain Q2 2018 Report. Retrieved August 14, 2019 from https://www.coindesk.com/research/state-of-blockchain-q2-2018?slide=72. Screenshot by Authors.
Figure 6-3: Domains within artificial intelligence. "Domains of AI." Reprinted courtesy of copyright holder. Copyright 2019 by Animal Ventures LLC.
Figure 6-4: Base Smart Contract for Dave's Coffee Shop. Screenshot by Authors.
Figure 6-5: Dave's Coffee Shop Smart Contract with daily earnings tracking. Screenshot by Authors.
Figure 6-6: "AI" Smart Contract uses an algorithm called "linear regression" to learn from data and make predictions. Screenshot by Authors.
Figure 6-7: The final Dave's Coffee Shop Smart Contract utilizing the functions from the "AI" Contract. Screenshot by Authors.
Figure 6-8: You need to set the Value field whenever you want to send wei to a contract. Screenshot by Authors.
Figure 6-9: Sales predictions for day 3. Screenshozt by Authors.

Glossary

51% attack – A condition in which more than half the computing power of a blockchain network is controlled by a single malicious miner or group of miners. If the attacker controls 51% of the network that makes them the authority on the network, giving them the power to spend the same coins multiple times, issue transactions that conflict with someone else's or stop someone else's transaction from being confirmed.

Address – Blockchain addresses are used to send or receive transactions on a network. An address usually presents itself as a string of alphanumeric characters.

"Agreed-upon and append-only" – These are two traits in the definition of a blockchain network. Blockchains are agreed-upon databases because blockchain software must stipulate protocols for how participants maintaining the network, come to consensus, or agreement, on the transaction history of the network. The verification process that all the nodes use to come to consensus is important because it replaces the authority held by a central administrator in a traditional database. Blockchain databases are append-only because the transactions being recorded and held locally by each node (or computer) can only be added to, not deleted. Records can be appended to reflect changes and the current state of the network, but the database is, in effect, immutable or permanent.

Application Program Interface (API) – A software intermediary that helps two separate applications communicate with one another. They define methods of communication between various components.

Artificial intelligence (AI) – The capability of a machine to imitate **intelligent** human behavior. These behaviors include reasoning, learning, speech, and movement.

Altcoin – Altcoins are any digital token that exist as an alternative to Bitcoin. Some altcoins are forks of Bitcoin with minor changes to the Proof of Work (POW) algorithm of the Bitcoin blockchain. One of the most prominent altcoins is Litecoin. Litecoin introduces changes to the original Bitcoin protocol such as decreased block generation time, increased maximum number of coins and different hashing algorithm.

ASIC chip – An "Application Specific Integrated Circuit" is a silicon chip specifically designed to do a single task. In the case of Bitcoin, the chips are designed to process SHA-256 hashing problems to mine new bitcoins. ASICs are considered to be much more efficient than conventional hardware (CPUs, GPUs). Using a regular computer for Bitcoin mining is seen as unprofitable and only results in higher electricity bills.

ASIC resistance – Protocols that are configured to resist the advantage given by ASIC mining chips and rigs.

Assassination market – A prediction market where any party can place a bet (using anonymous cryptocurrencies) on the date of death of a given individual, and collect a payoff if they "guess" the date accurately. These kinds of games or markets originated on the Dark Web.

Asset tracking – Asset tracking is using the ability of blockchain to create stored value and create an immutable record of ownership for that value. It is one of the most powerful use cases for blockchain. It could be used for land ownership, vehicles, or even supply chains more broadly.

Atomic swap – Atomic swap is a smart contract technology that enables exchange of one token for another without using centralized intermediaries, such as exchanges. For example, an atomic swap could be an exchange of litecoin for bitcoin.

Beachhead – In the development of a new product, a beachhead is a product entry point. For any given project, you can usually come up with many different beachheads that have different pros and cons associated with them.

BigChainDB – This is a scalable blockchain database. It's designed to merge the best of two worlds: the "traditional" distributed database world and the "traditional" blockchain world.

bitcoin – bitcoin is a cryptocurrency, otherwise known as digital peer-to-peer cash, that is secured by a network rather than a centralized authority. Bitcoin also often refers informally to the blockchain network that uses bitcoin as a cryptocurrency incentive structure. Bitcoin emerged in 2009 after the 2008 publication of a whitepaper by Satoshi Nakamoto. The Bitcoin blockchain represents the first secure and functioning blockchain for peer-to-peer transfers.

BitCore API – Maintained by BitPay, Bitcore is an open-source Node.js library for creating cross platform Bitcoin-enabled applications with a secure payment protocol and private key management. The BitCore API allows a method of Bitcoin integration using JavaScript. The API specifically enables an app to access private or public keys, perform peer-to-peer cryptocurrency transactions, manage networks, handle and convert bitcoin, and more.

Block (Bitcoin) – Data is permanently recorded on the Bitcoin network through files called blocks. A block is a record of some or all of the most recent bitcoin transactions that have not yet been recorded in any prior blocks. New blocks are added to the end of the record (known as the blockchain), and can never be changed or removed once written (although some software will remove them if they are orphaned). Each block memorializes what took place in the minutes before it was created. Each block contains a record of some or all recent transactions and a reference to the block that came immediately before it.

Block explorer – An online tool for exploring the blockchain of a particular crypto-asset/token, where you can watch and follow live all the transactions happening on the blockchain. Block explorers can serve as blockchain analysis and provide information such as total network hash rate, coin supply, transaction growth, etc.

Block header – A block header is used to identify a particular block on an entire blockchain and is hashed repeatedly to create Proof of Work for mining rewards.

Block height – Block height refers to the number of blocks connected together in a blockchain. For example, Height 0, would be the very first block, which is also called the Genesis Block.

Block reward – An amount of cryptocurrency or token a miner receives for processing transactions in a given block. Because creating (or "mining") blocks is so crucial to the security of the Bitcoin network and yet so hard, the Bitcoin protocol includes a mechanism to encourage people to mine: every time a block is added, the miner who found the block is given 12,5 BTC (this number will change at the next halving in 2020) as a block reward.

Blockchain – A blockchain is a *decentralized database that coordinates agreement on an append-only history of transactions across a peer-to-peer network*. Transactions in the network are secured through cryptography, time-stamped and stored in blocks of data that are verified across participating nodes. Each block is chained to previous blocks back to the "genesis" or first block of data and this creates a permanent, immutable history of events that is replicated and stored on each participating node. It is very hard to change this history, since there is no central authority or control for the network.

Basics of Blockchain

Blockchain 2.0 – This is the general term describing the evolutionary phase of blockchain that included smart contracts and distributed applications or Dapps.

Blockchain as a Service (BaaS) – Many large software firms are racing to deploy a version of blockchain that would take advantage of the cloud to create "on demand" blockchain networks. These companies include IBM, Microsoft, SAP, Amazon Web Services, projects like BlockApps, and even the Chinese retail giant Baidu. By hosting the blockchain network in the cloud, software companies can help smaller outfits get up and running on a blockchain quickly without the extreme cost of hiring hard-to-find blockchain developers.

Blockchain genomics – an emerging application of blockchain in genomics research, where blockchain is used to manage people's DNA data. Tokenization allows for controlled access to DNA data for purposes of research and provides for compensation to the individual subjects.

Blockchain hardware – This refers to how some startup companies are embedding blockchain encryption into the actual silicon chips. This will lessen the need for external nodes to verify the identity of the user of the device.

Casper – Consensus algorithm that combines Proof of Work and Proof of Stake. Ethereum is going to use Casper as a transition to Proof of Stake.

Centralized database – This is a database that is located, stored, and maintained in a single location. This location is most often a central computer or database system, for example a desktop or server CPU, or a mainframe computer.

Chaincode – A program that initializes and manages a ledger's state through submitted applications. It is the Hyperledger Fabric equivalent to smart contracts.

Chain linking – Chain linking is the process of connecting two blockchains with each other, thus allowing transactions between the chains to take place. This will allow blockchains like Bitcoin to communicate with other sidechains, allowing the exchange of assets between them.

Client – A server is a connection point for handling client requests such as getting data, while a **client** is software that allows a user to connect to a server and make a request for some kind of service, like retrieving a file.

Cloud mining – Classical crypto-asset mining requires huge investments in hardware and electricity. Cloud mining companies aim to make mining accessible to everybody. People can log in to a website and invest money in the company which already has mining datacenters. The money is managed by the company and it is invested in mining equipment. Investors get a share of the revenue. The disadvantage for the user is that cloud mining has low returns compared to traditional mining.

Coinbase – A secure online platform for buying, selling, transferring, and storing digital currency (a token exchange).

Coinbase API – This is a proprietary API from the Coinbase exchange that is designed to make it easier to integrate bitcoin, bitcoin cash, litecoin and ethereum into both new and existing applications.

Cold storage – This refers to keeping crypto-assets offline. Methods of cold storage include keeping them on a USB drive or other data storage medium in a safe place (e.g. safe deposit box, safe), or on a paper wallet.

Cold wallet – When a wallet is disconnected from the Internet. This prevents hackers from stealing crypto-assets through malware.

Colored coins – In 2013, a project to develop something called "colored coins" began as a way to represent real assets such as cars, real estate, precious metals, and stocks and bonds on the Bitcoin network. A change in the Bitcoin program was made in 2014, which made it possible to "color" a bitcoin by adding notes such as "this represents an ounce of gold" or "this represents a thousand euros."

Community of verifiers – Nodes on a blockchain network that function as verifiers of transactions on the network. In Bitcoin, they are referred to as "miners."

Compile – A compiler is a special program that compiles statements written in a particular programming language and turns them into machine language or "code" that a computer's processor uses.

Confirmation – A confirmation means that a blockchain transaction has been verified by the network. This happens through a process known as mining, in a Proof of Work system (e.g. Bitcoin). Once a transaction is confirmed, it cannot be reversed or double spent. The more confirmations a transaction has, the harder it becomes to perform a double-spend attack.

Consensus protocol – Blockchains use protocols to validate the current state of their data. Consensus algorithms or refer to the protocols used by a blockchain to validate or ensure agreement across their nodes that the data is the same. This is the method by which new data gets chained to older blocks. There are two main ways to come to consensus on a blockchain today: "Proof of Work" and "Proof of Stake," but others will likely emerge over time, as the fields of cryptography and distributed systems architecture evolve.

Consortium blockchain – A consortium blockchain is a blockchain where the consensus process is controlled by a pre-selected set of nodes; for example, one might imagine a consortium of 15 financial institutions, each of which operates a node, and of which ten must sign every block for the block to be valid. The right to read the blockchain may be public or restricted to the participants. There are also hybrid routes such as the root hashes of the blocks being public together with an API that allows members of the public to make a limited number of queries and get back cryptographic proofs of some parts of the blockchain state. These blockchains may be considered "partially decentralized."

Contract account – A special account for storing smart contracts on the Ethereum platform.

Conversational platform – The use of sophisticated chatbots for various industries such as healthcare and home energy advising.

Crypto-anarchist – Crypto-anarchists want to use cryptography to protect against government surveillance and censorship. They associated themselves with blockchain and cryptocurrency technology early in their development out of a desire to develop an alternative to the centralized banking and financial systems. They are similar to extreme libertarians. And by making it difficult to collect taxes and regulate commerce, they are hoping to reduce or even eliminate the power of the state over individuals.

Crypto-assets – Crypto-assets are the broadest concept of value on a blockchain. They are purely digital and transacted in the form of coins or tokens, but can represent anything from a store of value to a means of payment (or medium of exchange), to a physical asset. A useful way to think about all crypto-assets is across three broad categories that have some differences: cryptocurrencies, crypto-commodities, and crypto-tokens.

Crypto-commodities – Commodities are a class of assets that represent raw materials and different goods or things that bring value. Crypto-commodities are not that dissimilar – they are the digital way to represent commodities or physical assets on a blockchain. These tokens are also secured with the time, computational power and cost of electricity that cryptocurrencies like bitcoin require.

Cryptocurrency – A form of digital currency based on mathematics, where encryption techniques are used to regulate the generation of units of currency and verify the transfer of funds. Furthermore, cryptocurrencies operate independently of a central bank.

Cryptocurrency exchange – See Digital Currency Exchange (DCE)

Crypto-economics – Crypto-economics refers to the discipline of designing economic incentives in blockchains that optimize for fault tolerance, and resistance against attack and collusion of participants in the system. These incentives and dis-incentives are tied to a cryptographic token or reward structure.

Crypto-token – See "token."

Cryptographic hash function – The cryptographic hash function is a mathematical algorithm that takes a particular input which can be any kind of digital data (e.g. a password or jpeg file) and produces a single fixed-length output. Some examples of different hash function algorithms are MD5, MD4 or SHA256. The last one is used in the Bitcoin protocol. Main properties: (1) easy to compute hash value for any given message; (2) infeasible to generate a message from its hash except by trying all possible input combinations (brute force attack); (3) infeasible to modify a message without changing the hash; (4) infeasible to find two different messages with the same hash; (5) deterministic so the same message always results in the same hash. Cryptographic hash functions have many information security applications, notably in digital signatures, message authentication codes (MACs), and other forms of authentication. They can also be used as ordinary hash functions, to index data in hash tables, for fingerprinting, to detect duplicate data or uniquely identify files, and as checksums to detect accidental data corruption.

Cryptography – A method for securing communication using code. The main example of cryptography in blockchains is the symmetric-key cryptography used in the Bitcoin network. Bitcoin addresses generated for the wallet have matching private keys that allow for the spending of the cryptocurrency. The corresponding public key coupled with the private key allows funds to be unlocked. This is one example of cryptography in action.

Cryptojacking – Cryptojacking is the secret use of a device to mine crypto-assets. The first widely known attempt for cryptojacking was the torrent tracker Piratebay. They enabled an in-browser mining software so that whenever somebody visits the website, his/her computer will start mining cryptocurrency via the browser. Users started noticing the unusual behavior in their browsers and Piratebay took down the software. There have been many attempts for cryptojacking since then. The easiest way to find out if a computer is mining crypto-assets is to check the resources monitor for unusual CPU behavior or use the debug console of your browser and look for mining scripts. Developers also released Chrome browser extensions to protect users from mining occurring on their devices.

CryptoKitties – A blockchain-based virtual game developed by Axiom Zen that allows players to purchase, collect, breed and sell various types of virtual cats. It represents one of the earliest attempts to deploy blockchain technology for recreational and leisurely purposes, as well as for non-currency digital assets.

Cyberpunk – Cyberpunk is a science fiction genre in which the future world is portrayed as one in which society is largely controlled by computers, at the expense of daily life and social order. Literature, movies and video games of this genre point to a fear that the world may eventually be run solely by computers, including unusual scenarios where nonliving forms take on life-like actions and capabilities. Rebellion against large corporations and established organizations is a key aspect of cyberpunk.

Cypherpunk – A cypherpunk is any activist advocating widespread use of strong cryptography and privacy-enhancing technologies as a route to social and political change.

Darknet – An isolated area of the Internet that uses technology to avoid being searched and indexed. All darknets require specific software installed or network configurations made to access them, such as Tor, which can be accessed via a customized browser from Vidalia (aka the Tor browser bundle), or alternatively via a proxy configured to perform the same function. They are used for file-sharing, illicit goods, computer crime and for hiding political dissidents.

Decentralized application (Dapp) – A Dapp can be thought of as decentralized software – code that gets executed across all the nodes in a given blockchain architecture. A Dapp is very similar to the applications already in use today on smartphones, tablets, or desktops. The main difference is that the code is executed via smart contracts across a blockchain network, and therefore, the code maintains persistence.

Decentralized Autonomous Organizations (DAO/DAC) –Decentralized Autonomous Organizations or Decentralized Autonomous Corporations are a set of smart contracts that interconnect to run an "organization" automatically. We describe this as a "nexus of contracts" or conditional arrangements that combine to define the rules of the organization.

Decentralized Autonomous Supply Chains – An autonomous supply chain should have the capability to process a request to fetch a component from its location and to autonomously deliver this component to a specified delivery point, all without human intervention.

Decentralized database – A decentralized database doesn't have a single location, and instead, pieces of information are stored in different locations which are all connected to each other. Processing of the data in this type of database is distributed between different nodes.

Decentralized exchanges – A decentralized exchange is a set of protocols that allows a user to exchange across tokens with others without using a company in the middle. The centralized exchanges we know today are more readily targeted by attackers since they hold many accounts-worth of tokens at any given time. The functionality of decentralized exchanges is being built, but does not yet rival the centralized versions. They are harder to use and lack the liquidity of the larger, centralized exchanges. In the long run however, they should grow since they are designed to have less down-time, more privacy, and less censorship potential.

Decentralized intelligence – AI running on a blockchain can be thought of as a distributed group of intelligent agents collaborating on various problems. AI can run, train, and even make decisions on local devices in decentralized networks like a blockchain.

Decentralized storage systems – Blockchain projects in decentralized storage are pushing to improve upon existing storage provider services by reducing costs, improving security, or boosting functionality. These Dapps run on the premise that network users can offer their unused storage capacity across desktops, servers, and storage devices in exchange for tokens. This turns storage into a marketplace, where the nodes that store data receive a reward in return for their service. Companies providing decentralized storage Dapps suggest these services will cost a fraction of what centralized storage platforms are offering and can reinvent everything from consumer tools (e.g Dropbox) to enterprise cloud storage (e.g. Box) on alternate infrastructure.

Delegated Proof of Stake – Delegated Proof of Stake (DPoS) is a consensus algorithm maintaining irrefutable agreement on the truth across the network, validating transactions and acting as a form of digital democracy. Delegated Proof of Stake uses real-time voting combined with a social system of reputation to achieve consensus. Every token holder can exercise a degree of influence about what happens on the network.

Dfinity Network – Dfinity is a protocol that seeks to become an "Internet Computer." It was founded in order to address some of the scalability issues around running smart contracts on the Ethereum platform. While improving the execution speed of smart contracts, the network also claims to add more functionality so that longer Dapps can be run on its platform. Dfinity uses Threshold Relay rather than a traditional consensus protocol.

Digital cash – Various groups had been working on ways to create the concept of unique value in cyberspace for many decades. For instance, David Chaum pioneered early work on digital cash with his 1988 product "DigiCash" and Adam Back gave the world Hashcash in 1997. These efforts pre-dated the emergence of bitcoin, though did not solve the double-spend problem.

Digital coin – Representation of a digital asset built on a new blockchain. See also "token."

Digital Currency Exchange (DCE) – A digital currency exchange (DCE) is a market maker who exchanges legal tender for electronic currency, or who exchanges one electronic currency for another. Most exchanges happen online rather than at physical locations. DCEs are also known as crypto or cryptocurrency exchanges.

Digital notarization – A digital fingerprint of a document on a blockchain can be used to prove that the document, containing an idea, for example, was created at a specific point in time. With public/private key technology digital notarization can prove that you were the person that put the document there. Once it is there, any 3rd party can verify that the document was placed there by the person who holds the private key. It is also highly secure and global.

Digital signature – Digital signatures are a unique string of code that a user can produce that can be matched with his/her private key and public key. A recipient of a digitally-signed document can use the digital signature, document, and public key of the owner to prove that the document was signed by the owner and that the document has not been altered in any way.

Digital token – Another term for a digital coin. See "token."

Directed Acyclic Graph (DAG) – In mathematics, particularly graph theory, and computer science, a directed acyclic graph is a finite directed graph with no directed cycles. That is, it consists of finitely many vertices and edges (also called arcs), with each edge directed from one vertex to another. DAGs can model many different kinds of information. For example, a spreadsheet can be modeled as a DAG, with a vertex for each cell and an edge whenever the formula in one cell uses the value from another; a topological ordering of this DAG can be used to update all cell values when the spreadsheet is changed.

Distributed database – An additional form of information architecture is a distributed database, where all the nodes on the network contain information and they are equal and have equal rights. Blockchains are intermittently referred to as both decentralized and distributed, since they often have both qualities (independent nodes and full replication and rights).

Distributed Ledger Technology (DLT) – Distributed ledgers are a type of database that are spread across multiple sites, countries or institutions. Records are stored one after the other in a continuous ledger. Distributed ledger data can be either "permissioned" or "unpermissioned" to control who can view it.

Double-entry bookkeeping/accounting – This system of recording financial transactions dates back to 1340 CE when Italian bankers in the cities of Genoa and Florence began using this technique. It was a huge step forward because it provided an error detection mechanism for accounts. By making sure that the debits on the left side equaled the credits on the right, this ensured transparency for all stakeholders and allowed them to quickly see an accurate picture of a firm's financial performance at any point in time. 500 years later double-entry bookkeeping is still widely employed and is often credited with enabling the expansion of commerce during the Industrial Revolution and beyond.

Double-spend problem – This is the original problem that the Bitcoin blockchain solved allowing the creation of digital cash. The problem before Bitcoin was the inability to guarantee that someone making a purchase/transaction with digital cash would not be able to turn around and reuse the same tokens/asset to purchase again.

Edge computing – This is a distributed computing paradigm in which computation is largely or completely performed on distributed device nodes known as "smart devices" or "edge devices," as opposed to primarily taking place in a centralized cloud environment.

ERC-20 – This acronym stands for Ethereum Request for Comment followed by the assignment number. It is a technical standard for smart contracts that the majority of Ethereum tokens follow. This particular standard describes basic functions and events that a token contract built on Ethereum must have. It allows other people's Dapps to interact with a network's token contract, which is why it has been used by a large percentage of recent ICOs in raising funds for a project.

Ethash – Ethash is the Proof of Work function in Ethereum-based blockchain tokens. It uses Keccak, a hash function eventually standardized to SHA-3. These two are different, and should not be confused. Since version 1.0, Ethash has been designed to be ASIC-resistant via memory-hardness (harder to implement in special ASIC chips) and easily verifiable.

Ether – The primary native cryptographic token of the Ethereum network. Ether is used to pay transaction and computation fees for Ethereum transactions.

Ethereum – The Ethereum Project was one of the first blockchain networks developed as a more general-purpose blockchain. The project is run by the Ethereum Foundation and has the goal of growing into an ecosystem that functions as a worldwide trust-free decentralized computer. The network uses smart contracts, and in order to execute those contracts, a user needs to buy enough "ether" (gas for the network) which is the token that pays for the computing power needed to execute a contract. This helps guarantee the network is not spammed by infinitely running smart contracts or decentralized applications. Ethereum currently uses Proof of Work as its consensus mechanism, but is looking to switch to Proof of Stake.

Ethereum Foundation – The Ethereum Foundation's mission is to promote and support the Ethereum platform and base layer research, development and education to bring decentralized protocols and tools to the world that empower developers to produce next generation decentralized applications (Dapps). It is officially based in Switzerland.

Ethereum Improvement Proposal (EIP) – An EIP is a design document providing information to the Ethereum community, or describing a new feature for Ethereum or its processes or environment. The EIP should provide a concise technical specification of the feature and a rationale for the feature.

Ethereum Virtual Machine (EVM) – The Ethereum Virtual Machine (EVM) is Turing-complete and allows anyone, anywhere to execute arbitrary EVM Byte Code. All Ethereum nodes run on the EVM. The project is designed to prevent denial-of-service attacks. It is home to smart contracts based on the Ethereum blockchain.

Exchange – A place to buy and sell crypto-assets. In many cases an exchange charges fees for transactions, withdrawals, or deposits. Exchanges are a way to link a user's fiat funds to a location where the user can purchase crypto-assets/currencies. There are centralized exchanges for cryptocurrency (e.g. Coinbase) and there are decentralized exchanges that do not have a central authority or company.

Exchange trading – Looking at how many exchanges are supporting a token, and how trading is dispersed among them. This can be a metric used to help evaluate the value of a crypto-asset.

Externally-Owned Accounts (EOA) – Externally owned accounts contain a balance and are capable of sending transactions in the Ethereum network. Most importantly, an external account has no code associated with it. In contrast, a contract account is not controlled by a person and can store contract code.

Federated Byzantine Agreement (FBA) – In the Federated Byzantine Agreement protocol, each validator decides which other validators they trust. This creates a "quorum slice" which then overlaps with other slices on the network.

Federated learning – This is a machine learning setting where the goal is to train a high-quality centralized model with training data distributed over a large number of clients, each with unreliable and relatively slow network connections.

Federated protocol – This protocol is a mechanism to ensure that all participants in a network agree on a single transaction log. This consensus protocol is designed to be practically useful under a certain set of requirements and assumptions commonly encountered in permissioned blockchain networks.

Fiat money – Any money declared by a government to be valid for meeting a financial obligation, like USD or EUR.

Field Programmable Gate Arrays (FPGAs) – FPGAs were introduced to hardware in 2011 because they were faster, and required about one third the power to run as GPUs for high-powered machines performing computations.

Fog computing – Also known as fogging, this is an architecture that uses edge devices to carry out a substantial amount of computation, storage, and communication locally, and route it over the Internet backbone.

FOMO – An acronym that stands for "fear of missing out" and in the context of investing, refers to the feeling of apprehension for missing out on a potentially profitable investment opportunity and regretting it later.

Fork – The creation of an ongoing alternative version of a blockchain, by creating two blocks simultaneously on different parts of the network. This creates two parallel blockchains, where one of the two is the winning blockchain. The winning blockchain gets determined by its users, by the majority choosing on which blockchain their clients should be listening.

Frictional unemployment – This is the unemployment which occurs as people move between temporary jobs.

Fungibility – Fungibility is the quality of an item that makes it identical to another of the same kind. That means that one unit of a good is interchangeable with another. In economics, fungibility is considered one of the essential qualities of sound money.

FUD – An acronym that stands for "fear, uncertainty and doubt." It is a strategy to influence perception by spreading negative, misleading or false information about something, as opposed to reasoned criticism.

Gas – Gas is a measurement roughly equivalent to computational steps (for Ethereum). Every transaction is required to include a gas limit and a fee that it is willing to pay per gas; miners have the choice of including the transaction and collecting the fee or not. Every operation has a gas expenditure; for most operations it is ~3–10, although some expensive operations have expenditures up to 700 and a transaction itself has an expenditure of 21000.

General Data Protection Regulations (GDPR) – This is a new set of rules designed to give European Union citizens more control over their personal data.

Genesis block – The very first block in a blockchain.

Governance (for blockchains) – The administration in a blockchain network that decides the direction and rules of the company. This can be the social structures as well as the technical structures in place for making changes to a network.

Halving – A reduction in the block reward given to crypto-asset miners once a certain number of blocks have been mined. The Bitcoin block mining reward halves every 210,000 blocks.

Hard fork – A hard fork is a change to the blockchain protocol that makes previously invalid blocks/transactions valid, and therefore requires all users to upgrade their clients. The most recent example of a hard fork in public blockchains is the split between Bitcoin Classic and Bitcoin Cash. Ethereum also faced a hard fork which happened on July 21st, 2016, leading to the existence of both Ethereum (ETH) and Ethereum Classic, (ETC) which supports the old Ethereum protocol.

Hardware wallet – A physical device that allows you to interact with a computer that's connected to the Internet, yet still maintains a cold wallet by isolating the private keys. For the most part, these wallets are considered secure.

Hash function – A function that takes an input and outputs an alphanumeric string known as the "hash value" or "digital fingerprint." The hash is used to confirm coin transactions on a blockchain. Each block in a blockchain contains the hash value that validated the transaction before it and its own hash value.

Hashing – A one-way (non-invertible) function that maps a set of inputs to a set of outputs.

Hash chains – These are a cryptographic concept that allows for a recorded chronology of events (think of how GitHub runs its chronological versioning).

Hashrate – The number of hashes that can be performed by a Bitcoin miner in a given period of time (usually a second).

Hash value – A hash value is a numeric value of a fixed length that uniquely identifies data. Hash values represent large amounts of data as much smaller numeric values, so they are used with digital signatures. You can sign a hash value more efficiently than signing the larger value.

"History of transactions" – This is one of the traits in our definition of a blockchain. All of the transactions stored in a blockchain are visible to all of its participants. The events that have occurred in a network create a history of transactions that is easy to see because each transaction is "time-stamped." This time-stamping feature is part of the chronology of blocks and is crucial for allowing participants to accurately verify transactions.

Hot wallet – When a user's wallet is directly connected to the Internet 24/7. This is risky because it opens a user up to the potential of hackers stealing their coins.

Hyperledger – Started by the Linux Foundation, Hyperledger is an umbrella project of open-source blockchain software.

Hyperledger Composer – Hyperledger Composer is a Blockchain Application Development framework which simplifies the blockchain application development on Hyperledger Fabric.

Hyperledger Fabric – Hyperledger project hosted by Linux which hosts smart contracts called Chaincode.

Hypothesis – As with scientific inquiry in general, generating a hypothesis – or testable statement – is important for all product development. It is the statement or assumption that product iterations should test against. Verifying or falsifying a hypothesis gives you important data about the direction of your product.

Identity and Access Management (IAM) – Identity and access management is about defining and managing the roles and access privileges of individual network users and the circumstances in which users are granted (or denied) those privileges. Those users might be customers (customer identity management) or employees (employee identity management) or even citizens.

Immutability – An inability to be altered or changed over time. For blockchains, this refers to a ledger's inability to be changed by a single administrator or user. Rather than "deleting" information from a blockchain, information can be appended, or a fork can take place that changes the network going forward.

Initial Coin Offering (ICO) – ICOs are types of crowdfunding mechanisms conducted on a blockchain. Originally, the main idea of an ICO was to fund new projects by pre-selling tokens to investors interested in the project. Entrepreneurs often presented a whitepaper describing the business model and the technical specifications of a project before the ICO. They would lay out a timeline for the project and set a target budget where they describe the future funds spending (marketing, R&D, etc.) as well as token distribution (how many tokens are they going to keep for themselves, token supply, etc.). During the crowdfunding campaign, investors would purchase tokens with already established crypto-assets like bitcoin and ether. ICOs are a regulatory gray area, and are under scrutiny from the U.S. SEC.

Integrated Development Environment (IDE) – An application for software developers that primarily consists of a source code editor, build automation tool, and debugger.

Intelligent DAO – A combination of artificial intelligence on top of a decentralized autonomous organization. Intelligent agents could improve the decision-making of a DAO.

Internet of Value – This is sometimes what people call a blockchain-enabled Internet. Rather than only transacting information (messages sent back and forth) as our Internet does, blockchain technology unlocks unique value transfer digitally.

Internet of Things (IoT) – The Internet of Things is a system of interrelated computing devices, mechanical and digital machines, objects, animals or people that are provided with unique identifiers (UIDs) and the ability to transfer data over a network without requiring human-to-human or human-to-computer interaction.

Interoperability – Blockchain networks and crypto-assets are often isolated from one another, and need to be exchanged in order to be used. Blockchain projects like Cosmos, Polkadot, and Aion are looking to solve the interoperability piece by making different blockchains interoperable, or compatible with one another. This is especially important for smart contract

Interplanetary File System (IPFS) – The InterPlanetary File System is a hypermedia distribution protocol, addressed by content and identities. IPFS enables the creation of completely distributed applications. It aims to make the Web faster, safer, and more open. IPFS is an open-source project developed by the team at Interplanetary Networks and many contributors from the open-source community. It is a peer-to-peer distributed file system that seeks to connect all computing devices with the same system of files. In some ways, IPFS is similar to the Web, but IPFS could be seen as a single BitTorrent swarm, exchanging objects within one Git repository. In other words, IPFS provides a high throughput content-addressed block storage model, with content-addressed hyperlinks. This forms a generalized Merkle

DAG, a data structure upon which one can build versioned file systems, blockchains, and even a Permanent Web. IPFS combines a distributed hash table, an incentivized block exchange, and a self-certifying namespace. IPFS claims to have no single point of failure, and nodes do not need to trust one another.

IOTA – Refers to the token as well as the name of its open-source distributed ledger founded in 2015, that does not use blockchain (it uses a new distributed ledger called the "Tangle"). IOTA claims to offer features such as zero fees, scalability, fast and secure transactions, and so on. It is focused on the Internet of Things. It is based on the mathematical concept of the directed acyclic graph or DAG.

Key Performance Indicator (KPI) – a KPI is the indicator used to help measure the success of a project or hypothesis. It is often chosen ahead of time, in order to help orient evaluate a project using objective performance data.

Know Your Customer (KYC) – KYC is the process of a business identifying and verifying the identity of its clients. The term is also used to refer to the banking and anti-money laundering regulations which governs these activities. Almost all exchanges nowadays are expected to have this protocol implemented.

Latency – Latency is a networking term to describe the total time it takes a data packet to travel from one node to another. In other contexts, when a data packet is transmitted and returned back to its source, the total time for the round trip is known as latency. Latency is cited as a problem that many are trying to improve to advance the performance of a blockchain.

Layer 1 / Layer 2 – Blockchain layers describe some of the different functionalities as well as where and how to innovate for scalability. Base consensus protocols for networks like Bitcoin and Ethereum are considered Layer 1. Layer 2 approaches try to do more with the existing capacity of a network, rather than trying to increase the base consensus protocol's capacity. These approaches live "on top of" Layer 1, and are implemented as software that interacts with Layer 1 through smart contracts. Basically, Layer 2 solutions extend the utility of blockchains (bringing lower transaction costs and greater speed) by referring back to the security and finality of operations on Layer 1

Lightning Network – Lightning Network is an off-chain solution that can settle transactions without having to use the underlying blockchain. It opens up bidirectional payment channels between different individuals, allowing Bitcoin to process many more transactions per second.

Machine learning – Machine learning is a field of artificial intelligence that uses statistical techniques to give computer systems the ability to "learn" (e.g., progressively improve performance on a specific task) from data, without being explicitly programmed.

Maturity model – In the world of computing, a maturity model is an attempt to capture the current state of evolution of a particular technology such as blockchain or VR. These states usually range from "emerging" to "general adoption" and "usage."

Medium of Exchange – A standardized instrument or system that facilitates the purchase, sale, or exchange of goods between parties.

Merkle tree – A data structure used in cryptography and computer science that leverages a "tree" in which every leaf node is labelled with the hash of a data block and every non-leaf node is labelled with the cryptographic hash of the labels of its child nodes.

MetaMask – Is a tool that allows a user to view and run Ethereum Dapps in a browser without running a full Ethereum node. This helps simplify the overall development process.

Miner/Mining – Miners run nodes of a blockchain and are rewarded for validating the state of the blockchain. Usually the reward comes from mining, the process by which these nodes aggregate transactions to form a block.

Mining difficulty – Mining difficulty measures how hard it would be to find the next block. Every Proof of Work consensus algorithm has a mining difficulty which is also adjustable. Depending on how many miners join the network the difficulty might rise or fall. The aim of the difficulty is to keep the block times even and make the network secure. The average time for finding a Bitcoin block is set for 10 minutes. Litecoin is set for 2.5 minutes.

Mining pool – In a mining pool, different users organize together in order to provide computing power for a network. If, for example, a Bitcoin block is newly created, each of the users in the mining pool receives its fair share proportionately to his/her mining power. To become a member of a mining pool, a user needs to run software provided by the mining pool. The advantage of the mining pool is that block rewards get distributed across the pool providing more stable income.

Mining profitability – A measurement of the number of big and small miners and their profitability to help evaluate a crypto-asset's value.

Mining rig – A computer especially designed for processing Proof of Work blockchains (such as Ethereum) often consisting of multiple high-end Graphic Processing Units (GPUs) to maximize their processing power.

Monero (XMR) – Monero is a type of crypto-asset created in 2014 that is focused on privacy and scalability, and runs on platforms like Windows, Mac, Linux and Android. Transactions on Monero are designed to be untraceable to any particular user or real-world identity.

Moore's Law – The notion that our computing power doubles roughly every 12-18 months through IT development and advances.

Native token – Also called native coin or currency, is a token (see "token" for a definition) that runs on its own blockchain and is "native" to that network, offering some greater utilitarian or resourceful value within the network. Native tokens are often used within the network as an incentive for block validation or for a form of spam prevention in transaction costs. Examples of native tokens include BTC, ETH, NXT, etc. Native tokens are also referred to as "intrinsic tokens" or "built-in tokens."

NEO (NEO) – Refers to the crypto-asset and the name of China's first open-source blockchain that was founded in 2014 by Da Hongfei. It is similar to Ethereum in its ability to execute smart contracts or Dapps but has some technical differences such as coding language compatibility.

Network tokens – Network tokens are a broad category that encapsulates tokens created by their network, rather than by a Dapp. Usually you need these tokens to install software, run software, store data, pay for computation, or participate in governance on a given blockchain network.

Network Value to Transactions Ratio (NVT) – This measures the currencies market cap relative to daily transaction volume as a way to measure the value of a cryptocurrency.

New Institutional Economics (NIE) – New Institutional Economics is an economic perspective that attempts to extend economics by focusing on the social and legal norms and rules (which are institutions) that underlie economic activity, and with analysis beyond earlier institutional economics and neoclassical economics.

Node (full) – Any computer that connects to a blockchain network is called a node. Nodes that fully enforce all of the rules of the blockchain (e.g. Bitcoin) are called full nodes. Most nodes on the network are lightweight nodes instead of full nodes, but full nodes form the backbone of the network.

Nonce – A number only used once in a cryptographic communication (often includes a time-stamp).

Off-chain – Off-chain transactions refer to those transactions which move the value outside of a blockchain. Often, off-chain transactions will eventually settle on the original blockchain network chain.

On-chain – On-chain transactions refer to those transactions which occur on a blockchain – that is, recorded transactions of a blockchain – and remain dependent on the state of the blockchain for their validity.

OpenChain – OpenChain is an open-source distributed ledger technology. It claims to be suited for organizations wishing to issue and manage digital assets in a robust, secure and scalable way. Some features include instant confirmations, no mining fees, and security and scalability.

Oracle – Smart contracts on a blockchain cannot access the outside network on their own. Therefore, oracles sit between a smart contract and the external world, providing the data needed by a smart contract to prove performance while sending its commands to external systems. These are often thought of as external data feeds to a blockchain network.

Peer-to-peer (P2) network – The decentralized interactions that happen between at least two parties in a highly interconnected network. P2P participants deal directly with each other through a single mediation point.

Permissioned/Permissionless blockchains – People often interchange the words permissioned with private and permissionless with public. The general difference is that with permissioned chains you can create a barrier to access and delineate who can run a full node of the network. Whereas permissionless chains (like Bitcoin and Ethereum) are accessible to anyone, and anyone can choose to run a node of the network. By restricting access, you can create greater confidentiality, but you give up a certain amount of security and resiliency that comes from broader adoption and decentralization of a blockchain. You could imagine the differences here as similar to the differences between an Internet or an intranet. You can convert permissioned chains into permissionless chains over time, and there are many people working on the range of possibility regarding the permissioning of a chain.

Plasma – Plasma is a proposed framework for incentivized and enforced execution of smart contracts on the Ethereum network. It claims to be scalable to a significant amount of state updates per second (potentially billions) enabling the Ethereum blockchain to be able to represent a significant amount of decentralized financial applications worldwide.

Practical Byzantine Fault Tolerance – Byzantine Fault Tolerance is the characteristic which defines a system that tolerates the class of failures that belong to the Byzantine General's Problem. Byzantine Failure is the most difficult class of failure modes. With PBFT, nodes have to be recognized before they can participate on the network. These recognized validators send messages to the other nodes about the validity of a particular transaction. If over 66% of the nodes agree that it is valid, the transaction is accepted, and the database can be updated.

Prediction platform (for blockchain) – Blockchain platforms on which users can propose a topic for prediction and access the collective knowledge of the blockchain participants.

Private blockchain – a fully private blockchain is a blockchain where write permissions are kept centralized to one organization. Read permissions may be public or restricted to an arbitrary extent. Likely applications include database management, auditing, etc. that are internal to a single company, and so public readability may not be necessary in many cases at all.

Private key – Each time a user runs a wallet for the first time a public-private key pair gets generated. The private key is a randomly generated number which allows a user to transact over the blockchain. It is locally stored and kept secret. Each time a crypto-asset gets sent, a private key has to sign the transaction. This action is automatically executed by the wallet software. When a wallet asks users to do a backup what this means is that the users must secure their private keys. There are different types of wallets, such as online wallets, mobile wallets, desktop wallest, hardware wallets or paper wallets. The category of each wallet is determined by where private keys are stored. Online wallets are mostly provided by exchanges and keep a user's private keys on their servers. If the service provider goes offline users would lose access to their funds. Hardware wallets, on the other hand, store a user's private keys in a secure device which looks like a USB flash drive.

Programmable transactions – Coding the rules of various transactions into autonomous, if-then programs that a blockchain executes. Ethereum is thought of as the first network that extended blockchains to secure programmable transactions.

Proof of Activity – Proof of Activity is a mixed approach that marries the other two commonly used algorithms—namely, Proof of Work and Proof of Stake.

Proof of Authority – Proof of Authority is a modified form of Proof of Stake where instead of stake with the monetary value, a validator's identity performs the role of stake. Just like in Proof of Stake, in Proof of Authority consensus, identity as a form of stake is also scarce. But unlike Proof of Stake, there's only one identity per person.

Proof of Burn – Proof of Burn is a method for distributed consensus and an alternative to Proof of Work and Proof of Stake. It can also be used for bootstrapping one crypto-asset off of another. The idea is that miners should show proof that they burned some tokens – that is, sent them to a verifiably un-spendable address.

Proof of Capacity – Proof of Capacity allows the mining devices (nodes) on a blockchain network the ability to use empty space on their hard drives to mine available tokens. Proof of Capacity involves a two-step process of plotting and mining.

Proof of Concept (PoC) – A Proof of Concept is a common term in product innovation and startup building. For blockchain projects, PoCs are used to demonstrate the feasibility and practical potential of a project in a field such as Energy, Communication, Services, Insurance and Healthcare. A PoC is a prototype that is used for internal purposes in order to have a better understanding of a particular project before continuing to build.

Proof of Elapsed Time – Proof of Elapsed Time is a blockchain network consensus algorithm that prevents high resource utilization and high energy consumption, and keeps the process more efficient by following a fair lottery system.

Proof of Importance – Proof of Importance is a blockchain consensus algorithm that was first introduced by NEM. Proof of Importance is a reputation scoring used to determine which network participants (nodes) are eligible to add a block to the blockchain, a process that is known by NEM as "harvesting."

Proof of Stake – Proof of Stake is an alternate type of consensus algorithm for a blockchain. Instead of performing in a mathematical contest, miners or validators put up a stake of their tokens in return for the right to help guarantee/validate the network transactions in return for reward. Think of the stake as a nonrevocable security deposit.

Proof of Work – Proof of Work is currently the most utilized consensus algorithm for a blockchain. It is a set of protocols that helps validate the transactions on a blockchain. Every computer that runs a full node on a blockchain will compete against the other nodes to solve complex mathematical puzzles. Upon answering the puzzle, the winning node earns the right to write the next block of data and receives an incentive for that work. By "proving" their work to validate, they help keep the network secure. The downside to this method of generating consensus and securing the network is that it requires a large amount of computing power and therefore energy and cost. The more computer power at your disposal, the more likely you are to win the contest. Therefore, we have seen the rise of server farms or "mining" farms in several countries where energy is less expensive, as blockchain projects grow.

Protocol – A protocol in computer science is a function that defines rules and conventions, often at the network layer.

Provenance – The provenance use case is one of the most compelling uses of blockchain. For supply chains, blockchains allow a product to be documented in real-time as it moves from its original provenance through several touch points. Data provenance involves the ability to trace and verify when and who created information, how it has been used or moved among different data sources, and how it has been modified throughout its lifecycle while it has been exchanged.

Public address – A public address is the cryptographic hash of a public key. These addresses act as email addresses that can be published anywhere, unlike private keys.

Public blockchains – Public blockchains, like the Bitcoin network, allow anyone to write onto the blockchain or read from the blockchain. Essentially, participation is completely open and voluntary. In this sense, a public blockchain is similar to Wikipedia, since anyone can post or edit a page on the site. And like Wikipedia, there is a community of verifiers who reach a consensus about the validity of the transaction. If a member of the blockchain repeatedly tries to submit invalid transactions, the blockchain community will start ignoring that particular node.

Public key cryptography – Public-key cryptography, or asymmetric cryptography, is an encryption scheme that uses two mathematically related, but not identical, keys: a public key and a private key. The public key is used to encrypt, and the private key is used to decrypt.

Public-key identity – Public keys are also known as wallet addresses. This is a string of 34 letters and numbers. For blockchains, this address is stored in a table which links up to a complete history of all transactions that are linked to this address. When a miner validates a transaction, all it has to do is look up the public address in order to make sure that there is enough token in that wallet to complete the transaction and that it hasn't been spent already. Since no one necessarily knows the identity of the person behind any given public address, it does not matter if the whole network sees a wallet's contents and transactions. Each wallet address/public key has a corresponding "private key" of 64 letters and numbers. Given the encryption, no one can reverse engineer a public key in order to find out the private key.

Quantum computing – A quantum computer works with particles that can be in superposition. Rather than representing bits, such particles would represent qubits, which can take on the value 0, or 1, or both simultaneously. It represents a huge increase in computing power and thus, a major threat to current cryptographic standards used by blockchain.

Quantum-resistant blockchains – Post-quantum cryptography (sometimes referred to as quantum-proof, quantum-safe or quantum-resistant) refers to cryptographic algorithms (usually public-key algorithms) that are thought to be secure against an attack by a quantum computer.

Relative valuation models – Relative valuation models attempt to value cryptocurrencies relative to others. One such model is called the Equation of Exchange Monetary Model which attempts to put a value on the network, supply, and velocity of a cryptocurrency.

Release candidate – A release candidate (RC), also known as "going silver," is a beta version with potential to be a final product, which is ready to release unless significant bugs emerge.

Remix – Remix is a suite of tools to interact with the Ethereum blockchain in order to debug transactions. The Remix IDE is an IDE for Solidity Dapp developers.

Resiliency – Blockchain applications are said to be highly resilient since they don't depend on a single copy of the blockchain in order to function. Because each node has a complete copy, if one goes down there are many more replicated versions to serve as a backup.

Ripple (XRP) – A payment network built on distributed ledgers that can be used to transfer any currency. The network consists of payment nodes and gateways operated by authorities. Payments are made using a series of IOUs, and the network is based on trust relationships.

Satoshi – The smallest unit of bitcoin, equal to 0.00000001 BTC.

Satoshi Nakamoto – A person or group of people who created the Bitcoin protocol and reference software, Bitcoin Core (formerly known as Bitcoin-Qt). In 2008, Nakamoto published a paper on The Cryptography Mailing list at metzdowd.com describing the bitcoin digital currency. In 2009, they released the first Bitcoin software that launched the network and the first units of the bitcoin cryptocurrency, called bitcoins.

Scalability (for blockchains) – A change in size, or scale, to handle the ongoing demand for blockchain network resources.

Secure – Blockchains are often described as having great security. This refers partly to the fact that new blocks in a blockchain are cryptographically secured through hash functions, and when a new block is mined, the blockchain is immediately synchronized with the rest of the network. Tokens in a blockchain are also secured with the time, computational power and cost of electricity that these networks usuaully require.

Security token – Security tokens are digital tokens that are backed by real assets such as an equity, shares of a limited partnership company, or commodities. They are also subject to federal security regulations.

Segregated Witness – Segregated Witness (or SegWit) is a soft fork that happened within the Bitcoin blockchain. It solved congestion on the network by increasing the blockchain's block size limit and splitting blocks of data in two. It separated out the unlocking signature with the scripts that send and receive data with the transactional data. This allows the network to process more transactions per second so users don't have to wait as long for bitcoin transactions.

Self-executing – Functioning by itself, not controlled by any other party other than itself. Self-executing smart contracts would cut costs/overhead by removing the need for an arbitrator and trust towards a third party.

Self-policing asset – On an autonomous supply chain, a self-policing asset will have the ability to make decisions about itself and its maintenance, for instance.

Self-sovereign identity – This is a potential use of blockchain as a new technology layer that enables individuals and organizations to assert their own identity. A self-sovereign ID can be used to verify identity without needing an individual to produce numerous documents and paperwork each time they need their identity verified. Controlling its own data, a user could selectively allow visibility into references or credentials of its identity.

Server – A powerful central computer.

SHA-256 – The cryptographic function used as the basis for Bitcoin's Proof of Work system. This is from the SHA family of cryptographic functions, where SHA stand for "Secure Hash Algorithm." One can think of the hash as the fingerprint of the data. Hashes are one-way functions – they cannot be decrypted back. The only way to decrypt a hash is by brute forcing it. Brute force means to systematically try all the combinations for an input. Brute force attacks will always find the input, no matter its complexity.

Sharding – Dividing a blockchain into several smaller component networks called shards, capable of processing transactions in parallel.

Sharing economy – A sharing economy is an economic model where goods and services are often shared across a peer-to-peer network.

Sidechain – Sidechains are a way to increase interoperability between blockchains. Sidechains run in parallel to a main chain and contain a compressed version of the other blockchains that are to be linked. This will allow for checking the transactions stored on other chains and linking them to the transactions on the main chain. In the case of the Bitcoin network, sidechains are new blockchains which are backed by bitcoins, via Bitcoin contracts, just as dollars and pounds used to be backed by cold hard gold. You could in principle have thousands of sidechains "pegged" to Bitcoin, all with different characteristics and purposes, but relying on Bitcoin as the main chain that offers resilience and settlement.

Simple Agreements for Future Tokens (SAFTs) – Amidst the gray area of token regulation, some attempts have been made to self-regulate through projects like the **SAFT** (Simple Agreements for Future Tokens) framework to help those projects raising funds through an ICO to register with the SEC in the U.S. in order to be as compliant as possible. SAFTs essentially define investment contracts that allow investors to fund the technical development of token-based projects. No tokens are received in exchange for funds when using a SAFT, but they can be created later once a network is developed.

Simulated Ethereum Network – This is a testnet for Ethereum developers.

Smart contract – A smart contract is a small computer program that runs on a blockchain. You can think of a smart contract as an "if this, then that" program that executes upon its conditions being triggered. These are often called "self-executing" contracts because they guarantee the business logic that they represent, since the code runs automatically. Other phrases for smart contracts are "persistent scripts" and "autonomous software."

Smart object – A smart object or device is an electronic device, generally connected to other devices or networks via different wireless protocols such as Bluetooth, NFC, Wi-Fi, LiFi, 3G, etc., that can operate to some extent interactively and autonomously. They are part of the emerging Internet of Things model.

Soft fork – A soft fork is a change to a blockchain network wherein only previously valid blocks/transactions are made invalid. Since old nodes will recognize the new blocks as valid, a soft fork is backward-compatible. This kind of fork requires only a majority of the miners upgrading to enforce the new rules.

Solidity – Solidity is a programming language designed for developing smart contracts on the Ethereum network. Its syntax is similar to that of JavaScript, and it is intended to compile into bytecode for the Ethereum Virtual Machine (EVM).

Spoofing – Spoofing is an information security attack that involves masquerading an identity for illegitimate purposes.

Stablecoin – Stablecoins are crypto-assets pegged to a certain value or asset. For example, there are stablecoins that trade 1:1 with the U.S. dollar. These coins can be collateralized (or not) with other crypto-assets.

Staging environment – As a project or product is prototyped, part of its testing involves placing the product in a staging environment, which resembles the live network it will need to function in.

Steganography – The practice of concealing messages or information within other non-secret text or data. It has been claimed that steganography has been used to hide illicit images in blockchain data.

Store of Value – Considered a function of money, a store of value is anything that retains purchasing power and can be stored, retrieved, and exchanged at a later date.

Structural unemployment – Unemployment resulting from industrial reorganization, typically due to technological change, rather than fluctuations in supply or demand.

Suiches model – There are a number of "blockchain decision models," that help an enterprise or project determine whether blockchain would be useful technology for their use case. Along with the IBM model, and the Lewis model, the Suiches model is one such tool. Its focus begins with determining whether a database is needed for a project, and what kind of write access is needed.

Supply Chain Management (SCM) – In business, supply chain management is the management of the flow of goods and services. It involves the movement and storage of raw materials, work-in-process inventory, and finished goods from point of origin to point of consumption.

Swarm – A distributed storage platform and content distribution service, with a native base layer service of the Ethereum Web 3 stack. The primary objective of Swarm is to provide a decentralized and redundant store of Ethereum's public record, in particular, to store and distribute Dapp code and data as well as blockchain data.

Sybil control mechanism – Generally speaking, consensus is reached in a blockchain network by combining consensus protocols (or mechanisms) with Sybil control mechanisms. Proof of Work and Proof of Stake are both Sybil control mechanisms, and cannot achieve network consensus on their own. What they do achieve is a way to prevent Sybil attacks, which is when a single adversary controls multiple nodes on a network and has undue influence on that network.

Syntax errors – In computing, a syntax error occurs when a character or string is incorrectly placed in a command or instruction that causes a failure in execution.

Tangle – The IOTA Tangle is a stream of interlinked and individual transactions. These transactions are distributed and stored across a decentralized network of participants. IOTA uses a DAG instead of a blockchain to store its ledger, with the main motivation being scalability.

Testnet – A second blockchain used by developers for testing new versions of client software without putting real value at risk.

The DAO – The DAO served as a form of investor-directed venture capital fund that sought to provide enterprise with new decentralized business models. Built on the Ethereum blockchain, The DAO's code was open-source. The organization set the record for the most crowdfunded project in 2016, however, those funds were partially stolen by hackers resulting in an Ethereum hard-fork that created Ethereum Classic.

Third-generation blockchain – Computing technologies are emerging that push some of the components of blockchain further in new directions. Beyond evolving the existing platforms to handle greater transaction volume or interoperability, we are starting to see attempts at decentralized computing fabrics that do not fully resemble the early blockchains. See also "Web 3.0."

Threshold Relay – Threshold Relay creates a random group of validators on a network derived from a cryptographic beacon instead of crypto-economics (like staking). This changes some of the security threats that crypto-economic frameworks engender (e.g. relying on incentives built on the idea that participants won't want to see their holdings decrease in value).

Time-stamp – A digital record of the time of occurrence of a particular event. This is especially important for verifying transactions on a blockchain.

Token – (or crypto-token) In the context of blockchains, a token is a digital identity for something that can be owned. Tokens represent a smattering of assets in a blockchain environment. Besides currency and commodity tokens, today there are security tokens, utility tokens, and reputation/reward tokens. While these classification systems are not all mutually exclusive, it is helpful to think of how a token is being used in order to find terminology that helps people understand the purpose of the token. Modern tokens are often created using smart contracts with complex permission systems and interaction paths attached.

Tokenization – The process of converting assets to tokens that can be traded on a blockchain. Tokenization removes all aspects of the middleman institution. It enables online transactions through a decentralized system, breaking down power and access barriers. The "tokenization of everything" refers to how virtually any asset can be tokenized and transacted on a blockchain. Tokens can also be fractionalized, allowing for representation of assets at many levels.

Transaction – A transaction is a digitally-signed message authorizing some particular action associated with a blockchain. For a cryptocurrency, the dominant transaction type is sending cryptocurrency units or tokens to someone else; in other systems actions like registering domain names, making and fulfilling trade offers and entering into contracts are also valid transaction types.

Transaction fee (Bitcoin) – Fees may be included with any transfer of bitcoins from one address to another. Many transactions are typically processed in a way where no fee is expected at all, but for transactions which draw coins from many Bitcoin addresses and therefore have a large data size, a small transaction fee is usually expected. The transaction fee is processed by and received by the bitcoin miner. When a new Bitcoin block is generated with a successful hash, the information for all of the transactions is included with the block, and all transaction fees are collected by that user creating the block, who is free to assign those fees to him/herself. Transaction fees are voluntary on the part of the person making the bitcoin transaction, and represent an incentive to make sure that a particular transaction will get included in the next block.

Transactions per second – Along with other metrics, this is an especially important ratio for measuring how well a digital token is penetrating the consumer market.

Transparency (for blockchains) – Transparency refers to the ability to see all of the transactions and their history on a blockchain. This is important for engendering trust in a blockchain network.

Truffle – Truffle is a development environment, testing framework and asset pipeline for Ethereum, aiming to make life as an Ethereum developer easier. With Truffle, you get built-in smart contract compilation, linking, deployment and binary management.

Trustless – Does not require a third party to verify or manage. Smart contracts are primarily trustless, as they are meant to occur by themselves once the stipulations are met.

Turing-complete – A machine or language is Turing-complete if it can perform any calculation that any other programmable computer is capable of. All modern computers are Turing-complete in this sense. The Ethereum Virtual Machine (EVM) which runs on the Ethereum blockchain is Turing-complete. Thus, it can process any "computable function." It is, in short, able to do what you could do with any conventional computer and programming language.

Unbanked – This term refers to the population of approximately 2 billion individuals who do not have a bank account. Often, the unbanked are unable to access banking services because of a lack of identification or other government-issued documentation, leaving them to store and exchange value in less formalized ways such as cash.

Unit of Account – The unit of account is a term referring to one of the functions of money in economics. Essentially, currency offers a unit of account that allows for the comparison of unlike goods and services.

Use case (blockchain) – A use case is a specific description of business use for blockchain technology in a given industry. Developing use cases is sometimes a formal text description of a new application created at the beginning of the development process. It describes how users will interact with the application but is free of technical jargon. The more comprehensive use cases may even include some flow charts and/or financial projections in order to better make the case for that particular application.

User characteristics – This is another set of metrics that can be used to help determine the value of a token network by looking at the characteristics of the user base of the network, such as the distribution of token ownership throughout wallets.

Utility token – A form of crypto-asset or token. Utility tokens are like "coupons" for services by a specific company/network. They often carry utility such as the ability to purchase computing power of the network.

Value – Value in economic terms is generally referred to as a measure of the benefit of a good or service and is usually measured in units of some currency. The basic idea of blockchain is that we can use technology to disintermediate the institutions to transfer value directly.

Virtual Machine (VM) – A blockchain virtual machine is a higher abstraction than your computer itself. One way of thinking of a VM is to think of it as a special area within your computer either on your hard drive or in the cloud, where you can run different operating systems and applications. This is what allows you to function as a node on a blockchain and run the programs which you need to use to access the functionality of your blockchain. All of this happens separately from other applications running on your computer that might conflict with the global virtual machine running the entire blockchain.

Vyper – A Python-like programming language created to be a formal introduction to smart contracts on Ethereum.

Wallet – A wallet is a file that contains a collection of private keys and communicates with a blockchain. Wallets contain keys, not coins. Wallets require backups for security reasons.

Web 3.0 – Blockchain enthusiasts and developers have proposed that a new, blockchain-enabled Internet is the future technology stack of our world. This third-generation Internet is called Web 3.0. It will be more decentralized than today's Internet and blockchain will become embedded in the web technology stack.

Wei – Wei is the smallest denomination of ether, the crypto-asset used on the Ethereum network. It is roughly equivalent to individual steps in a program.

X11 – X11 is an algorithm for mining crypto-assets which uses 11 different hash functions.

Zero-Knowledge Proof – A cryptography mechanism for proving properties about encrypted data without revealing the data itself.

Made in the USA
Coppell, TX
20 July 2020